THE MAGIC OF CRUISING NORWAY
2024-25

Including a Russian Arctic Supplement

CONTENTS

Introduction	3
Cruising Options for Norway	6
Geography of Norway	11
A Norwegian History	19
Oslo - The National Metropolis and Capital	26
Stavanger	52
Haugesund	67
Eidfjord	77
Bergen - Norway's Second City	83
Sognefjord - Visiting Fläm, Gudvangen and Skjolden	104
Nordfjorden - Visiting Olden	121
Ålesund	133
Molde	149
Storfjorden - Visiting Hellesylt and Geiranger	161
Åndalsnes	179
Kristiansund	185
Trondheim	201

The Lofoten Islands - Visiting Svolvær	**218**
Harstad	**231**
Tromsø	**245**
Alta	**264**
Hammerfest	**275**
Honningsvag and Nordkapp	**287**
Cruising to Murmansk and Arkhangelsk, Russia	**299**
About the Author	**336**

The majority of maps used in this book are taken from Open Street Map contributors and are so noted for each map. For further information contact: *www.openstreetmap.com*

INTRODUCTION

A map of Norway and Svalbard

I have been cruising Norway for the past ten years, and have visited all of the major ports of call along its long and convoluted coastline, In 2017 I finally felt it was time to present a book on Cruising Norway. This volume is the third major revision, updating the material to be ready for the 2024-25 cruise seasons. Of all the places in the world where the cruise industry has developed itineraries, none can compare with the raw natural landscapes of intense beauty combined with the romantic Viking history that are found in Norway, one of the most sought after travel destinations for those who love to travel by ship. The major cruise lines with their mega liners can only visit the most important ports of call in Norway while the more upmarket or adventure oriented cruise lines operating smaller ships provide more comprehensive itineraries capable of including small ports of call that are not able to accommodate the large sea going vessels.

Early morning calm in Geirangerfjorden, so typical of the beauty of Norway

This title, which now comes in one combined provides you with an overview of Norway of its physical characteristics and challenging geography and a moderately detailed history to enable you to best appreciate the country without having to delve into complex academic treatises on either subject. Often my readers ask me to add more minute geographic or historic detail, but with the size limit Amazon sets for a book, to satisfy the wishes of so many readers I have now created this combined the former two volumes into one super edition. There is also a supplement on Murmansk and Archangelsk in Russia for those of you fortunate enough to add these Arctic ports to your itinerary. However at the time this book was being prepared for release, Russia invaded Ukraine and thus most, if not all, cruise lines have cancelled those visits.

The aim of this edition is to enable you to gain a sufficient understanding of the physical and cultural landscapes of Norway along with a look at the country's history to then focus upon the enjoyment of the ports of call your cruise includes, not to be able to pass a college exam on the subject.

A bright and sunny day in Geirangerfjorden, one of the most popular cruise ports along the Norwegian coast

I have included all of the ports of call visited by both the major cruise lines and the upmarket and adventure cruise companies. I have left out those very minor ports that can only be visited utilizing the local ferry boats or combined mail/passenger services that ply the hundreds of small fjords and bays, connecting nearly every village with the rest of the country. This book gives the reader the essentials on the ports that are likely to be a part of the itineraries of the majority of cruise lines.

I trust you will find this book both informative and sufficiently enticing to whet your appetite for a cruise along the coast and through the fjords of Norway.

Dr. Lew Deitch,
January 2024

CRUISING OPTIONS FOR NORWAY

Most of the major cruise lines offer summertime Norwegian Fjord itineraries. These cruise lines vary in price and of course in the levels of quality service and cuisine being offered. The itineraries vary from short one-week cruises to two weeks or longer. I strongly recommend cruise itineraries that are devoted only to the Norwegian ports and that begin and terminate either in Copenhagen or Oslo. In this way you are not spending days at sea between such starting or ending ports as Southampton, Edinburgh or Amsterdam. Why spend time at sea that could be better spent in Norway. You must choose your cruise line and the itinerary carefully to maximize how much of the country you will see, recognizing that Norway is so vast that you cannot get more than an introduction to its land and people on a single cruise even if it is two weeks in length. After ten years of cruising Norway, I believe I have now visited every port that is on a cruise ship itinerary.

Your choice of cruise line must be guided by the following factors to maximize your enjoyment:

* The amount of time you wish to spend on the cruise. The longer the time frame, the more ports of call and fjords you can visit. With the majority of cruises starting in Oslo, Copenhagen or Bergen, a minimum of two weeks is needed to explore well north into the Arctic region of Norway, a portion of the country that should not be missed because it offers a hauntingly magnificent landscape.

* The level of luxury and the number of on board amenities are important factors to many who cruise, often of equal value as the itinerary itself. The most luxurious ships are primarily found in the fleets of Silversea, Seaborne and Regent. These ships are relatively small and can offer more detailed itineraries that include ports seldom if ever visited by the larger cruise ships. The higher end cruise lines offer staterooms that are generally larger and better appointed than the mega ships belonging to the major mass market companies. There is also a higher ratio of crewmembers to passengers, thus giving more personalized and attentive service. Likewise the cuisine on the smaller up market lines is gourmet oriented, and often provides a taste of the countries being visited. But because these ships are smaller and carry fewer passengers their theaters and casinos are likewise not overly large and the entertainment is not as lavish. One must choose between having a more sedate and elegant atmosphere or "glitz" and glamour of the larger vessels.

* The level of detail that you wish to experience is a guiding factor. For the most intensive exposure to the more remote locations in Norway, there are a few adventure cruise ships that will offer itineraries that visit the most inaccessible ports or fjords that are not visited by either large or luxury cruise ships. Also Norway's Hurtigruten line offers the most extensive itineraries on its local mail runs and adventure oriented cruise ships. They also offer cruises during the winter months, a time when the majority of travelers are looking at tropical itineraries. Although the days are exceptionally short or even nonexistent above the Arctic Circle, the major attraction is the dramatic beauty of the Aurora Borealis or Northern Lights.

For those who are new to cruising or who have not traveled to Norway, here are some basic tips that will help to maximize your voyage:

* Always book an outside cabin if traveling on one of the larger ships that offer less expensive interior cabins, which have neither a window nor a veranda. Interior cabins can be quite claustrophobic because it is always necessary to use artificial illumination. At night these cabins are totally dark to where a nightlight is needed in the event you want to get out of bed for any reason. And without at least a window, you will miss so much of the local scenery in transit between ports of call. Much of the joy in cruising Norway is to just sit and soak in the passing scenery. Remember that daylight hours are extensive during the spring and summer months and much of the time you are close to the shore, traveling the inside passages or within the fjords.

* To economize, book an outside cabin with a window, as these are generally on the lower passenger decks where a veranda is not provided. One advantage in rough seas is that being lower down in the ship equals more stability when the ship begins to pitch or roll. There are often rough waters in the North Sea, especially on the transit between the northern tip of Denmark and the southern coast of Norway. And generally the weather is not conducive to wanting to sit outside on a verandah.

* Although forward lower deck cabins are offered at the lowest prices, be aware that the ship's maneuvering thrusters and anchors are forward. You will be exposed to a fair amount of noise when the ship is entering or leaving a harbor, rotating its position prior to docking and during docking maneuvers, and this can often interrupt your morning sleep, especially if you tend to be a light sleeper.

* If having the opportunity to enjoy fresh air at any time is important to you, then it is wise to book a cabin with a veranda even though you will not spend much time sitting out of doors. While traveling in Norway there is often so much scenery to be enjoyed from your cabin while in transit between ports.

* Whenever possible book a cabin in mid ship, as when a ship begins to pitch the mid-section acts like the fulcrum in that it experiences far less movement than either forward or aft cabins. The North Sea is noted for squalls that can cause the sea to become choppy. Once inside the fjords, the seas are generally exceptionally calm. But during transits between fjords or while en route from or returning to either Oslo or Copenhagen you may find that the conditions can be quite uncomfortable. I have seen waves of ten meters in the waters between Bergen and Copenhagen.

* If you should become queasy during periods of rough weather and pitching or rolling sea, it is best to go up on deck or out on your verandah and breath some fresh air. Also by staring off at the horizon the body surprisingly is less stressed by motion. But if you are unable to go out on deck because of the danger presented during really inclement weather, it is still possible to sit near a window and from time to time look out to sea, toward the horizon. Fear also plays a role in the way you feel during rough seas. If you become frightened that the ship may capsize or sink, it will only heighten your feeling of uneasiness.

Remember that ships can take a lot of punishment, and it is rare for a modern cruise liner to go down in rough weather. Starving one's self when feeling queasy will only make the condition worse. Dry crackers or toast along with hot tea is one way to calm an irritated stomach. And there are patches, pills or injections available from the ship's medical office to calm extreme discomfort.

Sailing out from Oslo it takes a few hours to reach the open sea

* Be prepared for sudden changes in the weather. During summertime, the average temperatures in Norway are in the teens or very low 20's Celsius, which is between 50 and 75 degrees Fahrenheit. Occasional summer rainstorms can drop temperatures and it is easy to become chilled or soaked if not properly dressed or carrying an umbrella. Dressing in layers is the best way to accommodate the changes that can occur on a given day. And yes there are occasional hot, humid days when the sky is blue, the sun feels strong and temperatures can climb up to between 25 and 30 degrees Celsius, which is between 77 and 86 degrees Fahrenheit, but these are the exception rather than the rule.

* Do not over indulge in eating or drinking. It is best to pace yourself and try and eat normally, as you would at home. Overindulgence only leads to discomfort and added weight gain. And even though meals are included on board ship, one of the delights is in having a meal ashore. Norway is noted for its fresh fish and seafood. And Norwegian cuisine is elegantly prepared and one of the delights of the country.

* When in port, weigh the option of going on organized tours against freelancing and visiting on your own. If you have any sense of adventure, a local map, public transit information and the names of basic venues make it possible to see as much, if not more, in a

relaxed atmosphere in contract to being shepherded around as part of a tour group. Also by striking off on your own you have more opportunity to mingle with and meet local residents. And in Norway most people do speak English as their second language, with many also speaking German. But in some of the more remote locations or smaller villages the only option is to take organized tours offered by your cruise line, as local tour operators, taxis or busses are few in number.

The newly minted Norwegian Kroner comes in the following denominations of graduated sizes and there are coins for values below 50 Kroner

* When starting a cruise, arrive at least 24 hours ahead of the departure and spend a minimum of one night in the port of embarkation. This enables you to recover from jet lag and to become acclimated to a new environment.

* When disembarking, it is also recommended that you spend at least one night in the final port of call before flying home. Two nights are preferable if your port of departure is either Copenhagen or Oslo.

* When on shore in Norway it is safe to eat without fear of gastrointestinal upset. The country maintains a high degree of sanitation, and good restaurants abound. And drinking the local water is totally safe even though most restaurants offer bottled water. You will also find that Norwegian cuisine is very palatable with a few minor exceptions.

* Violent crime in Norway is rare. The ports of call on the itineraries are exceptionally safe. However, pickpockets are found almost everywhere in the major cities such as Copenhagen, Oslo, Bergen and Trondheim where tourists will be seen in greater numbers. So wise precautions always apply regarding not keeping a wallet in a back pocket, not showing large sums of money and for women to keep a tight rein on their handbags.

* The use of credit cards is widespread at all major restaurants and shops. However, in Europe data chips are the norm. If your credit card has a data chip, insert it into the front of the credit card machine and follow the prompts. You will either enter a pin code or wait for the receipt to be issued and then sign it. Cards without a data chip will require a special pin code. Check with your credit card service before leaving.

* In Norway the national currency is the Norwegian Kroner. The use of the Euro, Pound or other foreign currency is rare, and only the occasional tourist oriented shop may be willing to accept other currencies. It is best to obtain Norwegian Kroner at an ATM or currency exchange at the start of your cruise. The easiest option is to order it in advance from your personal bank at home before departing.

* Returning to the ship is normally expedited by having your cruise identification card handy to be swiped by the security officers. Packages and large handbags are often put through an x-ray machine similar to what is used at airports. And passengers pass through an arch to screen for any major metal objects.

* Most ships offer hand sanitizers at the gangway and recommend that you sanitize your hands upon return. This is not mandatory, but it never hurts to be cautious. Norway is one of the cleanest countries in the world, but still a bit of extra precaution is a good policy.

GEOGRAPHY OF NORWAY

The topography of Norway with its coastline of fjords and offshore islands. (Maps of Europe, Creative Commons Attribution Share Alike 3.0 license)

Norway is the westernmost nation of the Scandinavian Peninsula with its southern coast on the Kattegat and Skagerrak, a waterway that is actually an extension of the North Sea. However, historically Norway, Denmark and Sweden have been interwoven throughout time and even today there are close bonds between the three nations that consider themselves to be the heartland of Scandinavia. Iceland is also geographically a part of Scandinavia, but it is located almost midway between mainland Europe and Greenland, yet

culturally it is a European nation. Finland, which was occupied by Sweden during much of its early history, is also considered to be a Scandinavian nation, however, linguistically Finnish is not a Germanic language, as are Swedish, Norwegian, Danish and Icelandic.

Geographically Norway is considered to be an elongated nation, essentially meaning that its shape has one axis that is far greater than the other. In this case, the north to south distance across Norway averages nearly 1,800 kilometers or 1,100 miles while its east to west extent in the south is less than 200 kilometers or 120 miles. In the far north there are locations where the country is less than 100 kilometers or 60 miles in width. Given its highly indented coastline and nearly 50,000 offshore islands, the total Norwegian coastline is nearly 22,000 kilometers or 13,620 miles in length.

The rugged mountains along the coast of Stortfjorden

The total land area of Norway covers 323,802 square kilometers or 125,000 square miles, which is approximately the size of the American state of New Mexico. But it is the elongated shape that makes the country appear to be so much larger than its total land area indicates. Norway extends over 13 degrees of latitude, extending north to just over 71 degrees North Latitude, making it the most northerly location in all of Europe. Approximately one third of the length of Norway extends north of the Arctic Circle, giving this region 24 hours of total daylight for nearly two months and then a reversal in winter with 24 hours of total darkness. In actuality, all of Norway experiences long summer days and long winter nights.

Norway's total population is only 5,360,000 in 2019. Over 1,000,000 live in the greater Oslo region. Another half million live in the greater Bergen area. This leaves only 3,800,000 for the remainder of the country.

THE NORWEGIAN LANDSCAPE: Norway is essentially a mountainous country, one of the most rugged countries in Europe with over 70 percent of the country consisting of mountain slopes. Only 2.7 percent of the country is considered to be arable, yet the Norwegians are able to develop pastures and orchards along with small garden plots on slopes that seem to be impossible to access. This is also a nation in which over 2/3 of the land is raw wilderness, so steep or so far north and cold that it has not been settled. And the combination of high altitude and high latitude, especially north of the Arctic Circle also means that much of the land is above the tree line, and sits bare and windswept. Once you are north of the Arctic Circle you will find that without snow cover during summer the land almost resembles a desert region because of its lack of significant vegetation. Geographers call these far northern lands polar deserts and you will understand why when you visit.

Small shelves of gentle land for farming on the offshore Lofoten Islands

The Scandinavian Mountains serve as the backbone or spine of the nation with spurs extending both east and west from the central ridges. The highest peak reaches an elevation of 2,469 meters or 8,100 feet above sea level. The median elevation of the land is just over 460 meters or 1,500 feet. These are old mountains that share a common thread with the mountains of the British Isles and the Appalachians of North America. It is believed that they once were part of the ancient continent of Pangaea prior to its breaking apart to slowly form the continents we know today. These mountains were heavily glaciated during the Ice Age or Pleistocene, as much of the land was buried under more than a kilometer of ice. As the ice advanced and retreated four times over several million years, it sculpted and gouged, deepening former river valleys along with grinding down and sharpening many of the highest peaks.

The spectacular beauty of Nærøyfjorden in central Norway

The landscapes of Norway are among the most spectacular and beautiful of any nation. This is a country of superlatives. The Scandinavian Mountains extend the entire length of the nation and are broken by deep valleys that once carried glaciers down to the sea during the four great glacial advances. In the far north, there are still many small active glaciers to this day. As the glacial ice sculpted these deep valleys, they were turned from "V" shape river valleys into wide "U" shape gashes through the scour and pressure exerted by the moving ice. Very steep nearly vertical walls leading up to the higher peaks are the hallmarks of glacially created valleys. As the sea level rose with the last glacial retreat, many of the high mountaintops were left standing as islands while these deeply carved valleys flooded with seawater to form the magnificent Norwegian fjords.

Present-day Norway has a coastline that is over 22,000 kilometers or 13,620 miles in length when one considers every mile of deeply indented channels called fjords and all of the islands. This same action occurred along the coastline of Alaska and British Columbia as well as in southern Chile and on South Island New Zealand. And today fjords are being carved by glacial action on Greenland and Canada's Baffin Island. But of all the glacially created fjords, none have the combined physical and cultural magnificence of those in Norway. This is not to say that the other fjords are not beautiful because of course they are. But there is a quality to the Norwegian fjords that is hard to match, even harder to put into words.

The upper reaches of the Valley of Fläm that was glacially carved

Most of southern and central Norway is covered in dense forest, the same coniferous forest that stretches into Russia, known as the taiga. Stands of spruce, pine and willow dominate the lower elevations, as at these northern latitudes the tree line is not very high above sea level. However, in the far north, above the Arctic Circle where the long winter climate is harsh, the landscape is one of tundra, essentially a polar desert. Norway's population clings to the shoreline and occupies the small valleys in between the higher peaks, but this leaves them with very little land that is good for farming. Yet the Norwegians are excellent farmer, working what they have to produce dairy products, fruits and vegetables.

The high glacially sculpted mountains above Olden on Nordfjorden

The rich Norwegian biosphere

Norway is rich in raw material resources. It is obvious that timber has been one resource, but the North Sea shoreline is exceptionally well endowed with reserves of oil and natural gas. There are also deposits of copper, lead, zinc and titanium that have added to Norway's overall mineral wealth. However, to mine these resources, the Norwegians have been forced exploit remote mountain areas, and for the extraction of oil and natural gas they have had to build some of the tallest off shore drilling platforms ever constructed. Norway is also well known for its shipbuilding and fishing industries, thus the technology was there to turn to building oil-drilling platforms. Many ocean liners and cargo ships have been built in Norway, and Norwegian corporations have invested heavily in the shipping industry.

THE NORWEGIAN CLIMATE: Norway is a country dominated over by winter. Around the Atlantic coastal margins rain rather than snow predominates because of the moderating influence of the warmer waters of the Gulf Stream. But even at sea level, the winter has periods of time that experience occasional heavy snow showers. The climate is said to be maritime, influenced heavily by the sea. The mountains and the interior experience cold winter temperatures and heavy snowfall. And most of Norway experiences little to no daylight for approximately two months in the middle of winter. Summer days are long; full 24 hours north of the Arctic Circle. And temperatures are mild, but along the coast there is still frequent rainfall, occasional fog and many days where there is no sunshine. Many coastal communities average only about 30 percent of the days in a calendar year during which there will be sunshine.

A thundering white water river flows past the village of Hellesylt

With a wet climate and high rugged mountain slopes, Norway is blessed with fast flowing rivers and streams, most flowing with tremendous force of white water rapids. Where rivers plunge over the glacially carved walls of the fjords, thousands of waterfalls add to the overall drama of the landscape.

At these northern latitudes during the long winter nights, Norwegians are treated to an incredible light show, as the Aurora Borealis; also known as the Northern Lights, dance across the sky. Many visitors wait until the deepest part of winter and willingly brave the cold, rain and snow to have an opportunity to witness this phenomenon so widely associated with Norway. But of course it is also visible in neighboring Sweden as well as in Finland, Russia, Alaska, Canada and Greenland.

Tourism plays a significant role in the Norwegian economy. During the summer, there are increasingly more and more cruise ships that offer tours along and through the fjords. Also the extensive Norwegian ferry system transports tens of thousands of European and American visitors along this spectacular coastline, some coming by automobile and combining road and ferry to explore even the most remote of those fjords that are serviced.

Summer with its extended daylight hours reaching a maximum of 24-hours per day north of the Arctic Circle in the height of summer is one of the spectacles that visitors find so magnificent. You will often see Norway advertised as "The Land of the Midnight Sun," and it is an experience you will long remember.

The inside passage north of the city of Tromsø at midnight

A NORWEGIAN HISTORY

To best understand the culture and the landscape of any country you visit, it is important to know something of its history. It is the course of history that molds the culture and creates the visual landscape with regard to both the physical and human elements seen. Architecture, transportation networks, land use patterns and the amount of natural forest or grassland are all impacted by the succession of events that took place in the past. Humans are players on a stage, interacting with the props that are available and creating an ever changing stage set. And for this reason history plays a major role in what the visitor encounters. In the case of Norway, this is an old country with its history extending back beyond the 9th century, yet as a modern nation, it only dates to 1905.

To many prospective visitors, the name Norway is often synonymous with those northern warriors known as the Vikings. In essence it is their history that is the starting point for any written account of Norwegian timelines, yet there were earlier fishing, hunting and herding tribes living along its shores dating back into prehistoric times long before our calendar. Despite the Hollywood image of the Vikings as warriors who terrorized and pillaged the shores of northern Europe, there were also merchants who engaged in legitimate trade, and colonists who set out from their cold, windswept lands to find more suitable homes.

The Sámi people still graze their reindeer on the Arctic islands and peninsula

Initially the Viking populace was scattered into tribal groups, each with its own chief of king. But in 872, much of the country was united under King Harald Hårfagre, this being the start of what would become a powerful force in Scandinavia. The Vikings adhered to their traditional "pagan" beliefs, but by the 11th century, Christian teaching had ultimately converted the majority, also helping to stem their raids on the nations along the North Sea.

Akershus Castle in Oslo dates to 1290 AD

The Kalmar Union, which was propagated by the Danes in 1350, ultimately united Norway and Sweden into one confederation, which was under the rule of the Danish king. But the Swedes rebelled in 1523 and left the Union because of their dissatisfaction with the power of the Danish crown. This break up was not without its share of bloodshed. Norway then became relegated to the status of a mere Danish province, something the Norwegians greatly resented. This displeasure festered until 1814, when Denmark, having lost a war with France, was forced to surrender Norway to Swedish rule. The Norwegians had drafted a constitution for their independence, but although forced into union with Sweden, many provisions of that draft were put into effect, as Sweden gave Norway a certain degree of internal home rule and its own separate crown, but the king was of Swedish nationality

Hanseatic League buildings in Bergen date to the 14th century

On the back streets of Bryggen in Old Bergen

The old village church in Geiranger

As a means of developing their nationalism, the Norwegian people turned inward and concentrated their efforts upon fostering greater interest in their cultural identity through the arts, music and other manifestations of what it meant to be Norwegian. But ultimately this led to a political interest in the creation of an independent nation, which finally came to fruition on 7th July 1905 when the Norwegian Storting declared the country separated from Sweden and that the Swedish crown no longer would be recognized. The Swedish government was livid and there were even calls for armed forces to be sent into Norway. But in the end, both countries held separate referenda, and Norwegian independence was approved.

Since there was no Norwegian royal house, it was decided to invite young Prince Carl of Denmark, son of King Christian IX, to become the king of Norway. Taking the traditional Norwegian name of Haakon, the new royal house was established. And King Haakon VII reigned until 1957. To the present day, King Haarald V is the true head of the royal family, but also shows pride in his close familial relationship to the Danish Royal Family.

Life for the average Norwegian during the 19th and early 20th century was hard, as the country's economy was based upon limited farming, timber extraction and fishing. Essentially Norway was a backward country and large numbers of the poor emigrated primarily to Canada and the United States. It has been estimated that well over half a million Norwegians left for the New World, and states such as Minnesota, North and South Dakota and the Canadian provinces of Ontario and Manitoba show significant Norwegian communities. As in many European countries, manufacturing plants were developing in the major cities, and for those peasants who left the land for the city, life remained hard, often more difficult because urban residents were not able to at least supplement their incomes with homegrown foods.

Interior of the old village church in Olden

Unlike many countries in Europe that industrialized, Norway did have one ready source of power, that being hydroelectric that provided clean and affordable energy for both industrial and domestic use. Apart from shipbuilding, manufacturing of paper products and a few fine quality metallic implements, Norway did not become one of Europe's industrial giants.

Although Norway was not drawn into the First World War, its economy did feel the same degree of contraction during the global depression of the 1930's. At the outbreak of World War II, Norway was invaded by Nazi forces from Germany because it offered two important resources. Its hydroelectric facilities, especially in the southern part of the country, were necessary for the production of heavy water, a vital component for the possible creation of nuclear weapons. And secondly was Norway's coastline that fronted on the major warm water trade route to the far north of European Russia. Nazi submarines and planes could harass allied shipping meant to aid the Russians in its fight on the Eastern Front once Germany invaded the Soviet Union.

Even far off Norway saw Nazi invasion during World War II and its few Jews were sent off to concentration camps

The German invasion of Norway overwhelmed the small Norwegian military and the country fell under Nazi occupation, but a strong resistance movement developed and was instrumental in thwarting many of Germany's strategic operations. Sweden offered refuge to the Norwegian freedom fighters along with Allied pilots and paratroopers who aided in operations against Nazi installations.

Germany established a puppet government under the leadership of Vidkun Quisling, a man whose very name became associated with being a traitor to one's own country. But the vast majority of Norwegians silently opposed German occupation even though Nazi propaganda tried to equate being Norwegian with being a part of their so-called "master race." The Viking heritage of Norway figured prominently into Nazi myth.

Modern Norway presents a totally different picture than it did in prewar years. After two decades of reconstruction and repair of many damaged bridges, roads and harbor installations because of the war, Norway was soon back to a level of economic stability. The country took its place in the modern world as a member of the United Nations and later of the North Atlantic Treaty Organization.

The biggest single boost to Norway was the discovery of oil and natural gas in large underwater reserves off the coast, but within Norwegian territorial limits. As a result, the country with its small population began to see great sums of money coming into its treasury. Rather than utilizing the money for infrastructure or squandering it on monumental constructs, Norway invested the money in global programs for the benefit of its citizens in a national pension program. Today Norway's pension program is the envy of the world, and every one of its citizens has a secure future ahead. Infrastructure development, medical and educational services and other government programs are financed through high levels of taxation while the pension program is the beneficiary of the petroleum and gas profits. Even with the current low prices for fossil fuels, Norway is secure. However, jobs in the petroleum and gas industry have diminished, and this has caused unemployment that then strains the government's welfare programs.

Overall life in Norway is good. There is equal pay for men and women, excellent health and welfare benefits, and the country has a strong educational system available to all citizens. Yet Norwegians are not overly indulgent and the average family lives a comfortable lifestyle without being extravagant, as seen among other oil rich nations. Norwegians hold the natural environment to be very special, and they enjoy their country's beauty and recreational potential. It is true that there is no "Eden" on this earth, but Norway is one of those countries where life can be described as almost idyllic.

OSLO - THE NATIONAL METROPOLIS AND CAPITAL

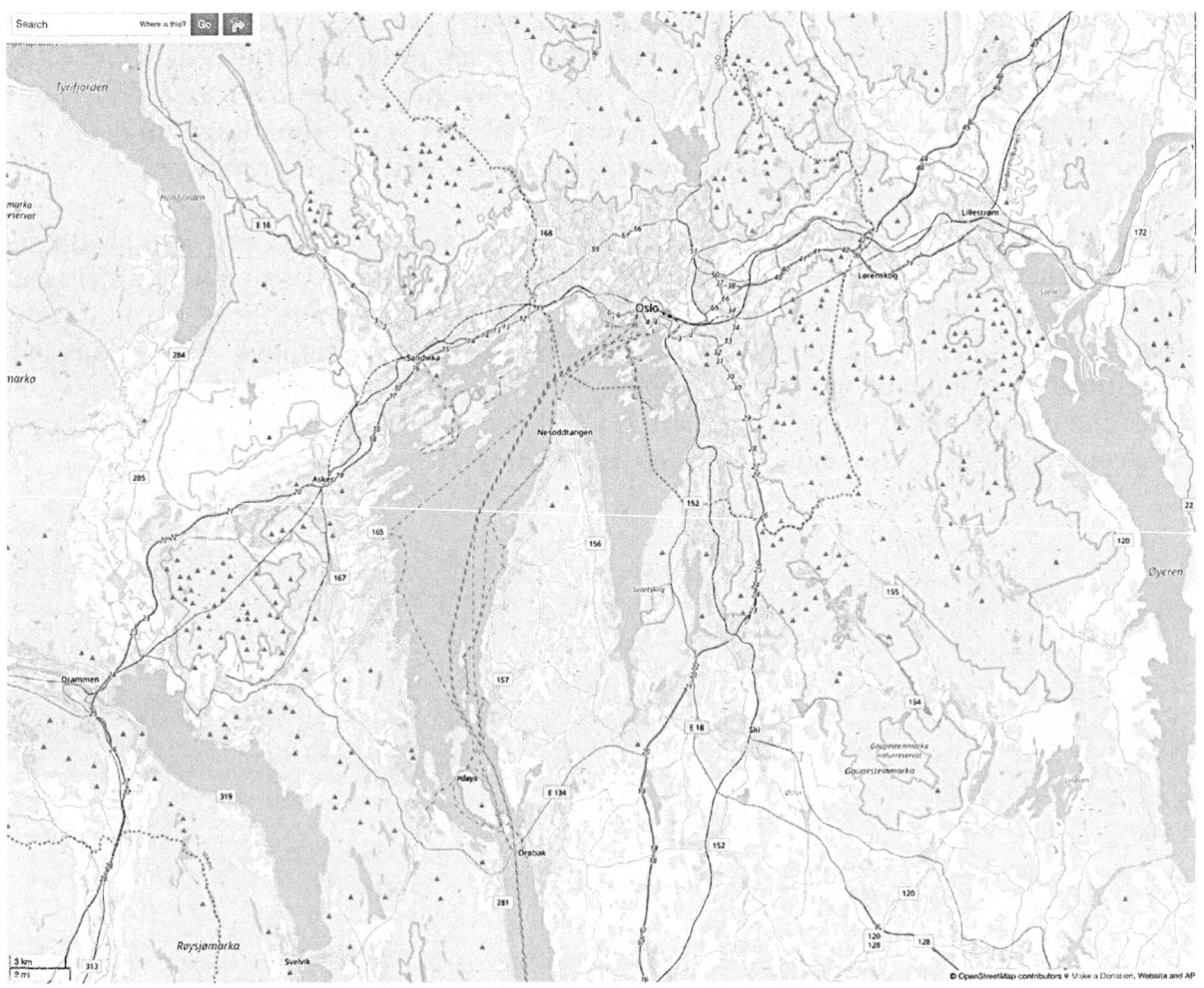

Oslo Fjord and the city of Oslo. (© OpenStreetMap contributors)

The majority of cruise ships do not visit Oslo as often as the other major cities of Scandinavia or the Baltic Sea region. Many cruise lines use Copenhagen as their port of embarkation for fjord cruises, as it is closer to the main travel route at sea. Oslo is actually not a convenient location to begin or end a fjord cruise because it is not on any major sea routes. The city's location is not as pivotal as Copenhagen or Stockholm in the planning of cruise itineraries. A visit to Oslo often involves one day or a half-day at sea at both the front and back end of the port call because of its location easily worked into a seven or 10-day cruise schedule.

THE SETTING FOR OSLO: Norway's capital is located approximately 130 kilometers or 80 miles up the long and narrow Oslofjord, which was created by glacial action during the Pleistocene or Ice Age. The journey up the fjord as well as back out after visiting the city is one of the highlights of visiting Oslo by ship. There are many small villages with their whitewashed wood houses that cling to the forested hillsides overlooking the fjord. It takes around three hours sailing time to reach the city or the Skagerrak on the return voyage. And if the weather is good, sitting out on deck and watching the passing countryside is richly rewarding, as it gives you a good glimpse into life in coastal life in the more populated portion of southern Norway.

One of the many picturesque villages along Oslofjord leading to Oslo

Approaching the city of Oslo by ship

Oslo occupies a crescent shaped bowl set amid thickly wooded hills at the upper end of Oslofjord. There are also numerous small islands within the fjord that belong to the city. Surrounding Oslo, the countryside is gently rolling and dotted with many fresh water lakes set amid mixed forests of broadleaf deciduous trees and conifers. Oslo is a picturesque, spotlessly clean yet modern city, reflecting both the past and forward look of the Norwegian people. Oslo has a population of only 560,000 and with its suburbs, it contain approximately 1,000,000 people, but the city gives the appearance of being a large town rather than a major city. The heart of Oslo hugs the shoreline at the top of the fjord, surrounded by spacious suburbs that extend into the surrounding hills and along both shorelines of the fjord. There are now a few high-rise buildings along the waterfront and in the newer east end of the city center. The city also possesses a myriad of parks and gardens, all combining to give Oslo the feeling of being far less urbanized than it truly is. Unlike Stockholm or Copenhagen, there are more single-family houses in Oslo than the other two larger capitals. The majority of the houses in Oslo, and for that matter in all of Norway, are constructed of wood siding, generally painted white. A front porch is commonplace and the houses are set in small, but impeccably landscaped lots that show how much Norwegians care about their homes. And it is this flavor rather than the proliferation of apartment blocks that lends the aura of being in a small city rather than a major capital. This illusion is especially noticeable after first visiting Copenhagen or Stockholm where the apartment block predominates.

Oslo summer weather is just about perfect with regard to temperatures that are in the 20's Celsius or upper 60's to mid 70's Fahrenheit. There are many rainy or cloudy and drizzly days, but around half the time the sky is blue and there is just a light breeze. However, winter weather can be cold, blustery with a mix of rain and snow. But there are no pleasure cruises at this time.

THE HISTORY OF OSLO: Oslo's heritage is that of the Vikings. Archaeological evidence shows that there were inhabitants in the area well before the end of the first millennium, yet Norse legend tells of the city having been founded in 1048 by King Harald Hardråe as a local trade center. So suffice it to say that Oslo is an old city. In 1261, King Håkon IV brought Norway to its golden age, forming a union with Iceland and Greenland. Oslo did not become the capital of the kingdom until the reign of King Håkon V (1299-1319). He is known to have been the first king to have actually taken up residence in the city, which was initially known as Christiana, later spelled Kristiana. The name was not changed to Oslo until 1925. To this day, the meaning of the name is unclear. It has been used as a boy's name but there is no single definition to its meaning. Several sources do say that it is taken from ancient Norse, and possibly means the meadow of the gods.

As Oslo grew in importance, its deep-water port closer to the interior heartland of the country with easier access first by road and later by rail slowly took away Bergen's significance as a port. And ultimately Bergen lost its role as the capital. Today Bergen is Norway's second city both in population and importance.

By the 14th century, Norway would be drawn into the Kalmar Union with Denmark. And in

1814, Norway became tributary to Sweden until 1905, thus the political significance of Oslo was far less important than that of Copenhagen or Stockholm. And this shows in the lack of many great stately buildings such as those found in the other two major Scandinavian capitals. The city was also primarily constructed of wood rather than stone or brick and it suffered numerous fires. The great 1624 fire actually caused the city to rebuild across the top end of the fjord where the city center is located today. The city rebuilt around Akershus Castle, which dates to the reign of King Haakon V who actually initially made Oslo the capital.

Akerhus Castle is adjacent to where cruise ships dock

There is a less pretentious air about Oslo, as it still maintains its small city flavor. In 1814, when Norway once again became an independent kingdom in personal union with Sweden, the city began to take on more the feeling of an important center with the development of many public buildings, but to this day, it never lost its lack of pretention. The Royal Palace was built in 1848 and the Storting (national parliament) was built in 1866, the two most prominent buildings in the city center.

In 1952, Oslo played host to the winter Olympic games. These were the first post-World War II winter games to be held. Norway was host to the 1994 winter Olympic games, held just north of Oslo in Lillehammer. This brought the focus of a lot of media attention to Oslo, as well as hundreds of thousands of visitors since the capital is also the major transport hub of the nation. Oslo was the city that Olympic athletes and visitors had to fly into, and then travel by train to Lillehammer. Despite its mountainous terrain, Norway does possess a significant railway system, and of course Oslo is the railroad hub of the country.

During World War II, Oslo became the seat of power for the puppet government under Nazi control. Freedom fighters were more active in sabotaging Nazi military installations rather than attacking many sites within the capital. But Nazi forces held a tight grip on the city, and its Jewish population, which was the largest in the country, was deported to concentration camps and few ever returned.

Since World War II, Norway has been considered one of the most peaceful and safest countries in Europe. But in summer 2011, a young Norwegian terrorist set off a large bomb in the government section of the city and then he opened fire on a group of young people at a summer camp on one of the islands in Oslofjord, killing 68 and wounding over 100. This was a catastrophic blow to national identity, as something like this could never have been anticipated in Norway. Fortunately there have been no further such homegrown terrorist acts committed in the country.

CRUISE DOCK IN OSLO: Depending upon your specific itinerary, your cruise may begin or terminate in Oslo or Copenhagen. Many Norwegian fjord cruises use Copenhagen as either their embarkation or termination port, often totally bypassing Oslo. The reason that Oslo is not always included is the result of its location. To enter or leave Oslo requires over three hours of sailing time into or out of Oslo Fjord whereas Copenhagen fronts on the Øresund, which is the main waterway connecting the Baltic Sea with the North Sea.

The vast majority of cruise ships dock alongside the western margin Akerhus Fortress, which is just steps from the very center of the city. Akerhus Fortress sits high above the water on a small peninsula that separates the beautiful Pipervika Harbor from the more commercial Rjervika Harbor on the eastern side of the fortress. There are very limited terminal facilities at either location. A third location is along the western edge of Pipervika Harbor at a dock
known as Filipstadveien, which also offers limited terminal facilities.

Despite having no grand cruise terminal, all three locations are just steps away from restaurants, coffee houses and the attractive city center. Thus no shuttle busses are needed. There is also adequate room at all three sites for tour coaches, taxis or private vehicles to drop off or pick up ship passengers.

HOTELS IN OSLO: If you are on a cruise that either embarks or terminates in Oslo, your cruise will not include any tours of the city. I strongly recommend that you plan to spend a minimum of one day, preferably two if possible, as this is a beautiful city worthy of your time. There are so many excellent sights to take in and its overall atmosphere represents the best of the urban lifestyle in Norway. To this end, I am recommending the following hotels as premier accommodation, offering the top level of comfort and elegance:

Along the Oslo waterfront in Pipervika

The Grand Hotel on Karl Johan Gate

* **Grand Hotel Oslo** - Located in the heart of the city on Karl Johanes Gate #31, this is the most famous and venerated hotel in the city, similar to that of the Grand Hotel Stockholm. It is an expensive hotel, but you must keep in mind that it offers all the five-star amenities one would expect. The hotel offers outstanding dining, room service, spa, fitness center and concierge services. It has always been my choice when staying in Oslo. I rate it *****

Seafood buffet at the Grand Hotel Oslo

* **Hotel Continental** - In the city center at Stortinsgata #24-26, this is a five-star property, but smaller than the Grand Hotel. It offers the same quality of dining with breakfast included in the room tariff. All the services one expects from a premier hotel are provided. The room rates are higher than most other hotels, but you must keep in mind this is based upon the quality of overall services offered.

* **The Thief** - This is another five-star hotel, but one that is quite modern in its overall decor. It is more of a boutique property with only 118 rooms and suites, located at Landgangen #1. The room tariff includes full breakfast. The hotel offers fine dining, a business center, indoor pool, concierge service and airport transportation. Its location in Aker Brygge is one of the most popular sections of the city for restaurants, bistros and clubs. This could be considered as the most "hip" part of Oslo for those into nightlife.

* **Thon Hotel Rosenkrantz** - Located in the city center at Rosenkrantz # 1, the hotel is right in the heart of all the major sightseeing and dining venues within a short walk of the

front door. This is a four-star property with rates that are slightly lower than the five-star properties noted above. Breakfast is included in the room tariff. The hotel offers fine dining, a fitness center and gym, full business center.

SIGHTSEEING IN THE CITY OF OSLO: When cruise ships are in port, their shore arrangements include city tours of Oslo, visiting many of the highlights. But if you choose to see the city on your own, you will find that public transport is quite good. Within the central part of the city there are numerous tramlines, and conductors can easily direct you to where you want to go since English is widely spoken. There is also an extensive commuter rail network that you can utilize to visit those few important venues that are out beyond the central city, especially the major Olympic ski jump facility in the hills above the city.

* **SIGHTSEEING OPTIONS:** There are numerous options for seeing the sights of Oslo from group tours to private touring. The options available include:

** **Ship sponsored tours** – If your itinerary calls for a port visit and Oslo is not the embarkation or terminal destination for your cruise, there will be a variety of motor coach and walking tours offered by the ship's tour desk. These are group tours, which do not enable you to pick the specific sights or schedule, but these excursions do give you a good view of the city and its lifestyle.

** **Private car and driver/guide** – If your itinerary includes a port visit to Oslo and the city is not the starting or terminal destination, you can have the shore excursion desk arrange for you to have a private car and driver/guide. I always prefer this option as it enables you to set your own pace and see what is of greatest interest to you. This type of more expensive touring gives you total control of your activities. To possibly save some money, you can go directly to other tour operators, but be warned that if at the time of sailing you have not returned, the cruise ship has no obligation to wait for you. Here are three reliable private tour operators you may wish to check for price and services: *www.getyourguide.com//*

*** Tours by Locals is a most reliable source and will tailor a tour to your taste and interest. Visit them at *www.toursbylocals.com/Oslo-Tours* for full details.

*** 8rental is a good source for private touring. Visit their web pages to learn about their services at *www.8rental.com/chauffeur-service-oslo* .

*** Blacklane is a very responsible company located throughout Scandinavia. For their services in Oslo visit them at *www.blacklane.com/chauffeur-service-oslo* .

** **Hop on hop off bus service** – There is a good hop on hop off bus service in Oslo that enables you to board right at the waterfront steps away from the cruise ship and then tour the city with numerous stops at all of the major highlights. Visit their web page at *www.getyourguide.com/Oslo/HopOnHopOff* .

** **Taxi touring** – There will be taxis at the dock and you can check with the drivers to see what rates they are offering for sightseeing by the hour. The major company is Oslo Taxi and you can check their web page at *www.oslotaxi.no* for specific details.

** **Public transit** – Oslo has a well-integrated system of bus routes, a Metro known as the T-Bane, commuter rail and ferryboats. For a good overview of all the services available check out Life in Norway at *www.lifeinnorway.net/public-transport-in-oslo* for full details.

** **Walking** is very pleasant, especially around the waterfront and through the city center, but you will miss many of the special venues that are beyond walking distance

* **MAJOR SIGHTS TO SEE:** Although Oslo is a comparatively small city as seen on the maps in this chapter, it is filled with wonderful museums, galleries and parks. Being compact makes getting around easier than in some of the larger cities of the Baltic Sea region. Most of the city's main attractions are close to the waterfront around which the central downtown is built. Many of the important landmarks of Oslo include:

** **Aker Brygge** – the city's main central square, which faces the quay and the busy harbor. The way Oslo's downtown area radiates out from the harbor; it shows the importance of the docks to the city's overall economic well-being. Today many modern apartment and condominium blocks have spread out along the waterfront from the main square. There are also many restaurants and bistros making this a very lively district at night. It has become very popular both with locals and visitors alike.

The cruise ship dock areas are all very much a part of Aker-Brygge, which means that you are in the heart of the city when you leave the ship.

Rush hour on the T-Bane, the Oslo Metro

A portion of Akershus Castle

** **Akershus** Castle – the great fortress palace that once defended Oslo. It dates to the days when warfare was a major fact of life. Most cruise ships dock along the waterfront right at the base of the fortress, making it an easy venue to visit either at the start or end of the day's activities. The castle is open daily from 6 AM to 9 PM, located right on the waterfront overlooking where cruise ships dock.

** **Domkirke** – the major cathedral of Oslo. Like all of Scandinavia, Norway is distinctly a Protestant country, primary Lutheran. As a Lutheran Cathedral you will not find the ornate décor that is so commonplace across Europe where the Catholic faith has been predominant. Lutherns believe in simplicity of design and decoration. Visitors are welcome except on days when there are special events or services, but no hours are posted.

** **Fram Polar Ship Museum** - This museum contains a major ice breaking exploration vessel and exhibits honoring Norway's polar explorations. Norway has been one of the world leaders in polar exploration given that a large portion of their country lies beyond the Arctic Circle. The address is Bygdøynesveien # 39. During the summer season the museum is open from 10 AM to 6 PM daily.

** **Holmenkollen Ski Jump and Museum** - Located in the hills above the city, accessed by train from the city's main station. this is a must see venue. The Olympic ski jump is dramatic to view from up close. On a clear day, the view from Holmenkollen is magnificent. And the ski jump is one of the world's best known. You will be able to see Holmenkollen from the ship when entering the harbor. It can be reached from Central Station commuter train to Kongeveien, a journey of 25 minutes. It is open between 10 AM and 4 PM daily.

The skyline of Oslo seen from Holmenkollen Ski Jump

Karl Johan Gate is the main shopping street

** Karl Johan Gate - **This grand boulevard runs from the heart of the city's shopping district past the Norwegian Parliament to Oslo University and the Royal Palace. The park along the west side of the street has a large outdoor cafe that is a popular spot for a cold drink or snack. It is a welcomed addition to the downtown Oslo environment.**

The famous Kon Tiki raft of Thor Heyerdahl

- ** **Kon Tiki Museum** – This museum is dedicated to the famous anthropologist Thor Heyerdahl, and this museum features vessels from his famous expedition in 1947. More on this important expedition is noted at the end of the list of attractions in Oslo. The address is Bygdøynesveien 36, reached by ferry every 20 minutes from the city hall pier. During summer the museum is open from 9:30 AM to 6 PM daily.

** **Museum of Norwegian Resistance** - For anyone with an interest in the role of the underground opposition to Nazi rule during World War II, this museum should be on your list. It is not well known, but it does document the role of the resistance fighters. The address is Bygning #21. It is open between 11 AM and 4 PM daily.

** **National Museum and National Gallery** - Here you will find a good assortment of exhibits on Norwegian culture and art. Among the works of art is the world famous, but controversial painting by Edvard Munch entitled "The Scream. The museum is located at Universitetgate # 13 and is open from 10 AM to 6 PM Monday thru Wednesday, extended to 7 PM and open from 11 AM to 5 PM on weekends. Thursday and Friday The gallery is at Bankplassen # 3 and open from 11 AM to 5 PM weekdays and Noon to 5 PM on weekends.

** **Norwegian Folk Museum** - Here you can learn about the folk culture and arts and crafts of the Norwegian people. Much of the museum is open air and gives you the feel of walking through a traditional village. The museum is located at Museumsveien # 10 in the district of Bygdøy and is open from 10 AM to 6 PM daily during summer. It can be reached by ferry from the waterfront opposite the Rådhusto the dock at Dronning.

** **Peninsula of Bygdøy** - site of the most fashionable residences of Oslo. If you are on your own, I suggest simply walking around and just soaking in the atmosphere. There are many fashionable restaurants and bistros and the district is home to several museum venues. You can reach the peninsula by ferry from the waterfront opposite the city hall.

** **Rådhus** – the brick city hall, which dominates the heart of Oslo. Red brick is a popular building material throughout Scandinavia, since quarried stone is difficult to obtain. The building is open daily from 9 AM to 4 PM and guided tours are offered for groups of 30 or more if pre booked. The building stands along the waterfront and is the most dominant structure on the downtown skyline.

The Royal Palace of Norway

** **Royal Palace** – This is the home to the King of Norway. There is a changing of the guard at midday and the palace gardens are open to the public. During summer guided tours are offered to the public. Tours in English are offered at Noon, 2 PM, 2:20 PM and 4 PM daily. The public entrance is off Slottsgården on the west side of the building. The palace sits at the upper end of Karl Johanes Gate.

** **Stortorvet** – the city's bustling market area, offering the visitor a glimpse into the rich diversity of seafood and produce. It is located at Stortorvet # 1 near the main cathedral and is open daily between 9 AM and 6 PM.

** **Stovnertårnet** – This is a new observation pathway of unique design to view the city if it is a clear day. And in autumn, the surrounding trees are ablaze in full color. The pathway is 260 meters long and winds its way to a magnificent crest overlooking the city. The lookout can be accessed via the subway on lines 4 and 5 to Stovner and then the start of the walk is a short distance from the subway stop.

Frogner Park and the Vigeland Sculpture Gardens (Work of Nick from Bristol, CC BY SA 2.0, Wikimedia.org)

****Vigeland Museum** - Adjacent to Frogner Park, this museum contains many of Vigeland's drawings and some of his marble sculptures. The museum is open Tuesday thru Sunday from Noon to 4 PM and is located at Nobeisgate # 32.

** **Vigeland Sculpture Park** – one of the city's major attractions with outdoor sculpture set amid lush greenery. Also known as Frognerparken, this massive park features hundreds of dramatic statues created by the master sculptor Gustav Vigeland. His view of mankind and its place in the world is quite distinctive and has won acclaim from art critics everywhere. The human figures depicted tell Vigeland's story of mankind, and you will either find that you can relate to his message or that you find it to be rather morose. There is little middle ground when it comes to the Vigeland Sculpture Park and how people react to it. The park is open 24-hours daily and is free to the public. It is easily reached by T-Banne traveling west from the city center to Majorstuen Station. The walk to the entrance into sculpture park will take only about five minutes

Frognerparken covers expansive grounds including the Viegland Sculpture Garden

** Viking Ship Museum** - This may be a small museum, but it does have several well-preserved examples of early Viking ships and other artifacts to help explain these energetic explorers. The museum is open between the hours of 10 AM and 4 PM daily and is located on the Bygdøy Peninsula at Huk Aveny # 35.

As you can see, Oslo is a city of museums. There is something for almost every taste, and I have not identified all of the museums. The most famous of the museums for those who were young when Thor Hyerdahl sailed in his flimsy raft from Peru to French Polynesia, proving a possible link between the two, a visit to the Kon Tiki Museum is an absolute must because it enables you to see Thor Heyerdahl's original raft, the Kon Tiki, that he sailed from Peru to French Polynesia in the mid 1900's.

Oslo is also a city of beautiful architecture, especially in the central portion where many of the older public buildings date back to the 18th and 19th centuries, reflecting a strong Swedish influence since Norway was joined to Sweden until the first decade of the 20th century. Residential Oslo has a more rural feel, as there is a high percentage of single family homes mostly constructed of wood, especially at the end of the 19th century. They exhibit a quaint and yet warm atmosphere, that more of a town than a major city. And Norwegians beautifully landscape their properties.

The old and new blend together in central Oslo

DINING IN OSLO: Norwegian cuisine is heavily oriented toward seafood. Atlantic salmon is one of the country's great delicacies. One distinct Norwegian treat is gravlax. It is salmon that has been rubbed with sugar and dill, giving it a very distinct flavor through the way it is cured. Also on the menu is herring, an essential staple in the Norwegian diet, as are the very crisp flat breads made from rye flour. Gravlox and herring are often eaten on these flat breads, topped with a piece of cheese. Fiskeboller is my favorite hot entree. It is made with chopped fish bound together with egg and breadcrumbs and then poached in fish broth. Fiskeboller can be served either hot or chilled. And poached salmon served with boiled potatoes and butter sauce is a basic staple during the summer months.

One Norwegian food item that many of us from the rest of the world may find difficult to accept is whale meat. I have tasted it by accident as part of a traditional buffet. It was prepared similar to meatballs. But when I tasted it and discovered that it was whale, I could not bring myself to eat it on general principle in that I believe whales are too magnificent to be slaughtered for food. But I must admit from the one bite I inadvertently tasted, it was very tender and flavorful, so I can understand why it is a popular food item. Essentially the much of the food of Norway is very similar to that of Sweden, but with a bit more emphasis placed upon seafood and of course the addition of whale meat. And as is true throughout Scandinavia, rich pastries and ice creams are a definite part of the

Norwegian dessert menu.

I am only going to recommend a few dining establishments that specialize in traditional Norwegian cuisine based upon my personal experiences. My friends and relatives all chide me about being a food "snob." That may be true, but I simply like dining at restaurants that offer the very best in quality and service. And in foreign countries I like to find excellent restaurants that offer the taste of that country. For Oslo I have these recommendations:

Poached salmon, boiled potatoes and cucumber salad at the Grand Hotel

* Grand Hotel Oslo - truly a grand hotel in every way, this venerable establishment is the city's number one hotel and it offers several world-class restaurants. For those on a cruise that will not be staying through the evening, I recommend the Grand Cafe, which faces out onto Karl Johan Gate. You have your choice of menu service or a buffet of delicious and traditional open face sandwiches. And when it comes to dessert, they offer a fantastic dessert buffet that will delight any sweet tooth. The cafe serves lunch and dinner. For a more elegant atmosphere, try Palmen, the main dining room for lunch or dinner. The cuisine is Norwegian and based upon the freshest ingredients of the season. Lunch, afternoon tea and dinner are served. The Grand Hotel is located on Karl Johan Gate opposite Parliament. Reservations are advised for dinner. It is best to have your ship or hotel concierge make the booking.

* Hos Thea - one of the finest restaurants in Oslo, specializing in Scandinavian dishes as well as cuisine from other parts of northern Europe. Hos Thea is elegant and the service is impeccable. However, unless your ship is staying late you may not be able to dine here, as they are only open from 5 to 11 PM for dinner. Located at Gabelsgate 11 in central Oslo. Have your ship or hotel concierge reserve a table for you.

* **Maaemo** - Located at Schweigaards gate # 15B, in the city center, this is truly one of the finest dining establishments in Oslo. It is elegant and expensive, but five-star quality food and service make it worthwhile. The traditional Scandinavian menu features a variety of meats, poultry and seafood all beautifully presented. Hours for dinner are Tuesday thru Friday 6 PM to 1 AM, Saturday 11 AM to 3 PM for lunch and 6:30 PM to 1 AM for dinner. Have your ship or hotel concierge call for reservations.

* **Fjord Restaurant** - In the city center at Kristian Augusts gate # 11, this is a very popular restaurant with a truly Scandinavian menu that is heavily oriented toward seafood. Their dishes are beautifully prepared and served in a warm, friendly atmosphere. They are open only for dinner between 5 and 11:30 PM Tuesday thru Saturday. But most cruise ships depart in the evening, so dinner is possible for many of you. Reservations are advised for dinner and the ship or hotel concierge can handle it for you.

* **Statholdergaarden** - A restaurant with 200 years of history located in an old house with nearly 400 years of antiquity, the atmosphere is superb, romantic for those who have that taste in mind. And the food is outstanding; once again they specialize in Scandinavian cuisine. Located in the central city at Radhusgata 11, and only open from 6 PM to Midnight for dinner. Ask your ship or hotel concierge to reserve a table for you.

* **VulkanFisk** - Located at Vulkan #5 in the district of Mathallen, this is a superb seafood restaurant featuring a broad menu of traditional Norwegian dishes all beautifully prepared. You will need to take a taxi to reach the restaurant, as it is too far northeast of the city center to walk. It is open Tuesday thru Thursday from 10 AM to 9 PM, Friday and Saturday from 10 AM to 10 PM and Sunday from 11 AM to 7 PM. They are known for their fabulous fish soup. And yes, as in so many seafood restaurants they do serve whale. A reservation is advised and your ship or hotel concierge can handle it for you.

SHOPPING IN OSLO: Oslo is an expensive city in which both to dine and shop. Norway has one of the world's highest standards of living and oil revenues have added to the overall expense of living in or touring the country. There are several shopping venues in Oslo, but North Americans in particular will find the costs quite high. Apart from the normal tourist kitsch, there are fine quality woolens, hand knitted sweaters and very excellent quality Scandinavian made clothing, but you will pay top Kroner. When I first started to visit Scandinavia every summer, I did not pay much attention to shopping, as few men do. But one summer I noticed that in all the cities there were major July sales. That year I bought several pair of Swedish and Danish made jeans and sport shirts. I was so pleased with the quality and style that now each summer when I am in Scandinavia, I make shopping for clothes a major activity. For men the Scandinavian brands such as Sand, Tiger, J. Lindberg and Johansen are outstanding and well worth the expense. Sorry I do not have any experience with women's clothing, but I have noticed that Scandinavian women always appear to be stylish and well dressed. I do know that Sand and J. Lindberg also produce a line of very stylish women's casual clothing. The major shopping venues are:

Saturday street life in central Oslo's shopping district

* **Eger Karl Johan** - a smaller, but very fashionable store offering clothing and accessories with an emphasis upon Scandinavian brands. It is located on Karl Johan Gate 23. Hours are from 10 AM to 7 PM Monday thru Wednesday and Friday, and from 10 AM to 8 PM Thursday. Saturday hours are from 10 AM to 6 PM.

* **Glas Magasinet** - the largest and oldest department store in central Oslo, this beautiful store offers a broad variety of merchandise. It also offers a department featuring traditional Norwegian handicrafts. It is located at Stortorvet 9 in the city center. Hours are from 10 AM to 7 PM weekdays and from 10 AM to 6 PM Saturday.

* **Karl Johan Gate** - This is the main shopping street, especially south of the Parliament.
* **Oslo City Shopping Center** - located opposite the central railway station at Stenersgaten 1, this is a collection of fashionable, but pricey shops. Hours are from 10 AM to 9 PM weekdays and 10 AM to 8 PM Saturday.

* **Steen and Strøm Magasin** - this is Oslo's other major department store that offers many fashionable Scandinavian brands for both men and women. It is located on Nedre Slottsgate 8 in the city center. Hours are from 10 AM to 7 PM weekdays and 10 AM to 6

PM Saturday.

Looking from the deck of a cruise ship at the Rådhus (city hall) dominating the central skyline with the shopping district just to the right

An

example of a typical small Norwegian wood house in Oslo

FINAL WORDS: Although Oslo is one of the smaller capitals of Scandinavia, it is a city that is rich in history, strong on pride and especially beautiful in a rather laid back manner. There are no grand boulevards or imposing monumental buildings, as is true in Stockholm. What Oslo lacks in grandeur it makes up for in charm.

It is quite easy for visitors to negotiate getting around Oslo on foot, using taxis and the local transportation. Most streetcar and bus drivers do speak sufficient English to be able to help guests from other countries.

The cruise in and out of Oslo along its long fjord is very picturesque and is in itself a part of your visit, so if the weather is good, it pays to remain out on deck and watch the countryside and villages as they pass.

The shoreline of Oslo passes, as the ship sails down Oslofjorden

OSLO CITY MAPS

MAP OF CENTRAL OSLO

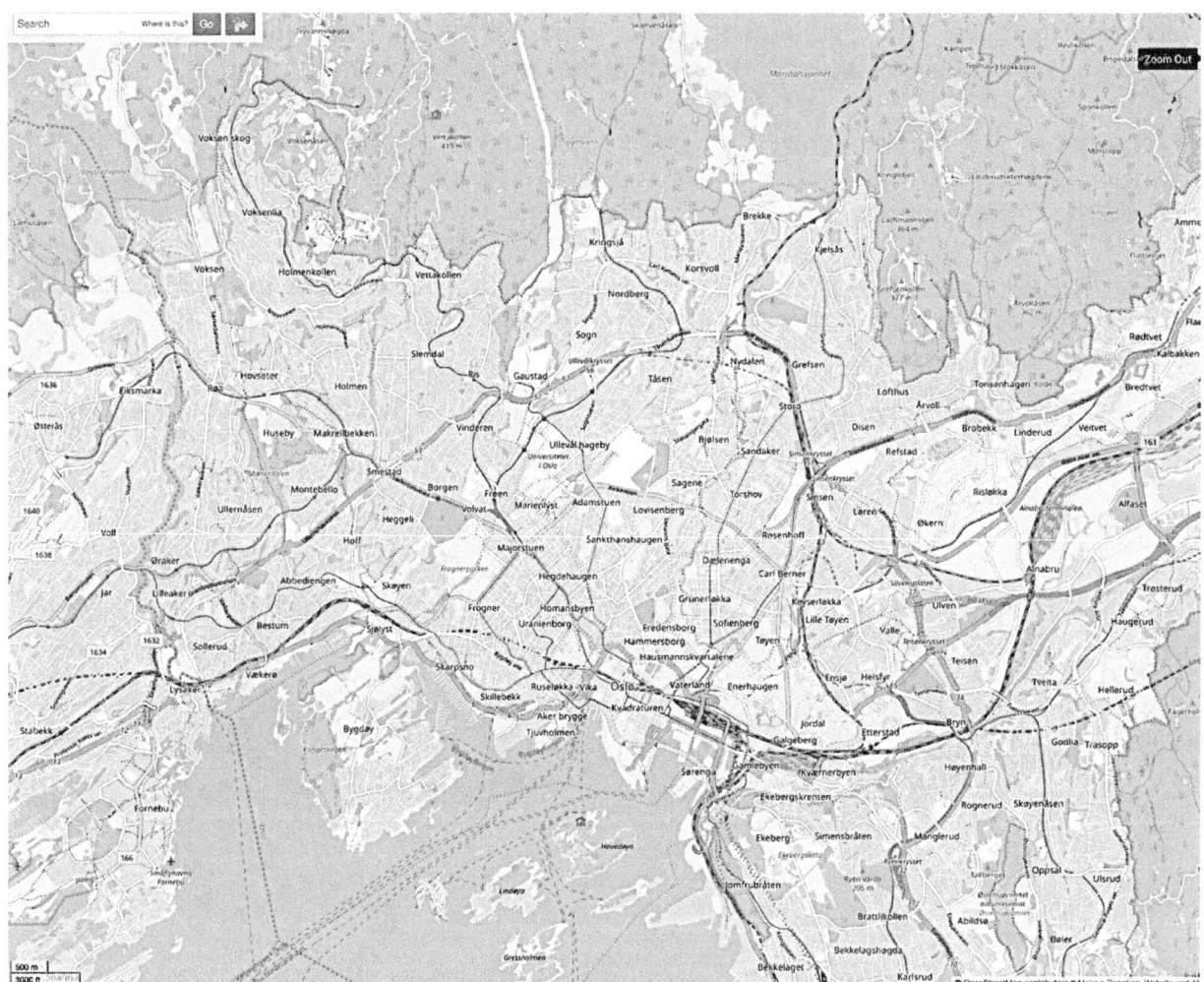

Central Oslo, (© OpenStreetMap contributors)

This map is best viewed directly from OpenStreetMap.com on your personal device where it can be expanded or one specific area can be enlarged. Given the format of this book, it is impossible to display maps with the level of detail you might wish to have while actually out exploring the city. But the OpenStreetMap maps used directly are the tool I always rely upon.

MAP OF THE INNER CITY OF OSLO

**The inner city of Oslo with stars showing cruise ship docks,
(© OpenStreetMap contributors)**

This map is best viewed directly from OpenStreetMap.com on your personal device where it can be expanded or one specific area can be enlarged. Given the format of this book, it is impossible to display maps with the level of detail you might wish to have while actually out exploring the city. But the OpenStreetMap maps used directly are the tool I always rely upon.

MAP OF CENTRAL OSLO

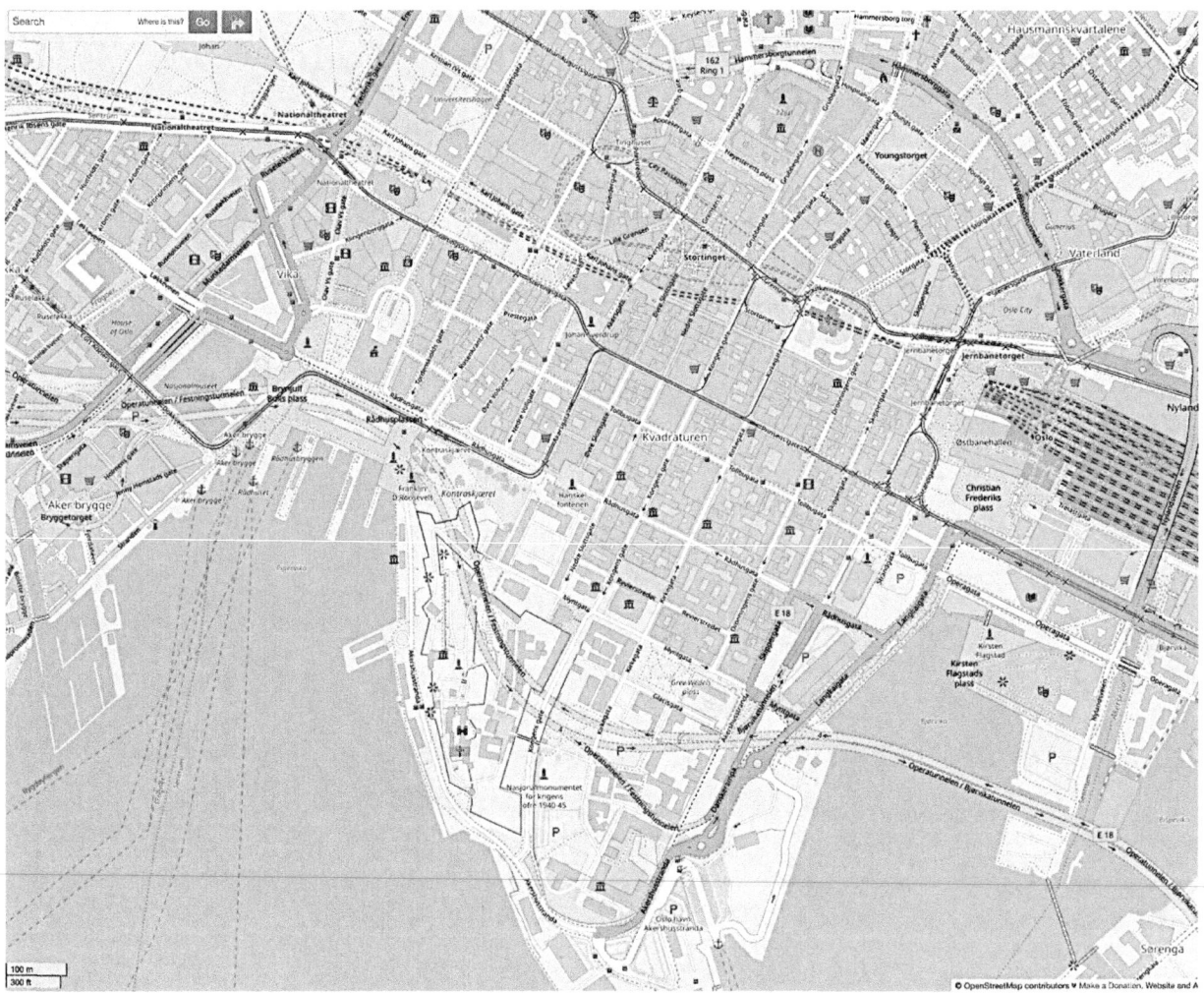

Central Oslo, (© OpenStreetMap contributors)

This map is best viewed directly from OpenStreetMap.com on your personal device where it can be expanded or one specific area can be enlarged. Given the format of this book, it is impossible to display maps with the level of detail you might wish to have while actually out exploring the city. But the OpenStreetMap maps used directly are the tool I always rely upon.

MAP OF VIGELAND SCULPTURE GARDEN AREA

Vigeland Sculpture Garden area

This map is best viewed directly from OpenStreetMap.com on your personal device where it can be expanded or one specific area can be enlarged. Given the format of this book, it is impossible to display maps with the level of detail you might wish to have while actually out exploring the city. But the OpenStreetMap maps used directly are the tool I always rely upon.

HOLMENKOLLEN SKI AREA

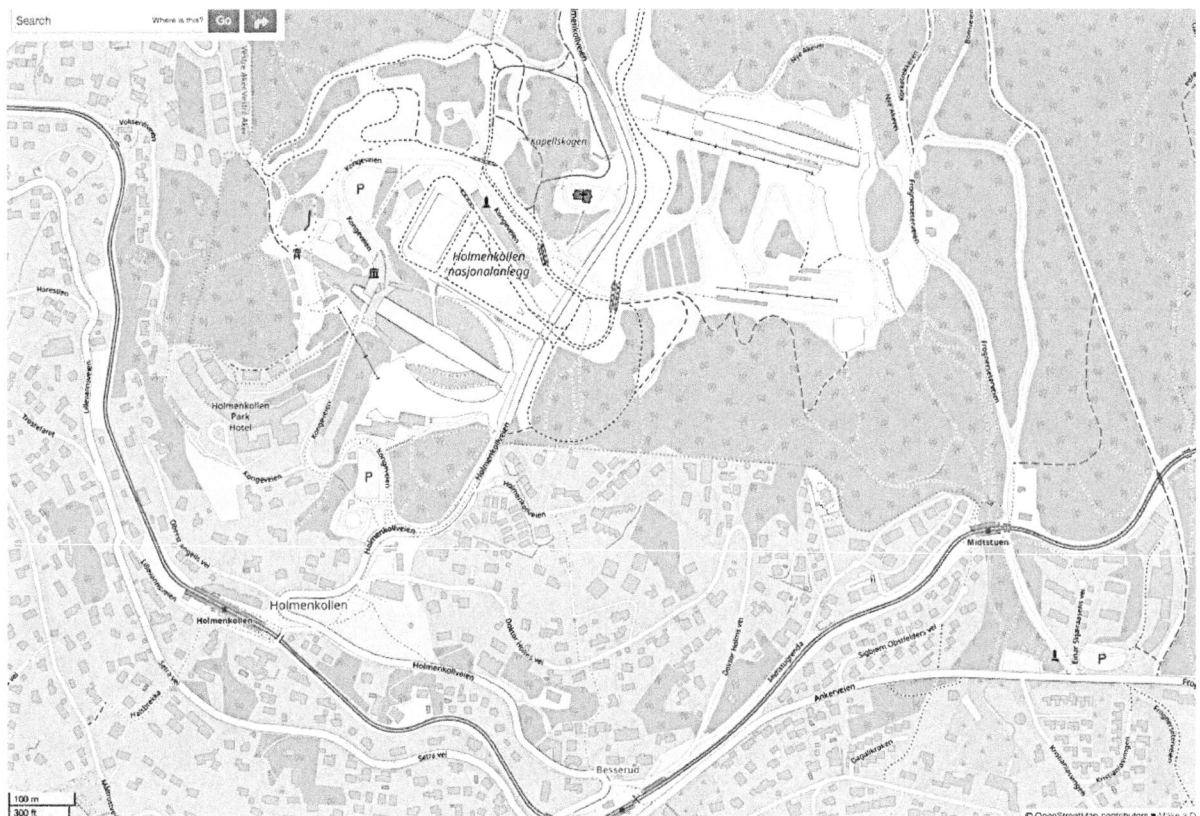

Holmenkollen ski area

This map is best viewed directly from OpenStreetMap.com on your personal device where it can be expanded or one specific area can be enlarged. Given the format of this book, it is impossible to display maps with the level of detail you might wish to have while actually out exploring the city. But the OpenStreetMap maps used directly are the tool I always rely upon.

STAVANGER

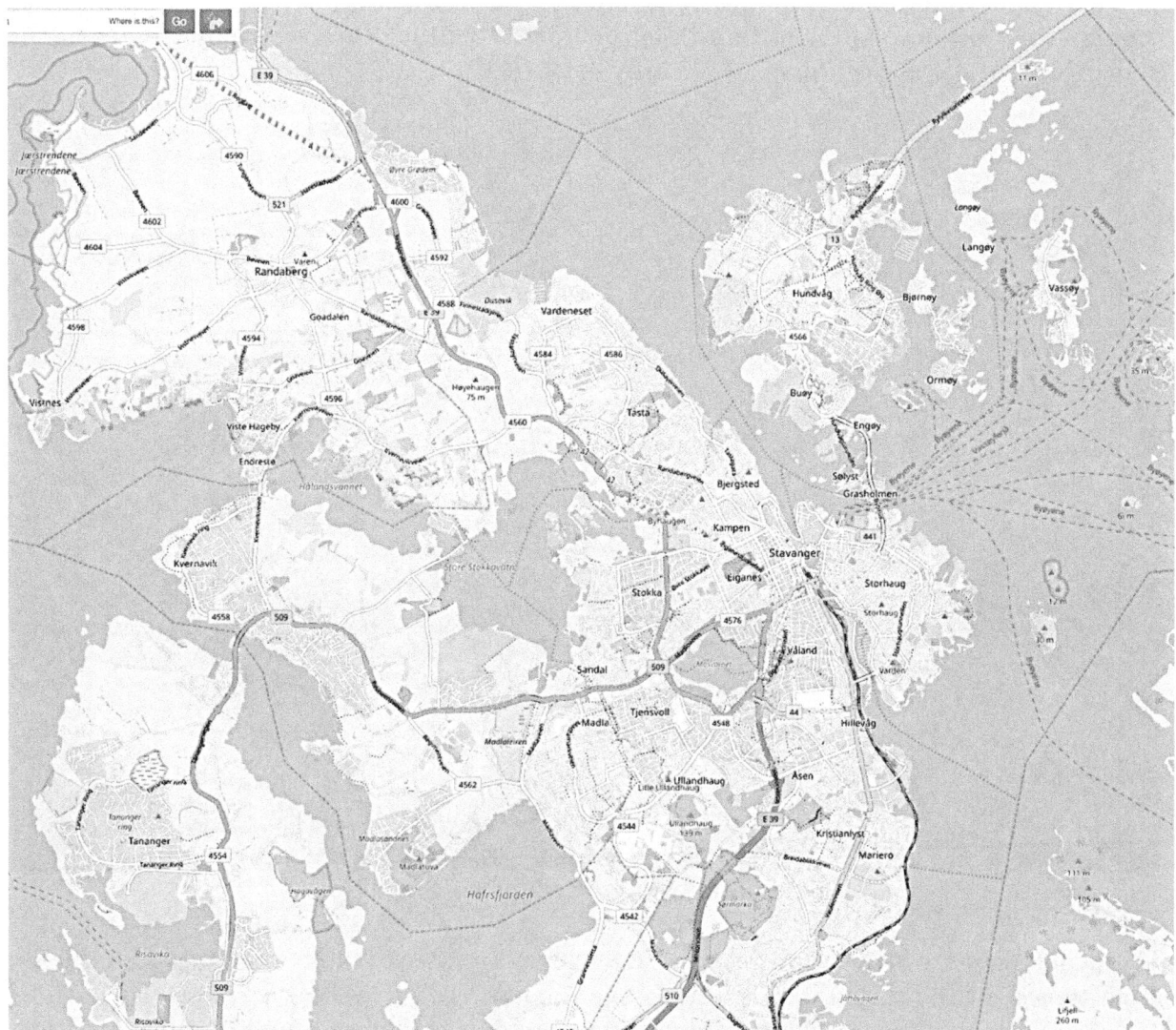

The greater Stavanger region. (© OpenStreetMap contributors)

THE CITY'S GEOGRAPHIC SITE: Stavanger is the fourth largest city in Norway with a current metropolitan population of approximately 300,000. Until recently, it was the third largest city in the country, but it has been slightly overtaken by the city of Trondheim whose local residents are very proud of their new ranking much to the dismay of Stavanger residents. There tends to be a healthy rivalry between the two cities.

The city is located on the west coast of Norway, facing to the storm prone North Sea in the southern part of the country. Stavanger sits on the more sheltered leeward side of a large peninsula that faces out into the North Sea. On the eastern side is the wide bay called Boknafjorden. This is essentially an outlet bay that was initially deepened by the coalescing of several smaller glaciers as they reached what was thousands of years back a lower sea level. The land is relatively low and gently rolling, the result more of glacial deposits rather than scour. And the region is also quite beautifully forested, the wooded areas interspersed with farmland that has been meticulously tended over the centuries. The magnificent fjord country that visitors expect to find in every port of call in Norway is found adjacent to Stavanger, but not in the immediate vicinity of the city.

A high altitude aerial flying over Stavanger

The peninsula on which the city is built does have a somewhat hilly and rocky character, often typical of the mixed debris having been deposited during the periods of glaciation. There are also numerous offshore islands that represent portions of the mainland cut off by the coming together of many glaciers before reaching the sea.

The climate is typical of the maritime coast of all southern Norway. There are few winter days with temperatures below freezing, but rather hovering in the low ranges combined with much rainfall to create a chilly, rainy environment. Summers are very mild and daytime high temperatures are in the 20's Celsius or upper 60's to mid 70's Fahrenheit, and rainfall is also prevalent throughout the so-called warmer season. Yet surprisingly this is a productive region agriculturally because of the longer daylight hours combined with mild temperatures and plenty of precipitation. The southern coastal region is not known for many days when you will find blue skies and brilliant sunshine. But on those rare days, the landscape definitely has an added sparkle to it.

Not that many cruise itineraries visit Stavanger, and if you happen to be on a cruise that will be including this major city, do not hold great expectations for a blue-sky day, as they are relatively rare. This same condition will also hold true in Bergen where rainy days predominate. The southwest coast of Norway is one of the wettest parts of the country with there being more rainy days than sunny throughout the year. But it is all this rain that gives the region its lush, green landscape.

An aerial of the Stavanger city center, (Work of EN:USER:GODZTISN,CC BY CC BY SA 3.0, Wikimedia.org)

SETTLEMENT OF STAVANGER: The area around Stavanger has a long history of settlement even predating the history of the Vikings. There is actual evidence of the town dating back to the 11th century, having become an important market center and seat of church activity once Christianity was established in southern Norway.

The official date of founding is the year 1125 when the beautiful Stavanger Cathedral was completed and the first bishop came to serve the area. But the community existed well before its official founding It remained an important center of religious administration until the Protestant Reformation. In the early years of the 17th century, the bishop relocated to Kristiansand, and Stavanger then came to rely upon its local market role combined with the addition of the herring fishing fleet by the 19th century.

During World War II, the airport at Stavanger was bombed early in the morning of April 9, 1940, destroying the small Norwegian air contingent based there to protect this coastal region of the country. Within hours the Germans landed troops and supplies, the start of making this an important base of operation because of its strategic position facing out to the major sea traffic lane north to Murmansk in the Soviet Union. One of the most distinctive aspects of the German occupation of Stavanger was that in 1945 after the surrender, German soldiers were required by Norway to remain and remove all of the thousands of landmines that had been laid during the war.

When the Norwegians began to exploit their offshore oil reserves in the 1960's, it was recognized that Stavanger had two advantages, namely its large and deep harbor and secondly its proximity to the developing oil reserves, which were west and southwest of the city. As oil exploration expanded, other centers such as Haugesund, Bergen and Kristiansund also became important service centers for the oil drilling platforms. But Stavanger was the first, and it is still vital to the petroleum production industry. However, the decline in oil prices and the essential overproduction has caused a major degree of disruption to the industry. This has also caused the population growth rate and the overall economic output of the city to stagnate. And this is of course to the delight of the people of Trondheim, allowing that city to gain the edge in that ongoing race to determine which is the country's third largest city.

Stavanger is quite hilly, (Work of Jerzystrzelcki, CC BYSA 3.0, Wikimedia.org)

THE CITY TODAY: Until recently, Stavanger was able to boast that it was the third largest city in Norway after Oslo and Bergen. It presently has a metropolitan area population of 319,000, but its city population is approximately 127,000. Trondheim is shown to have a city population of 176,000. But metropolitan Trondheim is still slightly below that of Stavanger according to most Norwegian sources. So in that ongoing race, the people of Stavanger still claim they are the third largest based upon metropolitan population.

As one of the oldest cities in Norway, there is a good degree of historic architecture, especially in the old town area. Although this was a well settled region during Viking times, as with all major Norwegian cities and towns, the emphasis architecturally is upon those elements of northern European tradition that were infused into the country with the coming of early Christian priests and merchant traders.

Typical wood houses of Stavanger. (Work of Holger Uwe Schmitt, CC BY SA 4.0, Wikimedia.org)

Stavanger sprawls along the water and into the hills behind the old city center. There is urban development on several of the small adjacent islands, connected to the central city by a network of small ferryboats. Most of Stavanger's residential districts are built of wood, a common building material in much of Norway because of the abundance of forests and the development of a forest industry. And the majority of the city's thousands of houses are painted white. Brick and stone tend to be reserved for public and commercial buildings rather than for individual homes.

Central Stavanger, (Work of Michael Spiller, CC BY SA 2.0, Wikimedia.org)

Today there are many modern moderately tall apartment blocks lining the waterfront and the city center does possess a few contemporary skyscrapers, but nothing that would be exceptionally tall. Remember that this is a small urban center by overall European standards. Norwegian cities do not exhibit many high rise buildings, especially outside of their central district. This is a country that still favors a more open plan for its cities given the small population of the nation.

CRUISE SHIP DOCK IN STAVANGER: When studying the map of Stavanger you will notice that there is a small cove between the modern city center and the more historic older city. It is along the western edge of this cove that there is a long dock capable of supporting two medium to large cruise ships. There is no terminal building simply because it is not needed. This location is essentially in the heart of the city just a very short walk to the center of Stavanger. Therefore no shuttle bus is needed to ferry guests to and from the ship. There is room alongside the ship for motor coaches, private vehicles and taxis to meet guests.

Old Town Stavanger, (Work of Zairon, CC BY SA 3.0, Wikimedia.org)

TOURING OPTIONS FOR STAVANGER: There are several options open to ship guests when touring Stavanger. These options include:

* **Ship sponsored tours** – Your cruise line will offer a variety of tours in and around the city of Stavanger, the majority being via motor coach and lasting anywhere from half day to full day, which generally includes a preset lunch.

* **Private car and driver/guide** – This option is more expensive but it gives you the freedom to see what interests you the most and at your own pace. The shore excursion desk on board can arrange for your private touring. But to possibly save some money you may wish to independently consider booking with the one service noted below:

** SVG is one of the very few limousine services in Stavanger that can offer a car and driver for private touring. Check their web page at _www.limos.com/airports/Norway/SVG_.

* Hop on hop off bus service is available in Stavanger. For details as to the nature of the service, routes, stops and cost for touring around the city you need to visit on line at _www.stroma.com/en-no/Stavanger/sightseeing/hop-on-hop-off_.

* **Taxi service** – There will be taxis waiting at the dock. You can ask about the charges for hourly or full day sightseeing. You can also go on line to the major taxi service to book in advance at *www.visitnorway.com/listings/stavanger-taxi* .

The traditional wood architecture of Old Norway, (Work of Ben Bender, CC BY SA 3.0, Wikimedia.org)

* **Public bus service** in Stavanger is another option. You will find that the city bus service covers most sites you may wish to visit. Check their web page, which is in English, found at *www.no* for details.

* **Walking** is an option for those who do not wish to do any extensive sightseeing but who still want to get a feel for the city. From the dock you can easily explore the downtown area and the historic older part of Stavanger on your own.

WHAT TO SEE AND DO IN STAVANGER: As a visitor off of a cruise ship, there are many interesting sights in Stavanger, and of course most cruise lines have a variety of tours planned. I personally prefer to get out on my own, but that is because I have been to Norway around 20 times in the last ten years. If this is your first cruise through the fjords, then of course a tour in a small city like Stavanger will enable you to see all the major sights either in the city or the surrounding countryside, depending upon your preference.

Here is my listing of the major sites worth your time while sightseeing within the city. And this is followed by the major locales outside of the city that can be visited within less than the usual six to eight hours that most cruise ships allow for Stavanger.

* **Museum of Archaeology** is located southwest of the city center, actually not too far south of the Cathedral. It is at Pedre Klowsgate #30-A and is also open only from 11 AM to 3 PM. Here you will find a good collection of artifacts and exhibits that portray the end of the glacial era along with the earliest evidence of human occupancy prior to the Viking culture. The museum also has a small cafe for quick meals.

* **Norwegian Canning Museum** - This museum presents the history of fishing for commercial canning and its role in the development of Stavanger. It is located along the narrow old harbor just north of the Old Town area at Oevre Strabdgate #88. It has limited hours between 10 AM and 4 PM daily.

In the heart of the older commercial center of Stavanger. (Work of Christian Bickel, CC BY SA 2.0, Wikimedia.org)

* Old Town Stavanger - The old sector of the city with its tightly packed whitewashed wood houses lining narrow streets so typifies the older cities found along the Atlantic coast of the country. There are also many small shops and restaurants that have opened in the old sector because this has become a focus of cruise tourism because of its proximity to the waterfront. Many of the streets are now reserved only for pedestrians, but some are rather steep since much of the Old Town climbs the adjacent hills, which typify so much of the urban landscape. There are many words to describe the old sector such as quaint, picturesque, romantic or even fairytale like. It does give you a good picture of what urban Norway was like even at the start of the 20th century.

* Skagenkaien - Here along the waterfront you will find much of the early maritime architecture of the city, dating back to the founding of the port. And like the Old Town area, you will find Skagenkaien heavily oriented toward serving the tourists, especially on days when ships are in port. This area is also very close to where cruise ships dock, so for those with limited mobility, this is the easiest venue to visit.

In Skagenkaien, (Work of Florian Pépellin, CC BY SA 2.5, Wikimedia.org)

* **Stavanger Cathedral** - Located at the edge of a beautiful parkland just to the southwest of the city center, this cathedral began as a Catholic center for the regional bishop. After an 18th century fire, the restoration of the main facade changed the entire look of the building, as under Protestant domination it was given more simplified lines. Originally this cathedral was closely tied to southern England, as it was English priests that first came to Stavanger in the 16th century. The cathedral is open during daylight hours for visitors unless there is a major event taking place.

* **Stavanger Maritime Museum** - Here you get a complete history with exhibits that relate Stavanger to the sea, and it is sure to please anyone who is interested in the role of sea commerce and the coast of Norway. It is located at the southern end of the old harbor at Strandkaien # 22 and also maintains limited hours from 11 AM to 4 PM daily. The museum does feature a good collection of replicas of small sailing vessels and early ships

* **Swords in the Rock** is an important monument to Norway's early history. It is located at Hafrsfjord on the southwestern edge of the city. The Norwegian name is Sverd i fjell. Without this being part of a tour, you will need to either have a private car or commission a local taxi on an hourly rate to get here. Or if you would like to try local transportation, city bus number 29 will bring you here from the city center. The monument consists of three hilts of old Viking swords that protrude from solid rock in the same fashion as the

famous Excalibur in the King Arthur legends. The monument celebrates a great battle fought in 872 in which Harald Harfagre was victorious and united most of the Viking tribes of Norway into a single nation. As an outdoor monument, it is open 24 hours a day all week and during summer with darkness coming around Midnight there is plenty of time to enjoy this monument.

* **Valbergtårnet** - This is the old watchtower standing on a high hill just to the east of the city center. In the days before any form of telecommunication, this was how the city protected itself by having watchmen on shift to look for the start of fires or even for the threat of outside invasion. Today it offers an outstanding close in view of the city center, giving the visitor some excellent photographic opportunities. Hours are from 10 AM to 4 PM weekdays and from 10 AM to 2 PM Saturday. There is a small entry fee.

EXPLORING OUTSIDE STAVANGER: For those who want to explore some of the natural beauty of the countryside outside of Stavanger, there are two prominent locations that you can get to either as part of a ship sponsored tour or on your own with a private car or taxi. My recommendations are:

* **Lysefjorden** - If your cruise line offers a boat trip into Lysefjorden and if you want to truly see some magnificent scenery, then this is an option I would highly recommend. This narrow fjord located across the broad bay known, as Boknafjorden is a short distance from the city, yet it is a world away, as the fjord is narrow and the walls are steep, offering some beautiful photo opportunities.

I highly recommend Lyseforden to those who are serious photographers and who want to capture some of the dramatic scenery of the fjords. It is best by boat despite there being good roads in the district.

The majesty of Lysefjorden, (Work of Falk Ladermann, CC BY SA 2.0, Wikimedia.org)

* **Vaulen Beach** - Located just south of the city on the east side of the peninsula, Vaulen Beach is not quite the rugged out of door environment since it is still within the greater urban zone. But it does offer beautiful scenery of a rather placid nature, having calm waters, small groves of trees and surrounded by low hills albeit there are still some houses in view. But it is a nice retreat from the heart of Stavanger and is easily accessed by private car or taxi.

DINING OUT: Depending upon your cruise company's itinerary you may or may not have time for lunch. Many people prefer to skip an actual restaurant lunch and simply have a quick snack so as to not loose time. But I personally think that the dining experience is part of the adventure. So if you want to enjoy a traditional Norwegian lunch, here are my choices:

* **Døgnville Burger** - Located at Skagen # 13 in Old Town, this is a typical American grille that is noted for its hamburgers, something you do not find as commonplace in Norway. They also do feature vegetarian dishes as well. For those American passengers here is a chance to have a taste of home, especially if you are not partial to seafood, which so dominates. Hours of service are from Noon to 9 PM weekdays and 2 to 9 PM Sunday. Reservations are not necessary.

* **Eg & Du** – In the heart of town at Eiganesvieien, this is an excellent traditional Norwegian restaurant with a varied menu, but with emphasis upon seafood. Their fish soups are a specialty. In addition to popular seafood dishes, they also have several dishes in which meat is featured in the local style as well as vegetarian dishes. They serve on weekdays from 11 AM to 7 PM and weekends from Noon to 6 PM. Call +47 51 89 51 80 to book a table.

* **Fisketorget** - Located in the city center at Strandkaien # 37 and open for lunch and dinner from 11 AM to 11 PM Monday thru Saturday, it is my first choice for traditional Norwegian seafood dishes. Two of the most popular dishes are a hearty fish soup and then followed by cod that has been sautéed with bacon. If cod is not to your taste, there are also choices ranging from salmon to whatever is the freshest catch of the day. They serve Monday thru Saturday from 11 AM to 10 PM. Call +47 51 52 73 50 to see if you need to reserve a table.

* **Renaa Matbaren** – This casual restaurant is located at Breitorget # 6 Oevre etasje, which is a fair walk from the dock. The restaurant serves traditional Norwegian and other Scandinavian dishes in a delightful atmosphere. Their menu also features many dishes that are typical of the rest of Scandinavia. They also serve vegetarian dishes. Hours of service are from 11 AM to 1 Am daily. Call +47 51 55 11 11 to reserve a table.

* **Restaurant SOL** - In the city center at Hetlandsgata # 6, this centrally located restaurant is noted as one of the best in Stavanger. Its menu features seafood, poultry and meats all prepared in a traditional manner and served in a charming atmosphere. It is so popular that it is best to have the ship concierge make a reservation. Their hours are Wednesday, Friday and Sunday from 5 to 10 PM, Thursday from 4 to 10 PM and Saturday from 1 to 3 PM and 5 to 10 PM. Call +47 977 22 201 to see if you need to reserve a table.

* **Sjøhuset Skagen** - This very traditional restaurant is located in the city center as well, its exact address being Skagenkaien #13. It is open from 11:30 AM onward and specializes in seafood, which is of course what one expects in Norway. Their fish soup is said by many to be the best in Stavanger, but of course you must be the judge. They also serve whale meat, a very traditional dish in Norway. I have tried it, and yes it has a wonderful taste, but somehow I could not bring myself to go beyond just a taste, knowing it was whale. But again that is a decision you must make. They are open from 6 to 10 PM Tuesday thru Saturday. Call + 47 904 17 327 to see if you need a reservation.

* **Tango Restaurant** - At Nedre Strandgate # 25, this is an excellent traditional Norwegian restaurant that again is heavily into fresh seafood. The dishes are beautifully prepared and served in a friendly, but casual atmosphere. They are open Tuesday thru Friday 6 PM to 10 PM and Saturday from 1 to 2:30 PM and 6 to 10 PM. Call +47 51 50 12 30 to see if you need a reservation.

SHOPPING: Stavanger is not really a major shopping destination for cruise passengers, as it has primarily souvenir stores in the Old City.

The most common item that people wish to buy is a hand knitted Norwegian sweater, and yes you will find a fair selection in the Old City area. But for a larger selection, I would recommend waiting until you get to Bergen unless you see something that you feel you absolutely must have. Be aware that the prices on these sweaters are quite high, but the majority are handmade and conserving the amount of labor that goes into the making of one, the price is not that great.

FINAL WORDS: Stavanger is a beautiful city that typifies the gracious, yet not ostentatious lifestyle of the people of Norway. And as the country's third major urban region, it does offer all of the important services for its people and those in the hinterland.

From a tourist perspective, there is a lot of historic architecture that will hold your interest. But there are few of what you might call memorable historic sites given that Stavanger was the focus of great historic events.

If you do love scenic environments and if your cruise line does offer any tours out into the hinterlands, especially to Lysefjorden I would highly recommend such a tour, as you will explore some lesser known landscapes not seen by thousands of visitors.

MAP OF CENTRAL STAVANGER

**The center of Stavanger with the star showing where cruise ships dock,
(© OpenStreetMap contributors)**

This map is best viewed directly from OpenStreetMap.com on your personal device where it can be expanded or one specific area can be enlarged. Given the format of this book, it is impossible to display maps with the level of detail you might wish to have while actually out exploring the city. But the OpenStreetMap maps used directly are the tool I always rely upon.

HAUGESUND

The Haugesund region (© OpenStreetMap contributors)

THE SETTING: Haugesund is located just north of Stavanger but not many cruise ships seem to pay a port call, which I think is a shame because it is a delightful small city with a picturesque setting, wonderful architecture and delightful people. If your itinerary is fortunate enough to include Haugesund, you will find it an enjoyable visit. Both Haugesund and Stavanger seem to be missing from the majority of cruise itineraries. Time is normally the constraint with many Norwegian itineraries because of the distances involved and the emphasis being placed upon visiting the fjords rather than urban ports of call apart from Bergen.

The city is actually in a very strategic location because it lies at the northern end of the Karmsundet, a rather narrow, but deep inside passage that begins across the opening of Boknafjorden. Once passing through this channel and passing Haugesund, ships need only be in the open sea for another short stretch before they can enter another inside passage all the way to Bergen. Given the severity of the winter weather on the North Sea and also the occasional summer storms that can bring rough seas, the inside passages along most of the

Norwegian coast has been a safe haven for ships plying the waters north and south between such ports as Arkhangelsk and Murmansk on the Barents Sea in far northern Russia and the Baltic Sea, which is reached after rounding the southern tip of Norway and passing through the Skaggerak between Denmark and Sweden.

Flying over Haugesund, (Work of Haugesund Avis Aerophoto)

The region surrounding Haugesund both on the large islands just offshore and the mainland is gently rolling to moderately hilly. The land where not cleared for agriculture consists of thick coniferous forests and the countryside is dotted with hundreds of glacial lakes while the coastline is indented with several fjords, both signs of intense glaciation. But although beautiful, it lacks the drama and majesty created by the higher mountains being closer to the sea, as found north from Bergen.

Climatically this area is within the maritime regime that dominates most of Norway until one gets beyond the Arctic Circle where a sub polar climatic regime begins. Winters are cold, hovering just around or above freezing and more rain than snow is commonplace. Thus blustery, damp and gray weather is the norm. Summers are very mild with daytime temperatures generally in the low 20's Celsius or upper 60's to mid 70's Fahrenheit., and with the warm offshore Gulf Stream, fog is quite common as the moist air loses its ability to hold the vapor, condensing it out into microscopic droplets suspended above ground level. The last time I visited Haugesund, it was a mild, almost warm August day with blue skies, but by midafternoon a bank of fog came in from the open sea and visibility was reduced to nearly zero in a matter of minutes. It was possible to just stand along the waterfront and watch the fog advancing like some alien miasma engulfing everything. It was quite hypnotic.

Haugesund is an important regional center for the surrounding farmland, fishing, servicing oil drilling platforms and fjord tourism. It is a very pleasant city with a population of 40,150 in its metropolitan area. The city presents both the feel of a small town, yet it has all of the important amenities of a city, including a well-developed business district, a beautiful cathedral, public buildings and parks. Like so many Norwegian cities, it is built on a series of hills, rising back from the waterfront and consists primarily of wood houses, most of them painted white. Public buildings are constructed of brick or stone, and many date to the late 18th and 19th centuries.

Looking along the main channel through the center of Haugesund

BRIEF HAUGESUND HISTORY: Like so much of southern Norway, archaeological evidence shows that there have been settlements in the region for many thousands of years, dating back to around 6,000 years ago. By the time of the Viking Era, starting in the 10th century, this was an important area for trade, including contacts across the North Sea to the British Isles.

The region surrounding Haugesund is known as Rogaland, and it was an important Viking stronghold. A great battle for control of Rogaland took place in 872 when King Harald

Fairhair was victorious and incorporated the area into his expanding Norwegian kingdom. The actual details of this victory are told in the Norwegian Sagas and some say they are as much myth as reality, somewhat like the stories of King Arthur and Camelot. A great monument, known as Haraldshaugen, was built in 1872 to commemorate the 1,000 anniversary of the great battle outside of Haugesund to honor King Harald, as the greatest early king of Norway. It is believed to be on the site where his burial mound exists.

During much of its history, fishing for herring dominated the local economy, but the stocks have been so badly depleted that they have not been viable since the early years of the 20th century. But since the mid 1960's, Haugesund, like Stavanger, has become a major center for servicing the oil drilling platforms off shore in the North Sea. Limited fishing still adds to the local economy, but nowhere near where it did a century earlier. In addition to oil drilling, Haugesund is a local trade center and does see a fair number of summer visitors who are exploring the surrounding countryside.

SHIP DOCK IN HAUGESUND: The few cruise ships that visit Haugesund dock in the port area on the small offshore island immediately adjacent to the city center. This port is primarily for the servicing of oil drilling platforms and often you will see one of these large constructs adjacent to your ship. The more upmarket cruise lines may offer a shuttle into the center of Haugesund, but the walk is quite interesting with good views over the narrow channel that runs along the city center. The distance is just over a kilometer or approximately 3/5 of a mile. During summer days when the weather is fine, the walk is quite enjoyable and gives visitors to amble through a residential quarter and dget a closer look at life in this small trade and oil service center.

TOURING OPTIONS IN HAUGESUND: As a small city that does not service many cruise ships your options for sightseeing are more limited than in Oslo or Bergen. Here are the options available to you in Haugesund:

* **Ship sponsored tours** – Your cruise line will off one or more tours of the city of Haugesund and some cruise lines may also offer a tour out into the surrounding countryside. These are motor coach tours, but it is also possible that a cruise line also offers a walking tour of the city center.

* **Private car and driver/guide** – This option is available in Haugesund on a more limited basis as a result of the small size of the community. You have the freedom of touring either in town or getting out into the beautiful surrounding countryside. To look into arranging such a tour on your own, you may wish to check on line with the only limousine service large enough to possibly offer a private tour. Visit *www.limos.com/airports/norway/HAU* to see if they can accommodate your needs.

* **Hop on hop off bus service** does not exist in Haugesund, as the market is too small.

* **Taxi touring** – There may be a taxi or two at the dock, but do not count upon this possibility. For taxi touring as an option you need to contact Haugland Taxi, which is the

main provider in Haugesund. The web page is www.visitnorway.com/listings/haugesund-taxi.

* **Walking** does enable the visitor to see much of the central city and visit the few places of interest.

SIGHTS TO SEE IN HAUGESUND: Many cruise lines choose to bypass Haugesund, especially if they stop in Stavanger because the two cities are so close to one another. But if you are fortunate enough to visit Haugesund, it most likely will be a short port call, either a few hours in the morning or afternoon, as rarely do any cruise ships spend an entire day. There will in most cases be at least one short motor coach or walking tour offered by your cruise line.

For those of you who want to go off on your own, here are my recommendations of places you really should see:

* **Arquebus War History Museum** is located at the top end of Førrestfjorden about 30 kilometers from Haugesund. This is one of those special locations that requires either a private car or taxi unless it happens to be part of a shi's tour. The museum is housed in a former German bunker, and is one of the best in Norway for telling the history of the Nazi occupation during WWII. The museum is open daily from 11 AM to 5 PM during the summer season.

* **Djupadalan** is an outdoor wooded area set aside for public hiking and recreation. If you are an outdoor type and would like to spend a few hours trekking through the woods on a well-marked path, this is the place to visit. It is located about eight kilometers east of the town center in the foothills and can be reached by private car or local taxi. This is a delightful walk that is suitable for all ages, and bicyclists often use this route, with bicycle rentals available in the city center.

* **Haraldshaugen** - This is the most recognized major site to visit within Haugesund. If your cruise line happens to offer a motor coach tour of the city, this will be considered the most important and historic site. But many cruise lines that stop in Haugesund do not offer any guided tours.

Haraldshaugen is located just north of the city and can be reached by private car or local taxi. You can also walk, as it is only two kilometers from the city center. Built in 1872, it commemorates the 1,000th anniversary of the famous battle fought in this area that ultimately unified southern Norway under the Viking King Harald Fairhair. He is also believed to be buried here according to the Norwegian Sagas. The monument is always open 24 hours per day.

Viking history and legend plays a major role in the historic background of this coastal region and also adds a colorful note to the whole story of these once mighty and feared warriors.

The Haraldshaugen Monument, (Work of Mark Köenig, CC BY SA 4.0. Wikimedia.org)

The Haugesund Our Savior's Church

* **Haugesund Our Savior's Church** dominates the skyline of the city center with its tall, red tower. The architectural style is very typical of 18th or 19th century major Norwegian churches found in the larger cities, but it was completed in 1901, being of more recent construct. The style is what is often called new or neo Gothic and it is faced in red brick, a building material that is not widely used in Norway.

The church, which can hold over 1,000 worshipers is open for visitors to take a look at the interior on Friday from 11 to 11:30 AM and on Sunday from 11 AM to 12:30 PM. If there are any services being held, visitors may be asked not to enter.

* **Steinsfjellet** - Located about 20 kilometers east of the city at an altitude of 227 meters or 744 feet above sea level, this observation point gives you a grand view of the city, surrounding woods, small lakes and the shoreline. If your cruise line offers a motor coach tour of the Haugesund area, this is often included as a photo stop. The drive is rather pleasant, but being outside of the city, you need to have arranged for a private car or hire a local taxi if you are on your own and would like to enjoy this panoramic view of the surrounding countryside and the city.

Along Haugesund's Strandgata

* **Strandgata** is the main pedestrian shopping street of Haugesund, and it gives you a good look at the basic lifestyle of the city, There are many interesting shops and cafes along this main street. Haugesund has a lively downtown area filled with interesting shops, cafes and food shops, giving the visitor a chance to take a close look at commercial life in a Norwegian trade center in contrast to the major cities such as Oslo and Bergen.

The Strandgata is a short distance from where your ship will dock and it is actually an enjoyable and somewhat scenic walk to reach the downtown core. The walk will take you over a high bridge that spans the main shipping channel and gives you a good aerial view of the center of the city.

DINING OUT: Unless your port call is for an entire day, you will either leave before the lunch hour or arrive afterwards. But for those who can spend an entire day in Haugesund, or for those who want a quick snack, I am providing my recommendations for two traditional Norwegian restaurants and one cafe that offers light snacks.

* **Brasserie Brakstad** - Located in the city center at Kaigata #2 and open from 11 AM to MIDNIGHT Monday thru Thursday, remaining open to 1:30 AM Friday and Saturday. Sunday hours are from Noon to 11 PM. this restaurant offers a casual atmosphere. The menu features a wide variety of Norwegian and general Scandinavian dishes featuring both seafood and meat entrees. Bookings are not needed. To reserve a table for lunch you can call them at +47 52 70 00 50.

Sunday summer crowds along the downtown waterfront

* **Lothus Mat & Vinhus** - On the city waterfront at Skippergata # 4, this is a very popular local establishment featuring traditional Norwegian cuisine, which includes many seafood dishes. Many patrons consider it to be the best restaurant in the city. Hours are from 6 PM to 1 AM Tuesday thru Saturday It is not necessary to book a table.

* **Naturbaskt** - Located at Haraldsgata and Skippergaten, and open from & AM onward, this is an ideal bakery/cafe where you can get a variety of sandwiches, soups and typical Norwegian pastries. This is my recommendation for a cafe that offers quick service and light meals. They are open from 7 AM to 6 PM Monday thru Friday, closing at 4 PM Saturday. On Sunday they do not open until 9 AM and close at 4 PM. It is not necessary to book a table.

SHOPPING: As in Stavanger, there are a few small shops selling tourist souvenirs, but the remainder of shops cater to local needs. If you are looking to invest in knitted sweaters or other local crafts, you will find the largest selection in Bergen.

FINAL WORDS: If you visit Haugesund and you are fortunate enough to have clear, sunny weather, you will find this a delightful community. But as noted earlier, weather plays a major role and when it is foggy there is less likelihood that you will dock if scheduled to do so. Ships can dock with little or no difficulty thanks to modern navigation equipment, but getting around to see the sights would be difficult if not impossible since Norwegian coastal fogs can be quite thick. But when you are able to visit, Haugesund, though nothing special, is just an enjoyable place in which to savor a bit of small city life Norwegian style.

THE HEART OF HAUGESUND

The city center of Haugesund with the star showing where cruise ships dock, (© OpenStreetMap contributors)

This map is best viewed directly from OpenStreetMap.com on your personal device where it can be expanded or one specific area can be enlarged. Given the format of this book, it is impossible to display maps with the level of detail you might wish to have while actually out exploring the city. But the OpenStreetMap maps used directly are the tool I always rely upon.

EIDFJORD

The village known as Eidfjord takes is name from the fjord on which it sits. Its location is quite dramatic with the narrow fringe of land including the village being backed up by mountains that rise dramatically. This is a classic fjord with its near vertical walls having been carved by glacial ice in the distant past, later melting and leaving this deep body of water with an average depth of well over 1,000 meters or 3,000 feet.

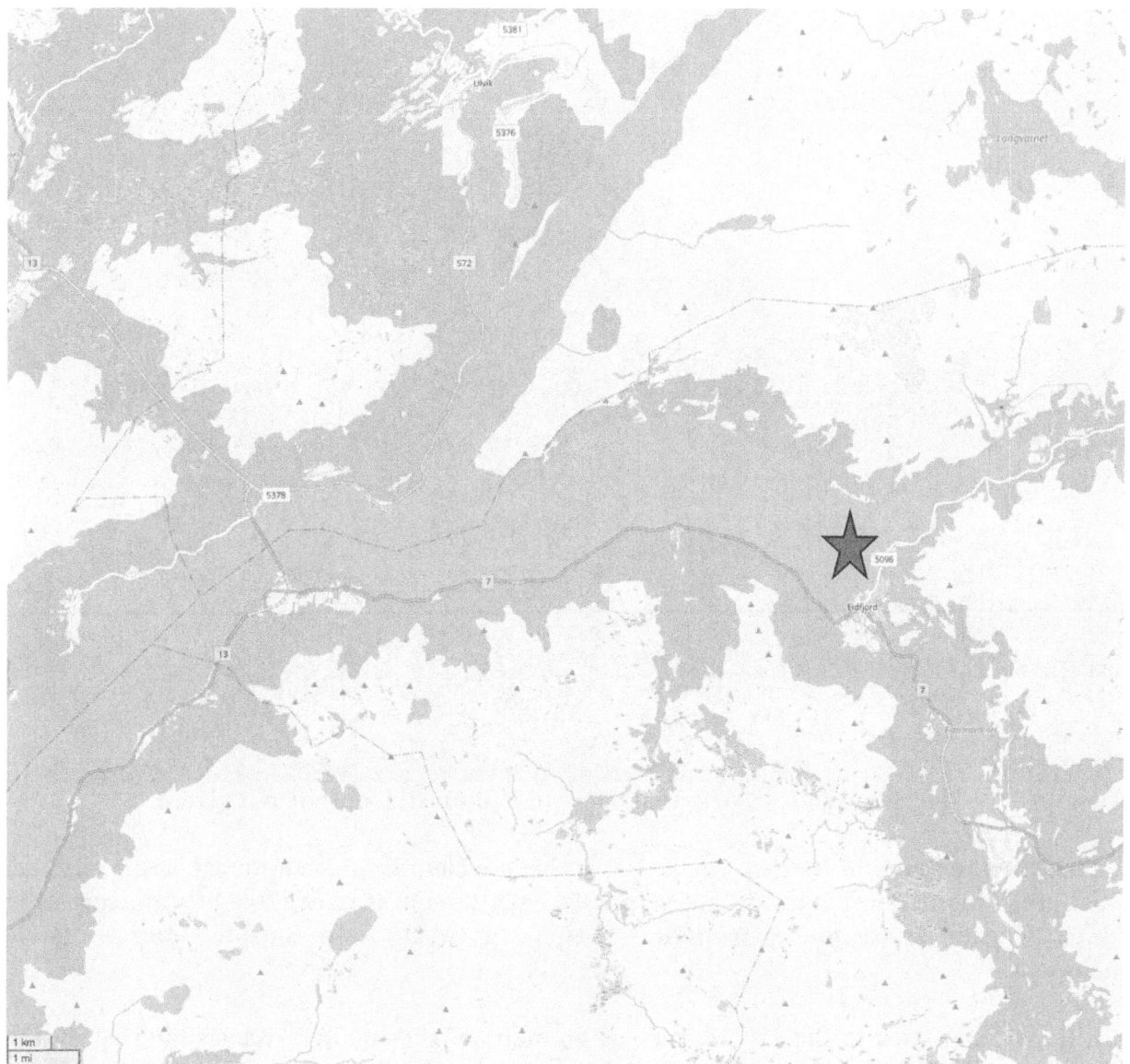

A map of the upper portion of Eidfjord showing the village location, (© OpenStreetMap contributors)

THE LANDSCAPE: Eidflord itself is part of a larger fjord system known as Hardangerfjorden and the village is over 110 kilometers or 65 miles inland from the open sea. It normally takes a cruise ship approximately three to four hours to travel from the sea or from Bergen, the nearest major city. The Norwegian coast presents a typical mix of islands and channels that have become the model for all glaciated coastlines worldwide.

The region is part of the Hardangervidda Plateau most of which is protected within the boundaries of the national park of the same name. In Eidfjord village the climate is tempered by the water and is moderately cold in winter and moist year around. This enables the region to project the most typical lush green view of a Norwegian fjord in the prime latitudes of the country.

The village of Eidfjord, (Courtesy of Wikimedia, author not given)

Given the proximity to Bergen, which is Norway's second largest and most scenic city, the vast majority of cruise lines do not stop here even though it is capable of servicing large ships. If your cruise line is including Eidfjord as a full stop consider yourself to be fortunate.

Eidfjord dates back to the 12th century as do many of the smaller villages high up on the Hardangervidda Plateau. And in the early years after Christianity arrived the its Viking ancestors became more pacified it was more closely tied both spiritually and economically to Stavanger to the south rather than to Berge, which is so much closer.

TOURING OPTIONS IN EIDFJORD: There are only limited touring options given that the village of Eidfjord only has 1,000 residents. These are the options available to you for your visit:

Looking down upon Eidfjord from the top of the Hardangervidda Plateau

* **Ship sponsored tours** – Your cruise line will off one or more tours of the village, including a walking tour given how small the community is. Depending upon the cruise line there may be one or two motor coach tours into the surrounding Hardangervidda Plateau And some cruise lines may offer either or both hiking and kayak adventure tours.

* **Private car and driver/guide** – This option may be available in Eidfjord on a more limited basis as a result of the small size of the community. You have the freedom of touring either in town or getting out into the beautiful surrounding countryside. To look into arranging such a tour on your own, you may wish to check on line with the only limousine service large enough to possibly offer a private tour in this more remote region. Visit *www.limos.com/airports/norway/HAU* to see if they can accommodate your needs.

* **Hop on hop off bus service** does not exist in Eidfjord, as the village is simply too small.

* **Taxi touring** – There may be a taxi or two at the dock, but do not count upon this possibility.

* **Walking** does enable the visitor to see all of the village and visit the few places of interest.

Eidfjord can accommodate larger cruise ships, (Work of Cavernia, CC BY SA 4.0, Wikimedia.org)

SIGHTS TO SEE IN EIDFJORD: The village is so small that it does not offer many venues of special interest. These are the only recommendations I can provide other than to simply enjoy this small community or to take one of the ship tours:

Eidfjord Church – This small community church with its distinctive history is not specifically geared to hosting visitors. But if it is open, you are certainly welcome to visit.

Galerie N. Bergslein – This is a delightful local gallery featuring the work of noted local artist N. Bergslein and a few other local artists. It is always open when a cruise ship is in port. It is located in town at Ostangvegen #20 in the heart of town.

Mabodalen Agricultural Countryside Museum – Located in the small outlying village of Ovre Eidfjord about five kilometers south of Eidfjord the only way to reach this local museum on your own is to take a local taxi if one is even available. Walking is an option if you are up to it. No hours are posted, but given the limited tourist traffic, it will be open when your ship is in port.

The dramatic landscape of Eidfjordt, (Work of Holger Uwe Schmitt, CC by SA 4.0, Wikimedia.org)

DINING: If you decide to dine in Eidfjord, which I highly recommend, these are my two choices for a fine Norwegian meal:

* **DYRAUNUT FJELLSTOVE RESTAURANT** – A delightful Norwegian restaurant in the heart of Eidfjord, located in the heart of town, featuring traditional cuisine from all of Scandinavia. They serve breakfast, lunch, brunch and dinner daily from 8 AM to 8 PM. This is a very popular eatery and has a diverse menu that will please a wide variety of tastes. Their quality, presentation and service are all top notch. Reservations can be made by calling +478 53 66 57 16, but they are not necessary.

RESTAURANT FJELL AND FJORD – This is another very popular local restaurant serving traditional Scandinavian cuisine in a delightful atmosphere. With its large glassed in atrium like environment it offers exceptionally charming surroundings. Centrally located at Laegreidsvegen #7 inside the Eidfjord Fjell & Fjord Hotel. Hours of service are daily between 3 and 8:30 PM. To reserve a table, call them at +47 53 66 52 64.

About to dock in Eidfjord, (Work of Rheins, CC BY SA 3.0, Wikimedia.Org)

The village of Eidfjord, (Work of Juanje 2712, CC BY SA 3,0, Wikimedia.org0

BERGEN
NORWAY'S SECOND CITY

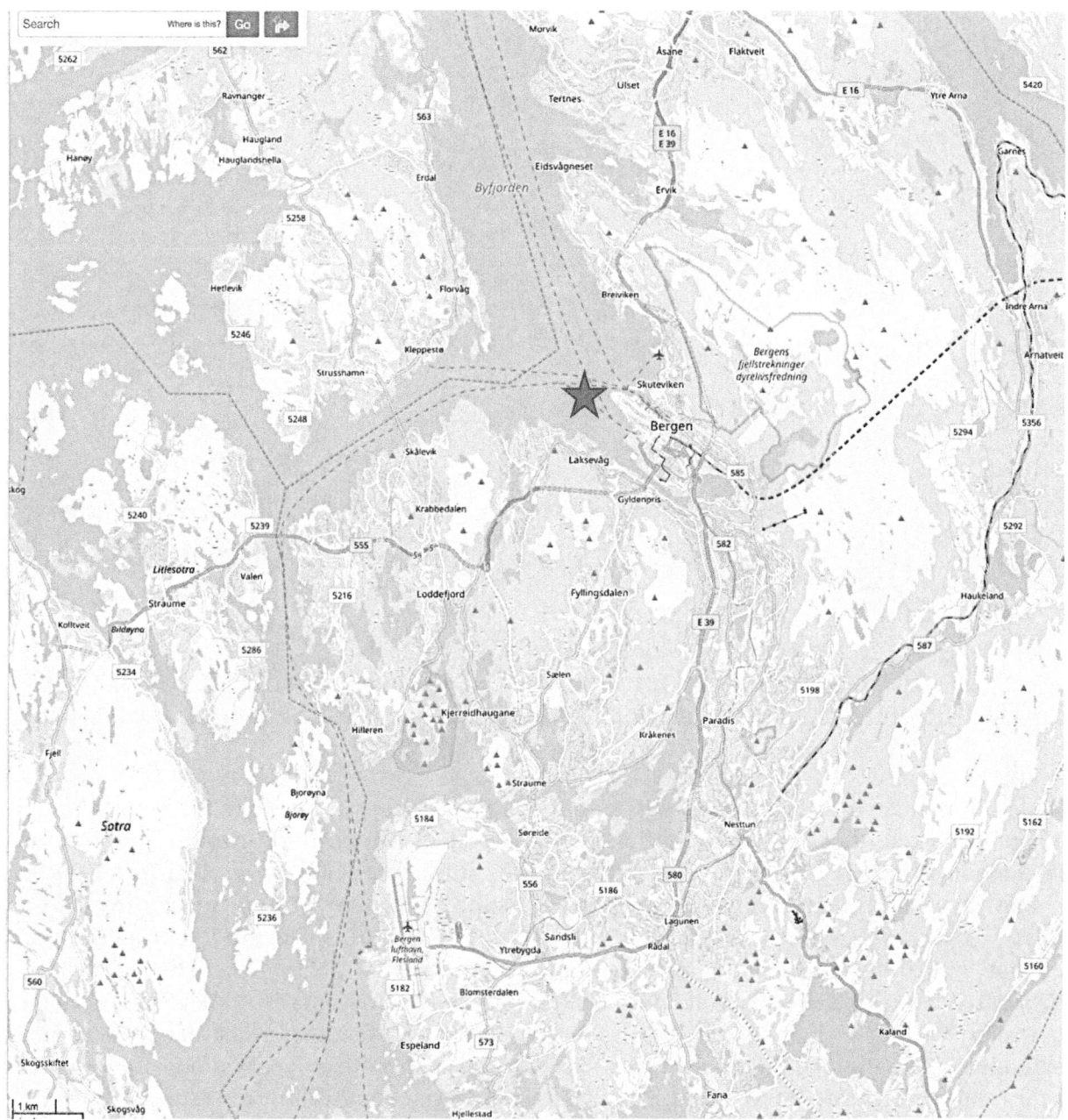

Map of Greater Bergen (© OpenStreetMap contributors)

A COMPLEX GEOGRAPHY: Bergen is the second largest city in Norway and for many cruise itineraries through the fjord country, it is the largest city that the ship will visit since few such cruises begin or end in Oslo. The geographic position of Oslo places it out of the mainstream for fjord cruises despite the city being on a major fjord. The spectacular mountain scenery that Norway is identified by actually begins just south of

Bergen and extends up into the region of the Arctic coast. Oslo is located in a gentle region of low mountains that are not spectacular.

The Bergen topography seen from the air, (Work of Tom G. Eriksen, CC BY SA 3.0, Wikimedia.org)

Today Bergen's population, including all of its outlying suburban reaches, is approximately 420,000. The city does not seem that large because of its physical geography. The first map in this chapter makes it easy to understand how the perception of size is affected by the urban layout. The city center is found on a small peninsula formed by two deep-water inlets, giving the city two distinct harbors. Mt. Fløyen rises up to the north of the main harbor, reaching a maximum elevation of 987 meters or 3,238 feet. The bulk of the urbanized zone stretches from the city center southward in a narrow valley that is formed between two parallel mountain ridges. In the south it reaches another deep-water inlet, extending to the international airport. There are also urbanized areas along the northern shore underneath Mt. Fløyen and extending around the northern and western edge of the mountains to the south of the central peninsula. Suburbs also spill out onto the large islands that protect the city from the full force of North Sea winters. A series of bridges connect the main islands to the heart of the city and for the smaller urbanized islands there is a fleet of small ferryboats. Bergen is so broken into small urban zones by its physical geography that it is very difficult to appreciate just how large the city is. The impression visitors receive is that of a moderate size city.

Sailing amid the islands to reach Bergen

This complex geographic interrelationship between land and water is again the result of glacial scour. Numerous tongues of glacial ice swept down former river valleys between the mountain spurs and their forward edges coalesced when they reached the sea, which at that time was much lower than today. After retreating the sea rose and it flooded these now deepened channels, creating the complex network of fjords and islands. The deep channels between the mainland and those pieces of land that now form the complex strings of islands along Norway's coast present a unique urban landscape where each neighborhood appears to be a village or town in its own right. Many small scoured basins amid the mountains filled with melt water and today comprise the thousands of glacial lakes that pepper the landscape.

The entire region is cloaked in thick coniferous forest, its growth heightened by the heavy precipitation that results from mild, moist air being forced to rise along the mountainous coast. This maritime climate begins to change in the vicinity of Bergen, as the more northerly latitude equates to shorter winter days, which end up being colder and thus snowfall down to sea level is more common that farther south at Stavanger. Summers are mild with daytime temperatures rarely climbing above the mid 20's Celsius or upper 70's Fahrenheit. Gray overcast and fog are commonplace, and Bergen is said to be the least sunny major city in Norway. With climatic changes, rainfall in Bergen has increased and today averages close to 2,280 millimeters or 90 inches per year. The city actually announces in its tourist brochures that it is the rainiest city in the country and chides itself in not having a sunnier climate. Thus when you visit Bergen you should not expect blue skies and sunshine, although during July and August there can be several consecutive days with absolutely beautiful weather that makes the city so amazingly photogenic. At times the temperature can climb into the mid 20's Celsius or upper 70's Fahrenheit. In my photos I have chosen from among my best taken over the past ten years of multiple visits. Perhaps that is not fair to those of you reading this book, as it gives a false illusion of Bergen's true weather. But at least knowing is being prepared. Bring an umbrella and a raincoat, but perhaps the Viking gods will shine upon you.

A view from Mt. Fløyen looking over central Bergen.

BERGEN 'S HISTORY: There is a bit of rivalry between the residents of Bergen and those of Oslo. Both cities date to within a few years of one another, so they are each among the oldest cities in Norway. But Bergen was the capital and most important city of Norway during its early years as a unified nation until the year until sometime during the reign of King Hakon V who moved the capital to Oslo sometime after 1299. Thus Bergen residents take pride in their early royal history while Oslo residents take pride in the fact that their city is now the capital and also the largest city of the nation.

The Bergen Domkyrken (cathedral) was built in 1150 and was the site of royal functions such as coronations, marriages and burials all through the rest of the 12th and 13th centuries. During its latter part of its time as the early capital, the Bergenhus Fortress, which stands watch over the northern harbor, served as a royal residence. During the 14th century, despite having lost the capital to Oslo, Bergen's trade in cod became so lucrative that if any other city wanted to develop its own cod fishing/drying enterprise, it first had to obtain permission of the king. Bergen was a minor trade center under the Hanseatic

League, but the surviving architecture along the waterfront of Bryggen lacks the distinctive ornamentation of traditional Hanseatic buildings. However, their unique character and wood construction has merited UNESCO World Heritage status.

The core of Bergen is compact nestled under Mt. Floyen

The 14th century loss of the capital to Oslo did hurt, but Bergen remained a significant Scandinavian city, and actually was larger than Oslo until almost the mid 19th century. It suffered the bubonic plague in the mid 14th century, was attacked by pirates in the 15th century and by a British naval fleet that was after a Dutch treasure fleet under city protection in 1655.

Like Oslo, Bergen also suffered from the ravages of fire because of the persistent use of wood as the primary building material. Various parts of the city experienced massive burning during every century until the mid 20th century. Today that danger still does exist in Bryggen and other older neighborhoods where wood houses are clustered together along narrow streets that often are very steep where parts of the city climb the surrounding hills, but modern firefighting equipment has negated the severity of the threat.

Bergen grew both as a port, but also as a major center for the catching of cod and the drying of the fish for export mainly to the Mediterranean. Bergen continued to grow as a trade port and ultimately by Norwegian independence from Sweden in 1906 it had become the second largest city of Norway. To the present day, Bergen is Norway's second largest city in population. But with regard to tourism, it is far more important than Oslo, as during the summer it is visited daily by numerous cruise ships while Oslo sees only a handful of cruises per week. It was not until the late 20th century the cruise industry discovered the Norwegian fjords, and ever since Bergen has been the major urban stop on almost all itineraries. During a typical summer day there can be three to four major cruise ships anchored in Bergen, generating thousands of visitors and significant revenue for the city's merchants and tour operators.

Bryggen along the waterfront, heart of old Bergen

Bergen was among the first cities in Norway to be attacked and then occupied by Nazi forces during April 1940. Because of its port facilities, it became an important German naval facility and was subjected to bombing by Allied forces. Given its strategic location along the major shipping lane for the Allies in their aid of the Soviet Union, Bergen was of prime value to the German navy.

CRUISE SHIP DOCK: The majority of cruise ships visiting Bergen dock opposite the western tip of the main peninsula that is home to the city's business district. The dock is across the street from the Rosenkrantz Tower also known as Bergen Castle. There is a terminal building but it is old and does not offer any special services, thus few cruise lines use the building, but rather set up portable desks near their gangways. However, there is a large parking area in front of the terminal where motor coaches, private cars, taxis and the hop on hop off busses all congregate.

Some of Bryggen's old buildings opposite the fish market

Parts of Bergen climb the sides of Mt. Fløyen from behind the cruise ship terminal

Most cruise lines do not offer a shuttle into the city center, as the distance is only around 1.3 kilometers or just under one mile. When there are more cruises in port than the dock can handle, the overflow uses the other side of the central city peninsula, and again there are no viable terminal facilities, but there is plenty of room for parking of motor coaches, taxis and other service vehicles. At times there can be as many as five cruise ships in port at the same time, which does present a bit of congestion along the wharf and the main road.

TOURING OPTIONS WHILE VISITING BERGEN: There are several options for exploring Bergen, which are detailed below:

* **Ship sponsored tours** – Each cruise line will offer a variety of tours around Bergen and possibly into nearby fjords. These are motor coach group tours and there may also be one city center walking tour depending upon the arrangements by your cruise line. And some cruise lines will offer an all-day motor coach tour into the fjord country south of the city, but I do not recommend it given the nature of the local weather. Likewise there is so much of interest in the city that would be missed and your itinerary will include other beautiful fjords.

* **Private car and driver/guide option** – For those who want the privacy and convenience of private touring at your leisure, the shore excursion desk can arrange for a private car and driver/guide, which has always been my preferred way to explore a city. To look into possibly saving money, you can check the following to see if they can offer comparable service at greater value:

** Tours by Locals is a widely respected company offering private touring. Check out their web page for Bergen at *www.toursbylocals.com/Bergen-Tours* for full details.

** Another service is 1 Cares found on line at *www.1cares.com/cars/rent-a-car-in-Bergen* for details on their offerings.

* **Hop on hop off bus service** is a very good way to get around the city since they stop right outside of the main cruise terminal. If more than one ship is in port, however, these busses do fill up rapidly and if you do not enjoy crowds while sightseeing, then I would advise against this service when crowded. To look into routes, times and fares visit *www.hop-on-hop-off-bus/bergen* .

* **Taxi service** is available and there are always a few taxis waiting outside the cruise terminal gates. However, to learn more about this option and also to make arrangements visit on line with *www.fjordnorway.com/things-to-do/private-sightseeing-by-taxi-p1708* for full details. Most taxi driver do speak English and are actually very good guides.

* **Light Rail** service exists between the central park in Bergen and the southern suburbs, and this is one way to visit the famous composer Sebelius' house. See the web page for details at *www.skyss.no/timetable-and-map/bergen-light-rail* .

The light rail route also takes you through numerous neighborhoods, which can be very interesting to anyone who enjoys exploring a city to see its daily life. You can essentially hop on and off the light rail trains.

* **Walking** is one way to see the central city. You can explore on foot or combine walking with public transport, but it will be far more time consuming and at the end of the day you will be exhausted, as Bergen has some exceptionally steep hills to negotiate. The disadvantage apart from the topography is that you will miss the wider scope of the city, which is beyond anyone's ability to cover on foot.

THE MAJOR SIGHTS TO SEE IN BERGEN: My recommendation for the must see sights in Bergen for those who are going to tour on their own includes (shown here in alphabetical order):

* **Bergen Fish Market** - Red is the color that best describes the Fish Market, located at the upper end of the north harbor, opposite Bryggen and at the start of the city's main shopping street, which is Torgallmenningen. Between the displays of fresh salmon, cooked crab and shrimp and the magnificent strawberries and raspberries, red dominates the Fish Market. You could not ask for any seafood or produce to be any more fresh than what is seen in the Bergen Fish Market. Personally, as a seafood lover, I would simply gorge myself on the fresh seafood if I lived in Bergen and had my own kitchen.

In the amazing Bergen fish market

The ready to eat meals in the fish market

Fresh summer berries found in the fish market

Jars of primarily salmon caviar are also available and make a popular souvenir item to take home. There are vendors selling cooked or smoked fish ready to eat on the spot or hot fish soup. And there are a few picnic tables at the market where you can sit and enjoy your fish. But most visitors come just to look and photograph the displays of seafood and berries. However, the locals do consider this an important shopping venue for their daily fish supply.

The fish market opens at 8 AM and during summer it remains open until 11 PM. However, most of the action is seen during the morning hours, as the fresh fish comes in and is quickly bought by local shoppers. But at the same time, this is the most crowded time of day with regard to tourists off various cruise ships. But by evening, if your ship is remaining late, there are far fewer tourists to contend with. This is always a popular place to stroll and experience the flavor of Bergen life, especially since in summer many locals come to the Fish Market in the evening after most cruise ships have departed.

* **Bryggens Museum** - This small museum located in the old city district of Bryggen at Dreggsallmenningen # 3 and open daily from 10 AM to 4 PM during the summer season presents a good look at life in Bergen in the days of the city's early development through the Hanseatic period.

Leading off of main square in the central part of Bergen

The lake in the center of Festparken is a gathering place for both waterfowl and people

* Central Bergen – The city's central downtown core begins at the Bergen Fish Market and extends over quite a large swath of the central city peninsula. There are few tall buildings, most being under ten stories and the majority of these low rise structures date to the 18th and 19th centuries with many beautiful examples of ornate architecture. The city center offers excellent shopping that includes one major department store and dozens of specialty shops, cafes and food shops. Many of the smaller shops do offer a varied selection of handmade knitted sweaters and jackets, which are a very popular gift item among tourists, but they are quite expensive and unlike many countries, in Norway bargaining is not an accepted custom. Norwegian woolen goods are a traditional item, also found in the shops of adjacent historic Bryggen.

* Festparken occupies a large square in the downtown area and is the focus of museums and other important civic venues. The park is noted for its beautiful fountain, its varied water fowl and its gazebo that sits amid a garden of flowers. Many important museums and galleries are gathered around Festparken. There is a massive fountain set amid a large manmade pool that is the focus of the park. It is frequented by a variety of wild waterfowl and is a source of amusement when one sits on a bench watching the children feeding the ducks and geese.

On Ole Bulls Plass in the central city connects Festparken with the Opera House

Festparken is situated just below Mt. Fløyen and visitors can capture some outstanding images of the unique structure of Bergen from the park.

A few of the more upmarket cruise lines do offer a shuttle bus, which normally brings guests to Festparken on the edge of the downtown core. The light rail trains begin or end their route on the north side of Festparken.

* **Historic Bryggen** - Here along the waterfront you will find the oldest surviving wood buildings in the city. Bryggen was once the center of the Hanseatic merchant's quarter and dates back to the 14th and 15th century. Many of the buildings today house fine arts and crafts shops, cafes and restaurants. This is the most popular part of the city center and is often crowded when two or more ships are in port. Most of the shops and cafes in Bryggen remain open well into the evening hours.

* **KODE - The Art Museum of Bergen** located along the southeastern edge of Festplassen, it is a significant art museum featuring many works by famous Scandinavian artists. It is open from 11 AM to 4 PM Tuesday thru Sunday.

A telephoto view of central Bergen from Mt. Floyen

* **Mt. Fløyen** - This is the number one tourist venue on anyone's list of places to see in Bergen. But there is one caveat - The weather must be good. Mt. Fløyen is reached by a funicular whose base is opposite the famous fish market at the upper end of the north harbor. The funicular will take you up to the observation level atop the mountain, 320 meters or 1,049 feet above sea level for a very dramatic view over the entire city and its surrounding mountains, water and islands. All of Bergen will be at your feet, but only if it is a blue sky day or if scattered clouds are above the level of the surrounding mountains.

If you are going on your own, I recommend as early in the day as possible because the crowds gather soon after 9 AM and the wait can be well over an hour, but it is worth the wait. If you are on a tour, your group will get special preference. The most critical factor, as noted before in visiting Mt. Floyen is the weather, as Bergen does experience so much cloud cover and rain. There is a teahouse and gift shop along with walking trails on top of the mountain. The funicular operates from 7:30 AM to 11 PM daily. The cafe atop the mountain is open from 10 AM to 6 PM daily, but the gift shop keeps longer hours from 9 AM to 8 PM daily.

The light rail line connects the newer outer suburbs to the south

* **Rosenkrantz Tower** - Often called the Bergen Castle or Fortress, it was begun in 1270 but not completed until 1560. It served as both a royal residence and a watchtower because of its position on the northern harbor. It is also part of the overall fortress defenses that once protected the city. During summer the fortress opens at 6:30 AM and remains open until 11 PM.

* **St. Mary's Church** - This beautiful Romanesque building dates back to the 12th century when Bergen was the first capital of a united Norway. It is where early Norwegian kings had their coronations, weddings and funerals. Located at Dreggen # 15 it is easy to spot from a distance by looking for its twin bell towers. The church is open between 9 AM and 4 PM Monday thru Friday. Between June 1 and August 31 there is a guided tour offered at 3:30 PM in English.

* **Suburban Bergen** – The city of Bergen is quite expansive and most visitors only see the central city and catch a glimpse of the size either when sailing between the outer suburban islands or from the top of Mt. Floyen. Those who have a private car and driver have more opportunity to explore the various sectors of the city, each with its very distinct character.

The suburban areas surrounding the city center for the most part date to the 19th century with their white wood houses climbing the steep slopes of Mt. Floyen and the other peaks surrounding the city center. The southern suburbs where Troldhaugen, the home of

Edvard Grieg is located extend well out from the city center and can best be appreciated by riding the light rail to its far end and back.

* **Troldhaugen** - This is the small house and estate that was home to Norway's most celebrated classical composer, Edvard Grieg. It is a museum dedicated to the famous composer and somewhat of a shrine to those familiar with the composer's music.

The house is open daily from 9 AM to 6 PM during summer, it is often offered as a special ship's tour on various cruise lines. This tour is especially popular with classical music lovers, as Grieg's music is so widely appreciated. If you go on your own and do not have a car, take the light rail from the city center at Festplassen and get off at Hop Station then follow the signs. It is a short and pleasant walk to the house and grounds.

Troldhaugen, (Work of Banja-Frans Mulder, CC BY SA 3.0, Wikimedia.org)

DINING OUT: Most cruise itineraries allow a full day and often many ships remain for much of the evening in Bergen. With the great variety of restaurants located in the city center, which is a short walk from where cruise ships dock, I highly recommend either lunch or dinner in the city. Many cruise itineraries allow the ship to stay well into the middle of the evening, so dining out in the city is possible for dinner. Here is a chance to enjoy great Norwegian food with a heavy emphasis upon fresh seafood. I have several restaurant recommendations primarily for lunch, but a few do remain open for dinner and in each case I have chosen a venue that specializes in traditional Norwegian cuisine.

* **Bare Vestland** is a traditional Norwegian restaurant that specializes in both seafood and meats prepared in the western Norwegian tradition. Their menu is very diverse and there will be a dish or two to please any taste, and they also have a broad selection of beers.

Open Monday thru Saturday for dinner from 5 to 10 PM. They are located close to the Fish Market at Vaagsallmenningen #2, this is a place that many locals patronize, so it is not strictly for tourists. Call +47 400 02 455 to see if they take bookings the day you wish to visit.

* **Bryggeloftet & Steuene** is a major restaurant on the waterfront in Bryggen. You cannot miss it because of its large marquee at the front. It is also in a prominent multi story brick building, which is not a common sight in Bergen. Open daily from Noon to 10 PM. You will find a very diverse menu, but the emphasis is upon seafood. And one of its specialties is a delicious fish soup, a Norwegian tradition. This is a top choice for either lunch or dinner and it is only about a 15 minute walk from where most ships dock. Call +47 56 30 20 70 for booking a table.

* **Daily Pot** - At Vaskerveien # 21, this is one of the most revered small restaurants with a stellar reputation. It is right in the center of the city. It is especially well known for its great soups, especially fish soup, which is such a Norwegian dish. The cuisine and service are superb. Soup and salad are the specialties and many dishes are fit for vegan tastes. They are open Monday thru Friday from 11 AM to 6 PM and on weekends from Noon to 6 PM. Call them at +47 450 75 373 to book a table.

* **Fjellskål** - Located on the waterfront just to the south and west of the Fish Market at Strandkalen #3, this is one of the city's most noted seafood restaurants. It is open Tuesday thru Thursday from 11 AM to 6 PM and Friday and Saturday from 9 AM to 10 PM. The array of fish and shellfish dishes is quite amazing, as are the fish soups. Freshness is the hallmark along with excellent preparation. And you are directly on the water where fishing boats are docking to unload their catch. Call +47 989 05 898 to see if they are accepting bookings for lunch.

* **Klosterette Kaffebar**- This casual restaurant is located near the heart of the city at Klosterette # 16 just off of Haugeveien, a short walk from the main square. It is easy to reach on the hop on hop off bus at stop # 5. It is noted for its excellent soups, especially the traditional fish soup. Fish cakes are a popular dish, but they also surprisingly do make a good burger for those who want something heartier. This is definitely a local cafe but one that does welcome the occasional tourist. Their hours are from 10 AM to 8:30 PM Monday thru Thursday, remaining open to 9 PM Friday. Weekend hours are from 11 AM to 9 PM. A reservation is not needed.

* **Restaurant Cornelius** - If you want to escape the city and the hordes of tourists, have the ship make a lunch or dinner reservation at this restaurant located on the island of Byorøya south of the city center in the main fjord along which the city is built. You will be given instructions as to where to meet their private boat that will take you to the restaurant and return you to the city. Here you will enjoy a fantastic seafood dinner pared with great wines in a setting that is idyllic and if the weather is nice, you can eat outside on their deck overlooking the water. They open at Monday thru Saturday between 6 and 10:30 PM, but a reservation is necessary since they must arrange transportation. Call +47 56 33 48 80 to book a table.

* **Restaurant Opus 16** - Located in the city at Vaagsallmenningen, which is close to the Festparken, this is a traditional Norwegian restaurant that places a high emphasis upon fresh seafood. Their quality and service are outstanding and the atmosphere is very serene. In addition to Norwegian dishes, they also feature a selection of other continental menu items. They are open Tuesday thru Friday between 6:30 and 10 AM and 5 and 10PM. Saturday dining is between Noon and 10 PM. On Sunday they serve between 7 and 11 AM. Call +47 53 01 22 00 to reserve a table.

SHOPPING: As a major city and also a center for tourism, there are many good shopping venues in Bergen, but only one that I felt was significant in its uniqueness. In addition, I note the downtown mall, but it does not measure up to what you would find in Oslo or other major Scandinavian cities. There are many small shops in Bryggen that sell the typical souvenirs and also the hand knitted Norwegian sweaters. But frankly none stand out as very unique. And you will find the same types of gift items, sweaters and kitsch all throughout your cruise. It is just that Bergen has a larger selection and better prices.

* **Galleriet** - This is the largest shopping mall in the city center, located at Torgallmenningen # 8 in the heart of the downtown. It contains a variety of shops and cafes on several levels, but it is nothing out of the ordinary if you have previously shopped in other major cities. But it does offer all of the basics, and when it comes to men's and women's casual clothing there are several Norwegian brands that are of good quality at reasonable prices. The mall is open weekdays from 9 AM to 9 PM and Saturday from 9 AM to 6 PM. And the mall is closed on Sunday.

* **Julehuset Christmas Shop** is a place where you can celebrate Christmas all year. It is located in Bryggen at Holmedalsgaarden #1 and open from 10 AM to 8 PM daily. On three floors you will find a wide array of souvenir items along with traditional Norwegian Christmas decorations and tree ornaments.
*

FINAL COMMENTS: Over the years that I have traveled through Norway, I have been to Bergen at least a dozen times. I always enjoy the overall flavor of the city, appreciating its antiquity mixed with modernity. It is exceptionally fresh and clean and has essentially an unhurried feeling even though thousands of tourists crowd into Bryggen and the Fish Market area. But you can take many quiet walks through its older residential areas, or ride the light rail out to quiet, leafy suburbs and come to understand what it is like to live in this coastal city.

The only real drawback can be the weather, which is so hard to predict. One never knows if it will be a rainy day, just overcast or if you will have blue skies. In July and August you will find the greatest chance of experiencing nice weather in Bergen, which unfortunately is the norm rather than the exception. But please do not let the weather limit your getting out and experiencing the city. Umbrellas should always be at hand.

MAPS OF BERGEN

THE INNER REACHES OF BERGEN

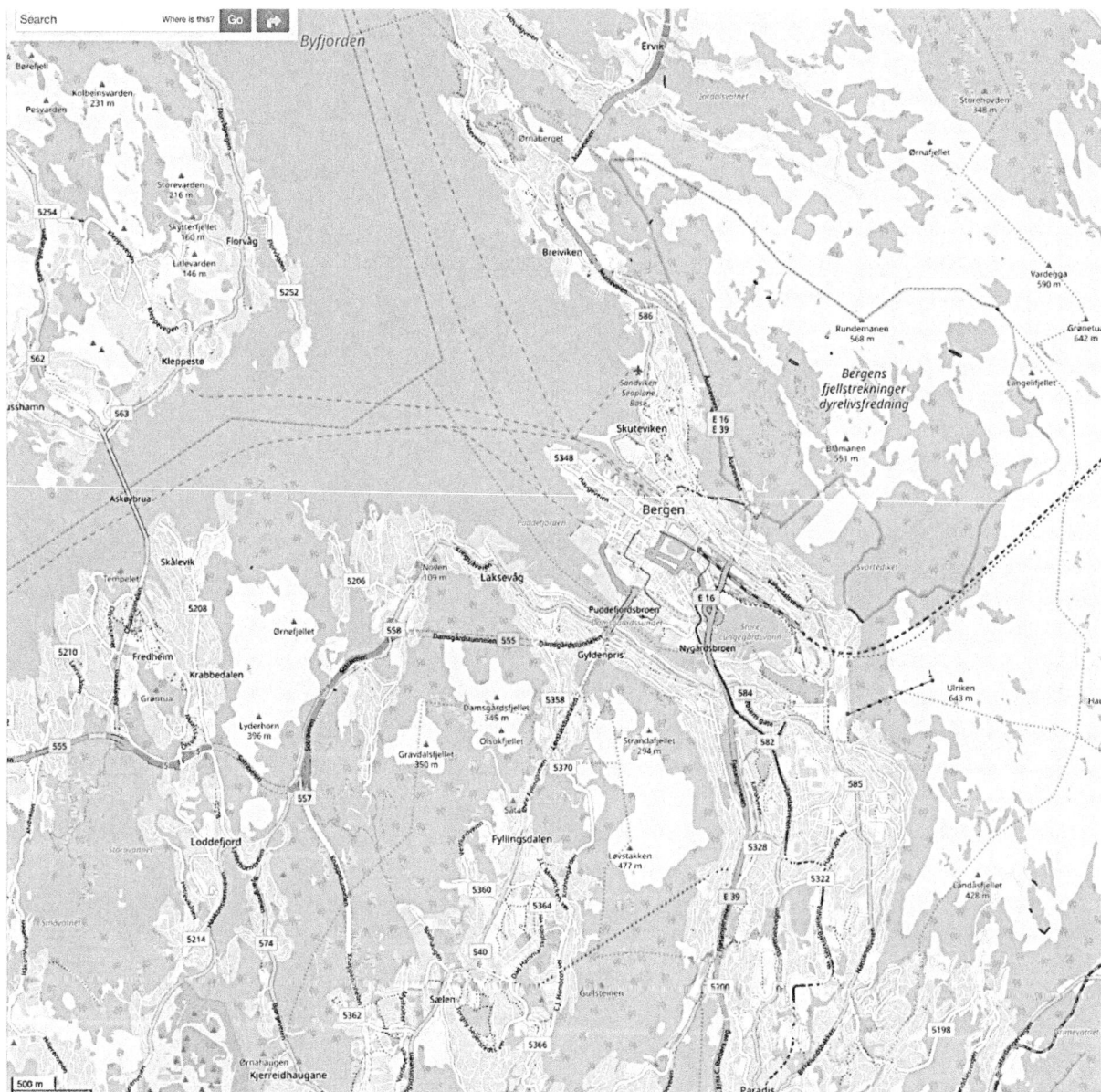

Inner reaches of Bergen, (© OpenStreetMap contributors)

This map is best viewed directly from OpenStreetMap.com on your personal device where it can be expanded or one specific area can be enlarged. Given the format of this book, it is impossible to display maps with the level of detail you might wish to have while actually out exploring the city. But the OpenStreetMap maps used directly are the tool I always rely upon.

THE CENTER OF BERGEN

Central Bergen with the star showing the cruise terminal, (© OpenStreetMap contributors)

This map is best viewed directly from OpenStreetMap.com on your personal device where it can be expanded or one specific area can be enlarged. Given the format of this book, it is impossible to display maps with the level of detail you might wish to have while actually out exploring the city. But the OpenStreetMap maps used directly are the tool I always rely upon.

THE HEART OF BERGEN

The heart of Bergen, (© OpenStreetMap contributors)
This map is best viewed directly from OpenStreetMap.com on your personal device where it can be expanded or one specific area can be enlarged. Given the format of this book, it is impossible to display maps with the level of detail you might wish to have while actually out exploring the city. But the OpenStreetMap maps used directly are the tool I always rely upon.

SOGNEFJORD
VISITING FLÄM, GUDVANGEN AND SKJOLDEN

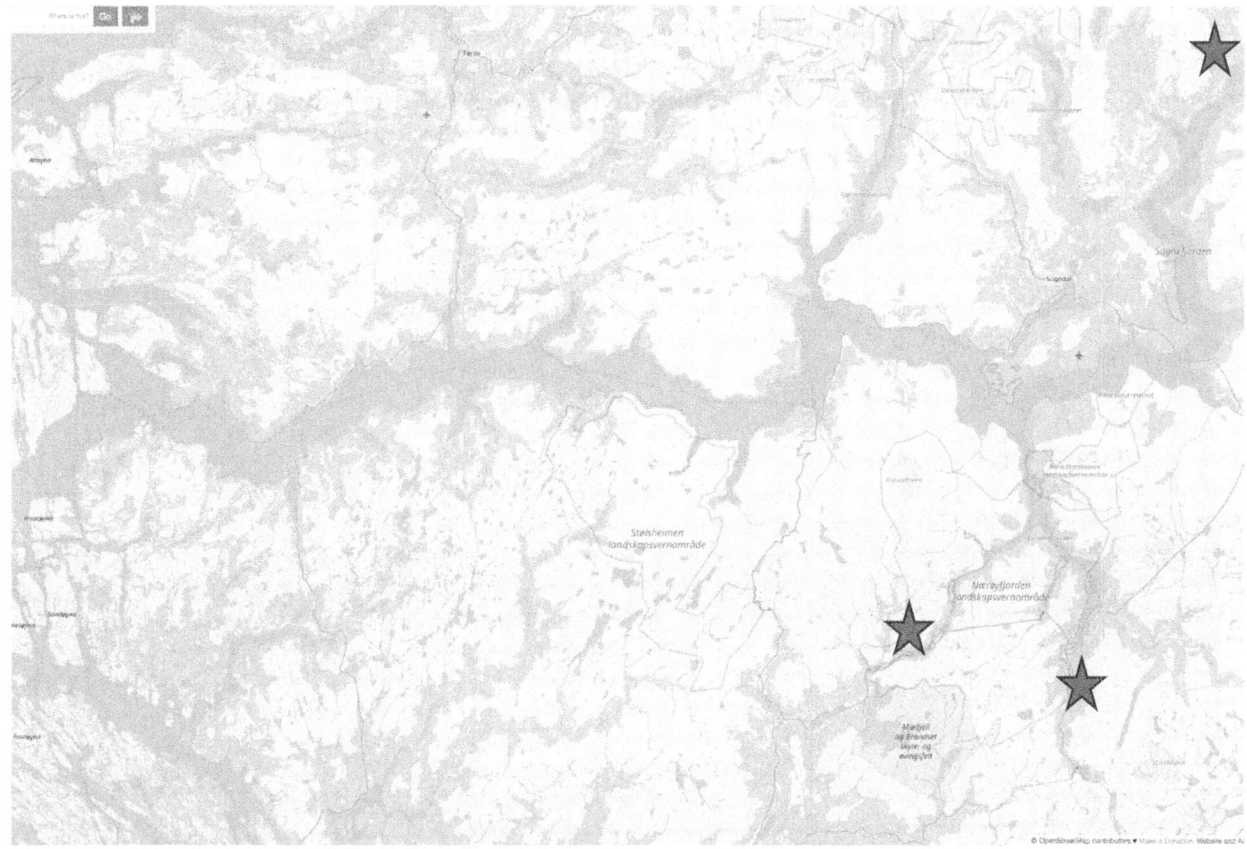

Sognefjord country, Fläm is the right hand star, Gudvangen the left hand star, Skjolden at the top right (© OpenStreetMap contributors)

Visiting Fläm, Gudvangen and Skjolden is often the highlight of those cruises that are not going all the way north into Arctic Norway. Skjolden is the least visited of the ports in the Sogjefjod country but is treated in this chapter for the benefit of those few readers who may visit since so few cruise itineraries include this small village.

It is very difficult to say which fjord system is the most beautiful. I have my favorites based upon their photogenic attributes, but in essence every fjord in Norway is special. And the Sognefjord system with its two major stops of Fläm and Gudvangen is hard to duplicate. Depending upon the amount of cloud cover vs. sunlight, the dappling of the landscape while sailing into these two small villages can simply be magical. There is no other word that seems to describe it. In all my years of visiting these two destinations, no two visits have ever been the same. The moods and shadows versus the brilliance of sunlight is everchanging. And for those few who get to visit Skjolden, the same comment will hold true – it is beautiful.

Remember that fjords are the result of pre glacial river systems having been scoured by glacial ice, often widened and definitely deepened most often with sheer vertical walls.

Every major fjord thus has tributary smaller fjords, presenting a rather complex landscape that can extend over 100 kilometers from the upper reaches to the sea. In the days before glaciation tiny creeks converged together and then formed the major pre glacial river system. Today they plunge directly down into the now deepened gorges, creating what amounts to hundreds of waterfalls. And given Norway's northern latitude and the altitude of its mountains, small glaciers still exist in the highest peaks and snow lingers along the tops of the fjords well into the summer, thus providing for sufficient water to keep the falls in full form.

Aurlandsfjorden in the early morning

The larger streams that were tributary to the main river were also gouged and deepened and today represent the branches of the overall fjord system. The two major southern branches of Sognefjord are Aurlandsfjorden, which is the location for the village of Fläm and Nærøyfjorden, home to the village of Gudvangen.

A NOTE ON TOURING OPTIONS: Given the remote location of these three villages and the brief length of time of most port calls, the only touring options you will have are those tours offered by your cruise line. Private cars with drivers, car rentals or hop on hop off bus tours are simply not available. If you elect to stay in port you will find that these are very small villages and you will be spending your time simply absorbing the beauty of the surroundings, but missing so much of the hidden depth of the landscape that will not be visible to you.

THE PORT OF FLÄM: Normally most cruise itineraries call for an early morning entry into Sognefjord, cruising slowly inbound for at least three to four hours before reaching Aurlandsfjorden, which is rather of short length. The journey is quite spectacular in the early morning light, of course providing the weather is relatively good. The best conditions are those when the sky is clear and there is a small amount of ground fog or mist swirling around the steep cliffs. I find that most often you can count the number of guests out on deck on one hand, as the majority are either sleeping or preparing for the day's activities.

To experience the beauties of Sognefjord and capture some of the greatest photos of your Norwegian Fjords cruise providing the weather cooperates, one must normally be out on deck at around 5:30 AM. But there is still an opportunity to enjoy a different perspective during the evening sail out from Gudvangen, as most ships will not reach the open sea until approximately 10 PM. My recommendation to those who really enjoy capturing fantastic scenic shots is for you to be out on deck for both the sail in as well as the evening sail out.

Sognefjorden and Aurlandssfjorden join

Arrival at Fläm is generally in the morning at around 8 or 9 AM. There is a single small dock that is capable of handling one medium size cruise ship, and it is available on a first come basis whenever the local car ferries are not arriving at the same time. Despite their smaller size, for obvious reasons the car ferries take precedence over a cruise ship. In the event the dock is occupied by a ferry or an earlier ship, your ship will drop anchor in the fjord and you will tender to and from shore by means of one of the ship's lifeboats. The only disadvantage is that such transfers can add up to half an hour to the time going to or coming from shore. This is especially the case on the larger cruise ships.

For those who remain in Fläm, usually only a handful of guests, there is very little to do. Fläm is a village with a few shops, a nice hotel and a several private residences. Apart from the port area there are very few places in which to walk. There are a few walking paths, but the time will pass slowly since the stop is around four hours duration and after an hour there will be nothing more to see or do. But if you wish to just relax and soak in the beauty of the surrounding mountains that tower above the fjord, this can be as enjoyable an experience as one of the tours. At least there is the hotel dining room where you can have breakfast or a late morning tea and relax in comfort.

Thus the most effective use of your time is to take one of the rail journey options. I can be bold enough to say that it should be an absolute must, as it is a journey of a lifetime with regard to the beauty you will see. In all my years of visiting Fläm I always take one of the rail journeys no matter the weather. Even on a gray and rainy day there can be some photo opportunities of a unique nature. Given the changes in elevation during any of the rail journeys, there can be drastic changes in what the weather conditions will be throughout the day.

The village of Fläm

The hotel patio in Fläm

THE FLÄMSBANA RAILROAD: Fläm is the coastal terminus of the Flämsbana, a railroad link of approximately 20.2 kilometers or 12.6 miles, but rising 867 meters or 2,844 feet in elevation. It connects Aurlansfjorden with the main railway line that links Oslo with Bergen. It is a vital link in the Norwegian transport system that connects main railway lines with ferryboats and highways, giving the country a more cohesive transportation network. This railroad is an amazing feat of engineering in a land so dominated over by deep and long fjords and high, steep mountains.

This train journey, which takes a little more than an hour each way, is the highlight of the day for most guests. It is one of the world's most spectacular rail journeys with a constantly changing panorama of the glacial valley, mountain peaks and a myriad of waterfalls. To accomplish the construction was a major feat of engineering, the line is a single track standard gauge with corresponding overhead electric cables to provide power. There are 18 tunnels on the line, which has an average 2.8 percent grade.

The views from the train are memorable beyond words or photographs. As a minimum, this short journey must be experienced. On the short journey the train reaches the summit and drops guests at the lodge in Vatnahalsen for morning tea and returns back down for Fläm about 90 minutes later after dropping off those continuing on the main line to Bergen or Oslo. I guarantee that you will treasure the memory of this short, but special rail journey.

The Flämsbana ready for departure from Fläm to the heights above

Heading up on the Flämsbana out of Fläm

One of the spectacular waterfalls of the Flämsbana route

Apart from hosting ship passengers for their excursions, the Fläsbana is a connecting railroad for ferryboat passengers who are connecting via the mainline railroad to Bergen or Oslo or other intermediate destinations. The railroad is one of the many links in the land and water transport network of coastal Norway.

The longest option offered by some cruise itineraries has guests transferring to the main line train at Myrdal where the Flämsbaha meets the mainline, as they are destined for Voss, located a short distance to the west. At Voss, guests board a motor coach for a dramatic journey back down the mountains, but continuing on to Gudvangen where they meet the ship later in the afternoon. This is a magnificent tour, but it is frankly a bit tiring for those of us over age 65. Also it does involve a lot of mountain driving and is not recommended for anyone who suffers from motion sickness.

This full day option includes a lunch break midway during the motor coach tour along with many scenic stops to enjoy panoramic vistas, breathtaking waterfalls and what to some might be considered 'hair-raising" mountain roads. It makes for a long day, and does involve a lot of very serious mountain driving with sharp curves and steep drops.

I offer a caution for anyone who has fear of heights and steep slopes with regard to taking this full day option to Gudvangen. But keep in mind that Norwegian drivers learn their trade on these roads, as do all Norwegian citizens, as there is no way to get around this rugged nation without negotiating steep curves, dramatic drop-offs and other aspects of mountain driving flatlanders never experience. So put your fears aside and trust the drivers.

En route down to Fläm and passing Undredal the scenery is dramatic

THE PORT OF GUDVANGEN: It will take your ship about two hours to sail back down Aurlandsfjorden and into Nærøyfjorden and the small village of Gudvangen. This is accomplished at midday, and on those days when it is sunny or even just partly cloudy, the voyage is nothing less than spectacular.

Most guests will crowd into the ship's observation lounges or be out on deck to absorb the raw beauty of this transfer between the two fjords. I have done this trip more than a dozen times, and each time is like the first. But unless it is extremely blustery or cold, I prefer to be out on deck to savor not only the views the freshness of the air. This is a part of the cruise that will live in your memory for all time to come.

I have also taken the rail-coach journey, meeting the ship in Gudvangen. Both options offer incredible vistas. On the shipboard journey the sheer walls of the two fjords, the small villages and farms tucked into every available shelf of land and the lacy ribbons of water flowing over the cliffs combine to say to you, "This is Norway at its Best." Despite being one of the most breathtaking of journeys, for those who are coming to Gudvangen via the overland train and bus route, they will miss this spectacle, but of course they will have as magnificent a journey of a different nature, one of high mountains and narrow valleys.

The view back to Gudvangen seen in midafternoon light

There is a quiet charm to the village of Gudvangen

Gudvangen is a small village located at the top end of Nærøyfjorden. It is essentially a residential village, but where car ferries dock, there is a nice visitor's center with a gift shop. And there are a few small hotels that cater to those who are traveling through the fjord country either by car, utilizing the combination of roads and ferryboat connections or the more physically active who are hiking, walking or cycling their way around the country.

The earliest hotel to open in Gudvangen was in 1830. Gudvangen is also connected directly to Fläm by way of the Gudvangen Tunnel that cuts through the mountain separating the two fjords. This has reduced the travel time by road by nearly two thirds and is an example of what the Norwegian government is doing in all settled parts of the country to shorten travel distances. As a prosperous nation, Norway invests heavily in its rail, highway and ferryboat transport grid, providing for excellent connections throughout the country.

In Gudvangen the dock is not large enough to accommodate any size cruise ship, thus it becomes necessary to anchor off shore and tender guests to the dock. Once in Gudvangen there is not much to do other than walk around the town and enjoy both its traditional wood architecture and the towering cliffs that surround it unless it is Viking festival time. The village is literally surrounded by waterfalls, a sight that is sure to please any camera enthusiast.

Gudvangen dates back to Viking times, and it has been a gathering place and small market center for approximately 1,000 years. Today there is a Viking festival held each year in late July or early August on the meadow located across the small river just east of the town. Locals dressed in traditional garb camp here in Viking fashion, performing traditional tasks, playing musical instruments and preparing food in the manner of their distant ancestors. There is a small admission fee, but this also entitles you to photograph the participants at your leisure if you are fortunate enough that your port call is during the time of the festival.

THE PORT OF SKJOLDEN: Only a handful of cruise ships make the longer journey up Lustrafjorden, which is a lesser fjord that joins Sognefjorden from the northeast. Skjolden is 123 kilometers or 76 miles north of Fläm by road, which is approximately the same distance by boat, however, there is no local ferry connection. The journey is in the opposite direction from Fläm and Gudvangen and would add an additional full day to the cruise itinerary if it was visited in combination with the two more famous ports. There are a few cruise itineraries that will simply visit Skjolden and then not visit Fläm or Gudvangen.

The village of Skjolden only has around 200 residents full time but surprisingly does have accommodation and dining facilities for visitors. For those traveling by automobile, this area offers a multitude of possibilities , especially at Breheimen National Park where small glaciers still exist. Skjolden is the farthest distance from the ocean of any town on the Sognefjorden system, approximately 200 kilometers or 120 miles, taking around four to five hours sailing time by cruise ship. Although there is a dock for cruise ships, the majority of cruises into the Sognefjorden system visit Fläm and/or Gudvangen because over the years these two villages have gained more fame. Fläm of course has the advantage of being the terminus for the world renowned Flämsbana Railroad.

The scenery in and around Skjolden is quite breathtaking, as being deeper into the Norwegian interior, the mountains are higher, giving the walls of Lustrafjorden greater height translating into taller waterfalls and more majestic scenery.

One of the many waterfalls surrounding Gudvangen

Aurlandsfjorden at the village of Undredal near Gudvangen

DINING OUT: Your time ashore in both Fläm and Gudvangen is so limited that there is no chance to sit and have a nice lunch. But you can have morning coffee with a pastry at the hotel in Fläm if you are not doing one of the rail journeys. If you do have any time for lunch, which is doubtful, I do recommend the main hotel dining room. The food is quite good as is the service.

Depending upon what services your cruise line has arranged, you may be limited to simply enjoying the village of Skjolden or there may be motor coach tours to Breheimen National park, which I would highly recommend if it is offered on your itinerary. Breheimen is a sizeable park covering 1,671 square kilometers or 675 square miles of rugged mountain landscape, including three active glaciers. The most noted is the Holåbreen Glacier. If you happen to be on a cruise itinerary that is including Skjolden and if that port call offers the opportunity to see the Holåbreen Glacier it will be an adventure you will keep with you for many years to come.

To fully enjoy the majesty of the park requires going on a hike or trek, which for most cruise ship passengers is not possible given the time constraints. But many cruise tours that do come into the park will include a small nature hike to give guests some appreciation for the natural beauty of the landscape.

The majesty of Aurlandsfjorden seen on the outward sailing

The village of Skjolden, (Work of Nisto, CC BY SA 3.0, Wikimedia.org)

The Holåbreen Glacier in Breheimen National Park, (Work of Frankemann, CC BY SA 4.0, Wikimedia.org)

The visit to Gudvangen is also quite short and occurs in the afternoon, well past the hour for dining. And there are no major hotel facilities or dining rooms in Gudvangen.

If your ship is stopping in Skjolden and you are staying in the village, I do recommend the Eide Gard Café for a late lunch or early dinner if your ship is staying past 4 PM since they are only open between 4 and 10 PM except Sunday when they do open at 2 PM. This small, but excellent café is expensive, but worthwhile. You will need to book a table in advance by having the ship concierge call at +47 951 09 643.

For a light lunch there is also the Lustrabui Bakery, which offers take away sandwiches and snacks with outdoor seating in good weather. It is open from 7 AM to 5 PM weekdays and on Saturday only until 2 PM, but closed Sunday.

MEMORIES: Every time I have visited both Fläm and Gudvangen I have found it to be a day filled with incredible, but ever changing scenery. The mood of the landscape will depend upon the weather, but even in the worst case scenario where it rains, there is still an aura of environmental magic to the entire length of Sognefjord and its tributary fjords depending upon where your ship is heading. Even on days when the weather is less than perfect, the fjords takes on a mood of their own that can be quite dramatic. Sometimes there is fog clinging to the water and at other times clouds gather over the mountaintops.

One of those clear mornings in Sognefjord

I do highly advise everyone to spend as much time out on deck, or if it is too cold then spend time in the observation lounge. Sailing into Sognefjord in the early morning hours can be quite a magnificent sight if you truly are willing to wake up extra early and be out on deck. I have done it many times and have found it a most enjoyable experience.

SOGNEFJORD MAPS

AURLANDSFJORDEN AND NÆROYFJORDEN

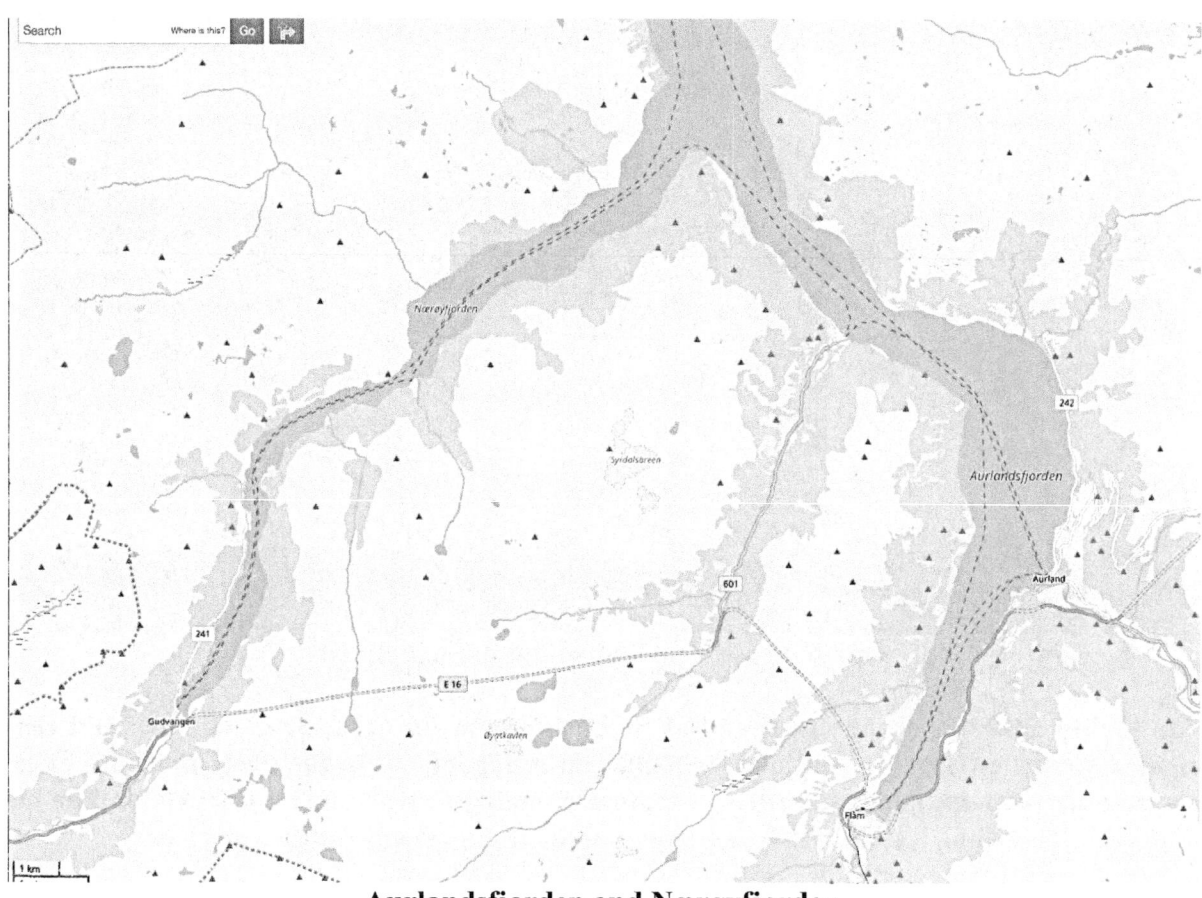

Aurlandsfjorden and Nærøyfjorden

This map is best viewed directly from OpenStreetMap.com on your personal device where it can be expanded or one specific area can be enlarged. Given the format of this book, it is impossible to display maps with the level of detail you might wish to have while actually out exploring the city. But the OpenStreetMap maps used directly are the tool I always rely upon.

LUSTRAFJORDEN AND SKJOLDEN

Lustrafjorden and Skjolden

This map is best viewed directly from OpenStreetMap.com on your personal device where it can be expanded or one specific area can be enlarged. Given the format of this book, it is impossible to display maps with the level of detail you might wish to have while actually out exploring the city. But the OpenStreetMap maps used directly are the tool I always rely upon.

NORDFJORDEN

VISITING OLDEN

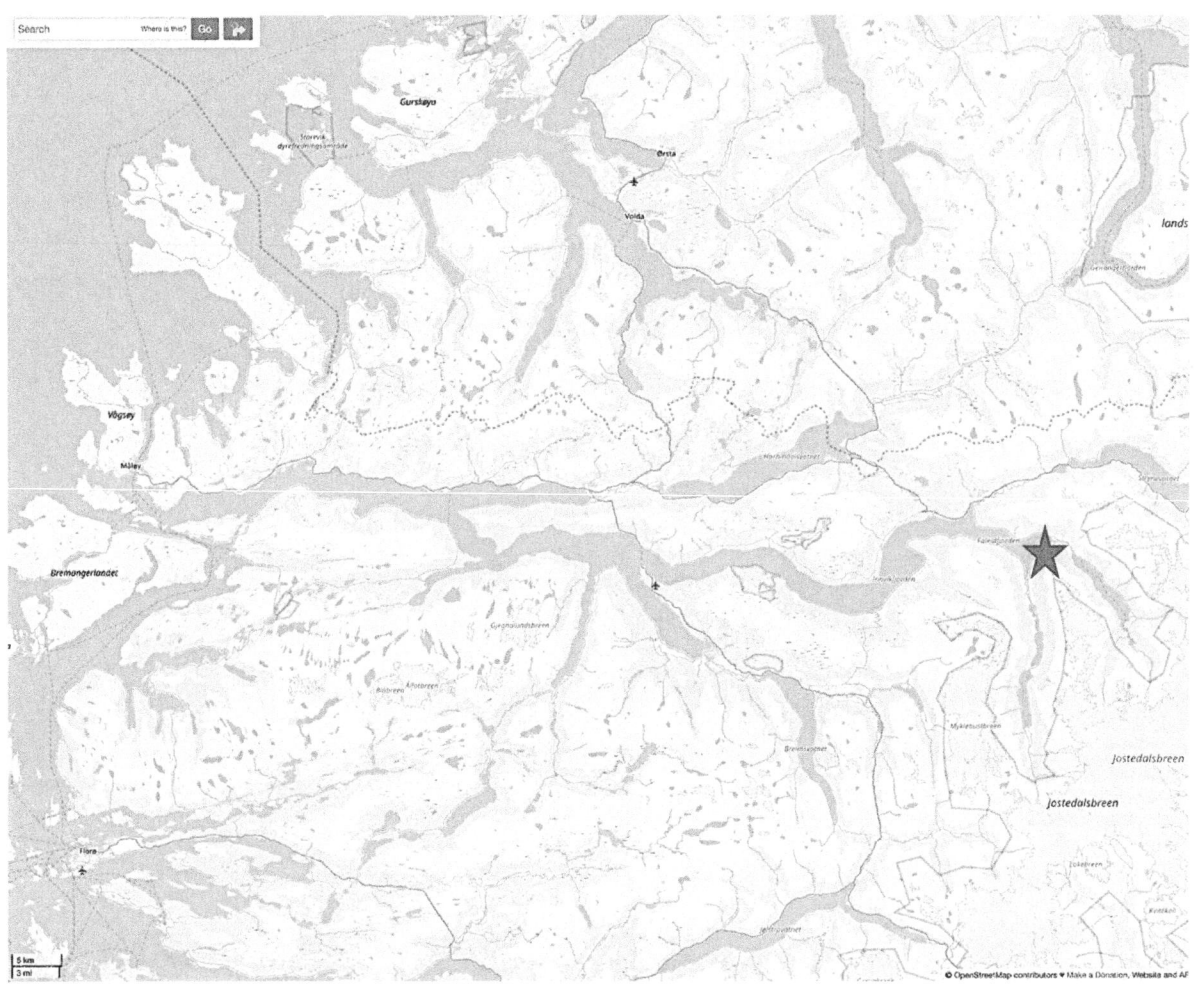

The Nordfjorden system and the location of Olden as per the star(© OpenStreetMap contributors)

Visting Olden after having sailed through the Sognefjord system the prior day (if you are sailing northbound) is almost reaching for sensory overload. Just when you thought you had seen some of the most beautiful scenery Norway has to offer, the next day you are waking up to a majestic landscape that rivals what you had just seen. If your itinerary is one in which you visit the Norfjorden system first and then sail on the following day to Fläm and Gudvangen, the same condition will apply. Which fjord system is more majestic? The answer to that question is purely subjective and a matter of taste. As one who has made the journey many times, I cannot give a definitive answer. Although I must say that the village of Olden and the chain of lakes south to the head of the Jostedalsbreen Ice Sheet is one of the most stunning landscapes in the country. And if you happen to visit on a day with dappled light, that is a mix of sun and cloud, you will experience the true glory of Norway.

Sailing up Norfjorden past the town of Loen at dawn

Norfjorden is among the longer fjord systems in Norway, its total length being just over 106 kilometers or 63 miles. Most of its runoff comes from the large Jostedalsbreen Ice Sheet, which some maps refer to as a glacier. Jostedalsbreen is the largest single mass of ancient glacial ice on the European continent, exceeded in size only by the large ice sheets of Iceland, which is a European country culturally, but not a part of mainland Europe geologically. Four small tributary fjords come together to form the primary Norfjorden. The village of Olden is located where the rushing waters of the Oldelva River flow into Faleidfjorden, a small extension or arm of the larger Norfjorden. The glacial melt comes from the Birksdalsbreen Glacier, which is a tongue of the larger Jostedalsbreen Ice Sheet. The glacier is located approximately 40 kilometers or 24 miles south of Olden, at the top end of the valley carved initially by the glacier thousands of years ago, and today fed by the Oldelva River.

Because of the depth of glacial scour, these fjords are especially deep, here where Faleidfjorden flows into Norfjorden it is 565 meters or 1,854 feet deep. There is no ship in the world that would have any difficulty navigating in water this deep, however, the largest cruise ships cannot be accommodated with docking facilities and the town of Olden cannot handle thousands of ship guests at one time. So the limiting factor in whether your itinerary includes a stop in Olden is not determined by the act of navigation, but rather by the inability of small villages to service the needs of large numbers of visitors at the same time. Thus if you truly want to enjoy cruising through most of the fjords of Norway, you are best off in choosing a smaller size and lower tonnage ship that carries 500 passengers or less.

DOCKING AND VISITING OLDEN: It takes around four hours to sail all the way through Norfjorden to the village of Olden. Once again I recommend that you be out on deck if the weather is good or even just partly cloudy, as the vistas of mountain crags, swirling mist and layers of cloud will offer up some incredible scenes. Last time I sailed into Olden it was one of those majestic mornings with a mix of dappled sunlight, some patchy fog and calm waters. The scenery was breathtaking and there were only two other guests out on deck to enjoy this natural spectacle. Everyone else was still in bed or just starting to stir, and they missed it all. There is a single dock, and given that this is not a major cruise destination, it is doubtful that more than one cruise ship will be in port at a given time. Being able to dock on the very edge of the village does make the visit easier, as you do not need to spend time waiting for and then riding the tender boat to or from shore.

The Olden area is surprisingly old with regard to settlement. Evidence shows that pre Viking settlement can be traced back to the Iron Age. But the actual village of Olden is relatively young by Norwegian standards with settlement dating back to the mid 1600's, but there were scattered households at the top end of the fjord as far back as the early 1300's. The old church located in the heart of the village was built in 1759, but on the same site there was once an old stave church built back in the 1300's.

Sailing into Olden on a spectacular morning

Within the Olden region, back in 1905 and again in 1936, there was a massive avalanche of rock that toppled off of Mt. Ramnefjelt into Lovatnet Lake, creating a massive series of tsunami waves that killed 102 people in the two disasters combined. This to date is the largest loss of life from any natural catastrophe in the history of Norway. Some cruise operators do offer a hike to Lovatnet Lake, not with the past disaster in mind, but for guests to simply enjoy the breathtaking scenery.

Although the village of Olden only has a resident population of 500, it is becoming more oriented to the cruise industry. There are a few local tour operators and a hop on hop off bus that meet the ship and offer affordable tours through the town and to the front of the Birksdalsbreen Glacier. And most cruise lines also offer one or more scenic tours. Apart from some cruise lines having a hike to Lovatnet Lake, most offer a coach tour to visit the Birksdalsbreen Glacier. These tours do involve a bit of hiking in order to reach viewpoints that are advantageous in seeing the glacier. And some cruise operators offer a longer coach tour to visit the more massive Jostedalsbreen Ice Sheet. Visiting Olden is all about the natural landscape, as the village itself offers only the old church and its lovely houses, sights that can be enjoyed in a matter of minutes.

The road to the village of Olden

SHIP DOCK: There is a small dock in Olden capable of handling a single cruise ship of medium size, but it is doubtful that there would ever be two ships in port at the same time. And because Olden is so small, the very large cruise ships could not be accommodated with the volume of service its guests would require.

TOURING OPTIONS FOR OLDEN: Olden is too small and too isolated to be able to offer the cruise passenger the total array of services found in the larger or more heavily visited ports of call. Because services are so limited, the cruise lines that visit rely upon the local services as detailed below:

The fast flowing Oldelva River through Olden

* **Local village tour** - There is a local bus with an open top to tour people around the small village and to take the Olden Lakes drive, which is approximately 15 kilometers or 9 miles in length and absolutely spectacular. When the weather is perfect, which is quite frequent during summer, you will have photos that will be great treasures of this day.

This slow drive with photo stops brings you within photographic distance of the still active Josteadal Glacier. The driver will offer narration during this tour and will even make extra stops if someone wants to get a particular view of the passing scenery. Tickets can be purchased on shore for the several round trips that will be made during the time your ship is in port. .

* **The Briksdal Glacier Shuttle** is a three hour tour up to the beautiful Birksdal Glacier where you are dropped off for approximately 1.5 to 2 hours of exploration on your own. There is a small shop and refreshment stand while at the shuttle drop off. For details visit on line with *www.fjordnorway.com/things-to-do/briksdal=glacier-shuttle-bus-olden* . Once again there will be a representative to sell tickets for this tour upon the arrival of your ship. Normally there will only be one tour during the day because of the time consumed with the drive to the glacier and back.

* You can simply walk around the village of Olden, but this will occupy you for no more than an hour, but be sure to also include the village church and cemetery while you are walking around the town. I do advise one of the bus tours to appreciate the magnificent

scenery of this special fjord. And you will still have some time left during which you can wander around the village, as the dock is less than a ten minute walk from the heart of the settlement.

The old 17th century church in Olden

DINING OUT: Olden is such a small village, and choice is very limited. Lunch is possible if you do not go on a group tour, but the majority of guests generally return to the ship given the meager selection of restaurants.

* **Molla Gjesthus** - Located opposite where the ship docks, is a small guesthouse with limited offerings of food and drink. It is very expensive, but it does provide local color and has a friendly staff. However, if you research the guest house on Trip Advisor you will find the reviews to be quite mixed. I personally found lunch to be quite acceptable. The dining room is open Sunday thru Thursday from 2 to 9 PM, Friday and Saturday from 2 PM until 2:30 AM. Reservations are not necessary.

* **Yris Kafe** - Located in the heart of Olden, and often showing up in guide books as Per's Cafe, this small establishment offers light lunches and the prices are reasonable by Norwegian standards. It is open from 11 AM to 9 PM Monday thru Thursday, remaining open until 10 PM Saturday. Sunday hours are from Noon to 9 PM. Reservations are not required.

The Oldelva River in whitewater south of Olden

FINAL WORDS: Again I find it hard to put into words how magnificent the scenery is when visiting Olden. The sail into this tiny village and the sail back out in the late afternoon can provide some of the most incredible photographic opportunities if there is the right mix of cloud and sun.

Many visitors want perfectly blue skies, but they do not realize that a mix of sun and cloud produces shadows that can heighten the majestic quality of photographs. But this being Norway, it can often be very cloudy, rainy or the fjord can be shrouded in fog. It is always a gamble. But even when there are patches of low clouds or fog, the good photographer considers this a benefit. If you notice many of the photographs in this book were taken by me on days that so many visitors would consider to be less than perfect.

The beauty of the lower Oldelva Lake

The magnificent beauty of Upper Lake nearest the glacier

Sailing out from Olden in the late afternoon

The beauty of Oldelva Lake on the return into Olden

An idyllic Olden village house

MAPS OF THE OLDEN AREA

THE VILLAGE OF OLDEN

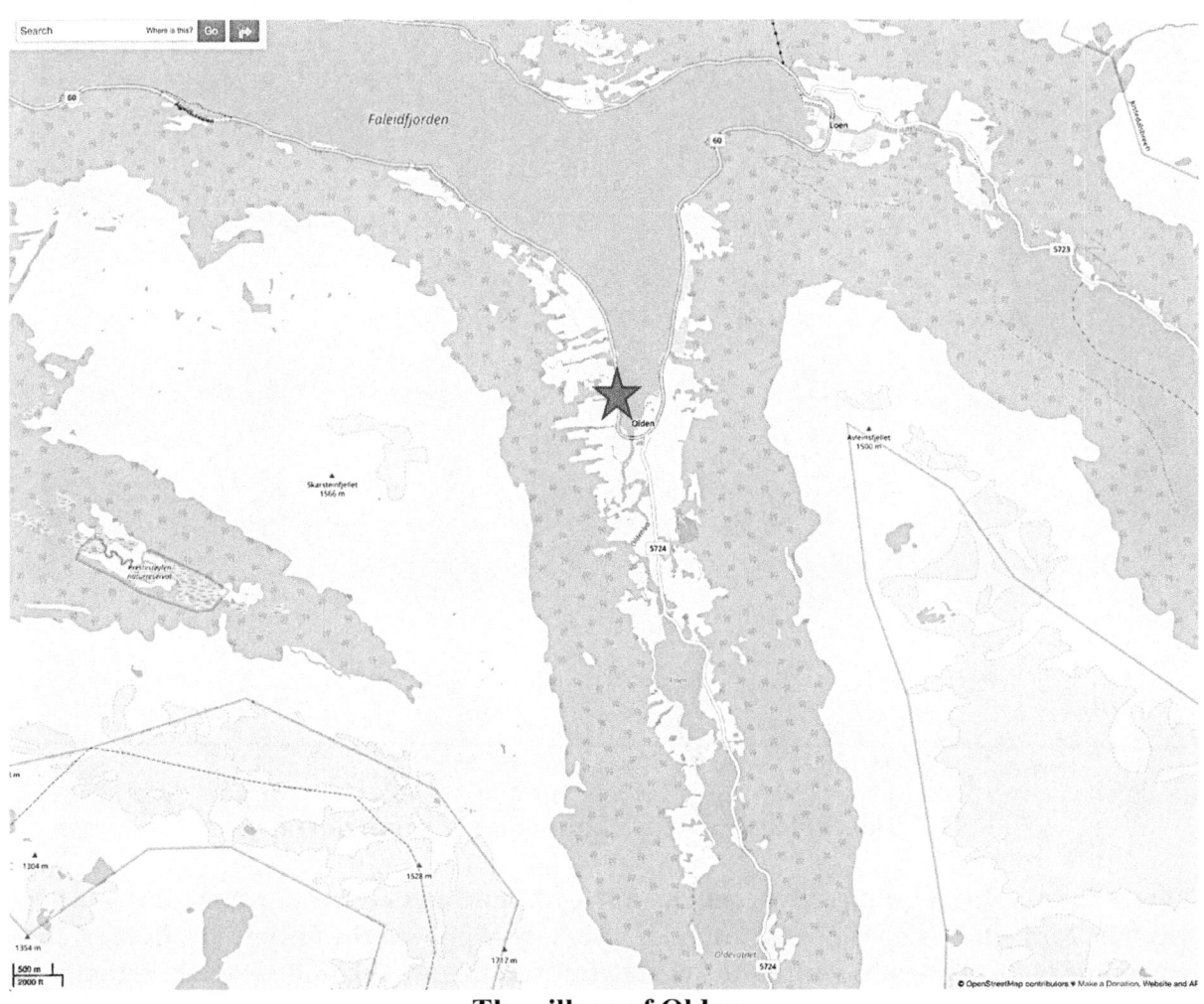

The village of Olden

This map is best viewed directly from OpenStreetMap.com on your personal device where it can be expanded or one specific area can be enlarged. Given the format of this book, it is impossible to display maps with the level of detail you might wish to have while actually out exploring the city. But the OpenStreetMap maps used directly are the tool I always rely upon.

THE OLDELVA RIVER LAKES

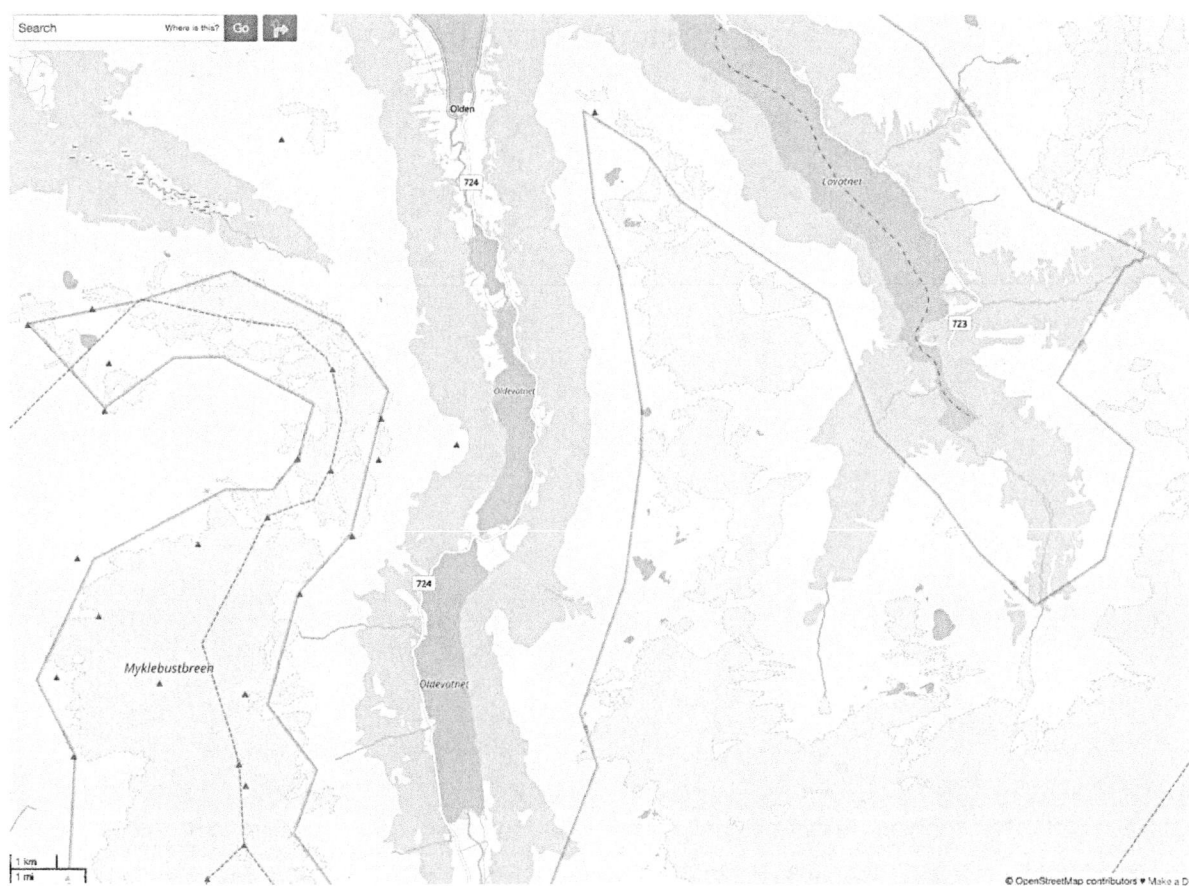

The Oldelva River and its chain of lakes south of Olden

This map is best viewed directly from OpenStreetMap.com on your personal device where it can be expanded or one specific area can be enlarged. Given the format of this book, it is impossible to display maps with the level of detail you might wish to have while actually out exploring the city. But the OpenStreetMap maps used directly are the tool I always rely upon.

ÅLESUND

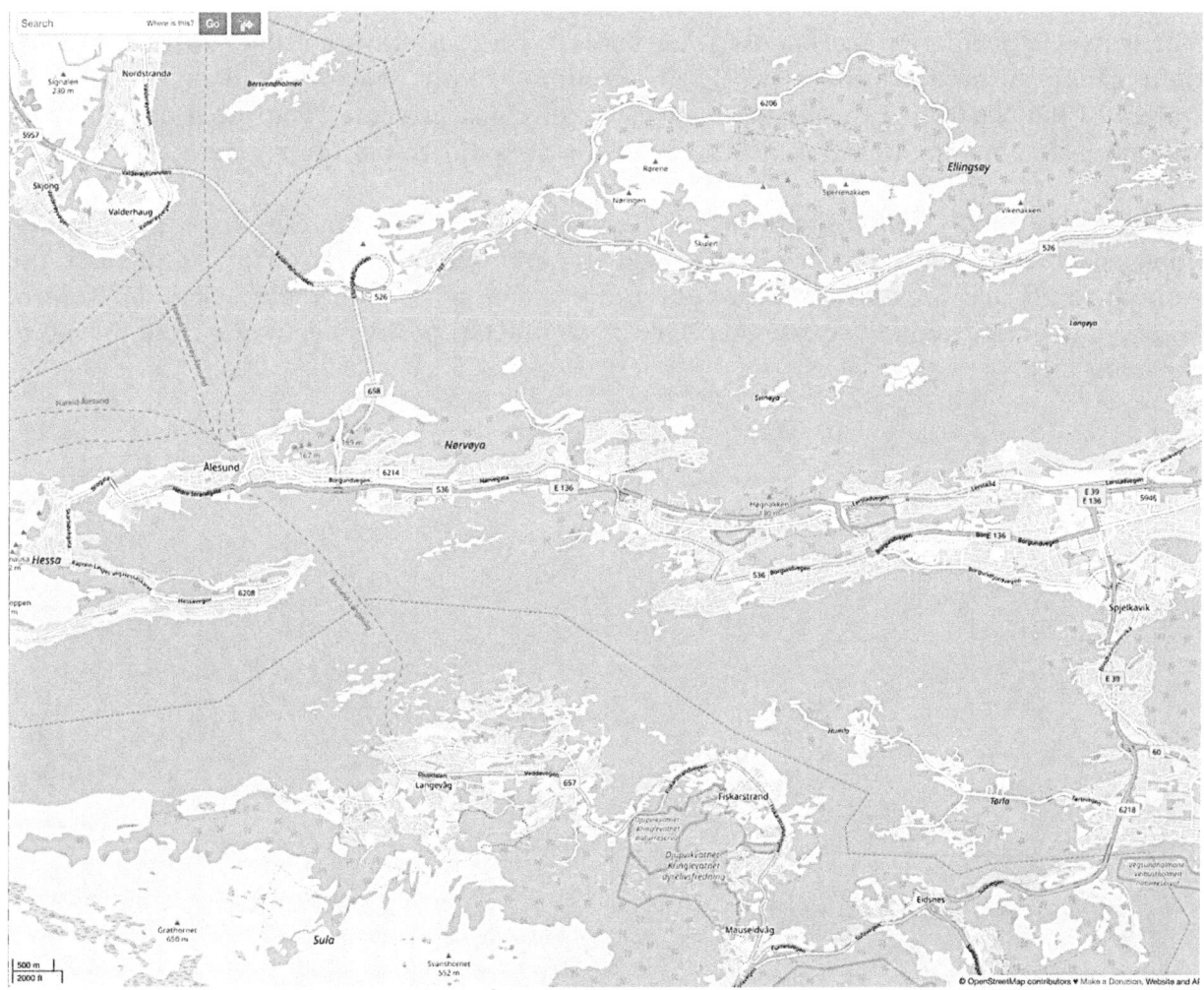

A map of the region of Ålesund (© OpenStreetMap contributors)

A visit to Ålesund comes as quite a surprise to those who are simply expecting another Norwegian town or village. Ålesund is a significant coastal city with a metro area population of approximately 49,000 residents. Both the physical setting and the architecture of the city make it quite distinctive and to some degree unique among the coastal ports of Norway. It may be a small city, but it visually presents as a significant port of call with a nice and inviting downtown core.

THE PHYSICAL LANDSCAPE: Ålesund is a city of islands. It is located at a junction of several fjords that came together during the last glacial advance, carving up the landscape in such a way that when the ice melted back and sea level rose, numerous rugged offshore islands were created. Ålesund is connected by one of the channels between the islands to the entrance of Geirangerfjorden, the most visited of all of the fjords of Norway. The city actually occupies portions of seven different islands. The surrounding islands, including those that are a part of Ålesund are rocky, but not very prominent. And as is true in most of Norway below the Arctic Circle they are thickly covered in coniferous forest or woodland. The higher mountains from which the fjords originate are visible from Ålesund and their snow-covered peaks add to the overall beauty of the landscape.

The waters immediately surrounding Ålesund are calm most of the time, but can become quite choppy when the wind picks up at any time of year. Once beyond the islands, the waters of the North Sea can be quite stormy, especially in winter and often during short summer gales, making the approach to the urban area difficult at those times.

The region still falls within the maritime climate regime similar to that of Bergen and the other ports to the south. But being that the high mountains are a bit farther to the east, the rainfall totals are slightly lower and there are a few more sunny days than in Bergen, Haugesund or Stavanger because there are no significant peaks to generate rapid lifting of the moist air.

Center of Ålesund from the viewing platform atop of Aksla

A BRIEF HISTORY: Viking legend dates back to a famous warrior in the 10th century named Rollo who came from a village just northwest of present day Ålesund, showing that the area has a long history. But the city of Ålesund itself only dates back to the early 19th century, being founded as a town in 1838. The city center of today, however, owes its unique existence to a great fire that occurred in 1904, destroying most of old primarily wooden town because of very strong winds that fanned the flames into a conflagration.

Prior to the great fire, Kaiser Wilhelm of Germany used to vacation here and when he heard about this terrible fire, he sent building supplies to build shelters that would temporarily house the community. The actual rebuilding was done after initial shelter was provided, and it was decided to utilize the Art Nouveau style, which was so popular, especially in Germany. Architects and builders trained in the style were brought from Germany in to help in the rebuilding, making Ålesund a classic example today of Art Nouveau. It is so well recognized and it has an interpretative center and it is active in the Europe wide network to preserve this as an important architectural style. It is one of Europe's best examples of Art Nouveau. style

Examples of Art Nouveau style along the Ålesundet

What fed the Ålesund economy until the mid 1930's, was fishing, in particular for herring. But the local fishermen ultimately destroyed their bounty by devising better ways to catch the fish. By the mid 1930's, the stock became so depleted that the industry died. Today there is limited fishing, but it no longer is the mainstay of the Ålesund economy.

During World War II Ålesund was a major hot bed for resistance, much of with close ties to the British who aided in getting many people out of the country despite the Nazi occupation. The invading military did not use Ålesund for any major activities and most allied raids were on installations farther to the north, thus sparing much damage to the city's precious architecture or infrastructure.

The dock at Ålesund is in the heart of the Art Nouveau area

After the war, as Ålesund began to assume more of a regional role, new business and bank buildings in the city center led initially to the destruction of numerous of the old Art Nouveau buildings. And although they were the pride of the city, there was little to no attempt to spare them. There were even those in the community that openly welcomed the new developments as a sign that Ålesund was modernizing. By the 1970's, as more demolition took place to bring in further development a backlash developed and there were demonstrations against the ongoing destruction of the city's unique architectural heritage. As a result, today Ålesund is very protective of its post 1904 fire revival, and Art Nouveau is very much a selling point in the community. The city has continued to grow and the modern development is now seen east of the city center in areas that have grown out of the former woodland and farms, and this has been welcomed, but no longer at the expense of the city center. Much of the thanks for the sparing of this architectural treasure goes to cruise ships, as Ålesund became a popular port of call because of its distinctive architectural style and this added greatly to the economy. And this spared more destruction of this valuable resource. There is no other city in all of Scandinavia that possesses a city core filled with Art Nouveau buildings, giving Ålesund a unique position.

One infrastructure development that did bring total approval was the linking of the various islands within the city and beyond by means of bridges or tunnels, bringing a more cohesive transportation pattern into being. As a result, today most of the inhabited portions of Ålesund are linked together without the need for the use of ferryboats. The transport network helps to make Ålesund a major regional center with easy access to the mainland.

The dock for cruise ships in central Ålesund

SHIP DOCK IN ÅLESUND: Two medium to large size ships can dock right in the heart of central Ålesund just a few steps from the most beautiful of the city's Art Nouveau and Art Deco buildings. There is no terminal, but a large parking area permits tour busses, private cars and taxis to greet guests. And for those not on any tour, it is very easy to walk through the heart of the city.

TOURING OPTIONS FOR VISITING ÅLESUND: Depending upon your cruise line, there may be several tours offered to either some of the outlying islands or to the mountainous interior, as each cruise line has its own agenda as to what they choose to provide. These are the various options available in Ålesund:

* **Ship sponsored tours** will include both motor coach tours to the outlying islands that make up the greater Ålesund region and also walking tours to show you up close the architectural styles for which the city is famous.

* **Private car and driver/guide** service is available in Ålesund either arranged through the shore excursion desk on board ship or on your own. If you attempt to save some money on private touring, you might first check out:

** _www.toursbylocals.com/Alesund_, which is a very popular and reliable service in Norway.

* **Hop on hop off bus service** is available in Ålesund operating on a single route daily between 9 AM and 4 PM with eight stops. For further information as to their service check on line at *www.city-sightseeing.com/alesund* for details.

* **Taxi services** are easily obtained on the dock and many drivers will offer hourly or daily touring rates. Check with *www.alesund-taxi.no/sightseeing* for details.

The very heart of Ålesund

* **Walking** is one way to see the beautiful Art Deco and Art Nouveau district of the city. The entire city center is within easy walking distance of where the ship is docked. And there are numerous restaurants and cafes where you can either dine or have light refreshment. There is also a small indoor mall along the waterfront.

By just walking you would miss the view from the top of Mt. Aksla unless you are prepared to climb over 400 hundred stairs on the side of the peak. It is a rather steep climb and you need to be in good condition or do not even attempt it.

There are several attractions that would be beyond your reach without being on a tour, having a private car or taxi. Most of the taxi drivers do speak English and actually are very willing to serve as your guide for an hour or two at a flat rate.

MAJOR SITES TO VISIT: In visiting Ålesund there are numerous attractions worthy of our attention. The major sights include:

* **Ålesund Museum** is also in the city center, located at Rasmus Rosennebergsgate #16 and open daily between 11 AM and 3 PM daily, but closed on weekends, which would be unfortunate if your ship were to dock on Saturday or Sunday. Allow at least an hour or more. The museum is devoted to the history of Ålesund and also to the importance of the fishing industry in the city's growth.

The Alnes Lighthouse (Work of Tolpost, C, CC BY SA 3.0, Wikimedia.org)

* **Alnes Lighthouse** is a very popular attraction. It is located on the outer island of Godøy, which is reached by way of a series of bridges and tunnels, showing you the way in which these settled islands are all linked to Ålesund. The ride there and back is worth the visit alone. You will need to be on a tour, providing one is offered, or you can negotiate a rate with a local taxi for the drive there and back.

The modern lighthouse dates only to 1936, and its architectural style is unique in that it built with four flat, angular walls capping out at 225 meters or 738 feet in height. The lighthouse also has a small museum to help you understand its role, and it is still active in its function as a beacon for mariners. There is a cultural center adjacent to the lighthouse and a small cafe that provides refreshments and light meals.

* **Atlantic Sea Park** is usually the second most popular attraction, but it is not located in the city center. It is at the western end of the city via a bridge that connects central Ålesund with Hessa. It is walkable, about five kilometers or three miles, but again it is easiest to take a taxi. Again most of the tours will include a stop at the Atlantic Sea Park. The focus is the aquarium that highlights the sea life of this region, and their outdoor exhibits do include penguins even though they are from the Southern Hemisphere and were never found in Norway. The park does put on a show with their seals, which both adults and children find very endearing. The park is open from 11 AM to 4 PM daily, and remains open to 6 PM on Sunday.

* **Fjellstua Overlook** is the number one visitor attraction in Ålesund, especially during clear weather. Rising up just east of the city center is the mountain known as Aksla where the Fjellstua Lodge is perched with its outdoor deck providing a dramatic view over the city and well out to sea or eastward into the fjords.

You can reach the top on your own, as previously noted, but only if you have the strength to negotiate 418 steps that will climb the side of the mountain. Or you can hire a taxi to take you to the top, wait for the short time you will spend viewing the panorama and then return you to the city center. But all of the city tours that the various cruise lines offer do include a drive to the top of Aksla to enjoy the view.

The viewing deck is open 24 hours per day. The Fjellstua Lodge restaurant is open Sunday thru Tuesday from 11 AM to 5 PM, Wednesday thru Saturday from 11 AM to 10 PM.

Standing in the heart of Ålesund

Looking down on the Ålesundet from Aksla

Along the Ålesundet running through the heart of the city

The center of Ålesund is snug against the mountainside

* **Giske Kirke** is a small regional church on the island of Giske, which is en route to the Alnes Lighthouse. The church dates to the 11th century and is well preserved, giving you a glimpse into early Christian life in Viking Norway. The church is open Monday thru Saturday from 10AM to 5 PM and on Sunday from 1 to 5 PM.

* **Jugendstilsenteret and Kunstmuseet Kube** is the most important museum to visit to learn about Ålesund after the 1904 fire and the development of Art Nouveau. It is just steps from where the ships dock, located at Apotekergata # 16. It is open from 11 AM to 4 PM on days when the ship is in port. This is in effect two museums for the price of one admission. A visit gives you the story of the city of Ålesund and of the Art Nouveau movement. And there is a small, but interesting museum shop. A visit then makes the architecture of the city center far more meaningful.

The Sunmore Museum

* Sunmoere Museum is located a short distance east of the city and you will need to have a taxi or be on a tour to visit, but it is well worth the effort. During summer, the museum is open daily from 10 AM to 4 PM and Saturday from Noon to 4 PM with Sunday hours being from 10 AM to 4 PM. This is essentially a spacious outdoor museum that recreates Norwegian life through a number of houses and buildings along with having a display of Viking relics. The setting is very conducive to strolling about and each building presents a glimpse of life as it was. Many visitors consider this to be the best sightseeing venue in Ålesund.

This is not an exhaustive list, but presents you with the most important sights in Ålesund. But during your one day stop you must allow a couple of hours simply to wander the streets of the old inner city and soak up the architectural flavor. If your cruise does stay overnight, and if the weather is favorable, the city takes on a very beautiful glow when the sun is low in the western sky. During summer there is only a brief hour or two of darkness, but Ålesund looks so especially rich during the golden hours of late evening sun.

DINING OUT: Unless your ship should just happen to stay overnight, which is rather rare on fjord itineraries, but not unlikely, as I have stayed overnight there twice, you will be able to at least have lunch in Ålesund. Here are my recommendations for traditional Norwegian restaurants in Ålesund.

The rugged nature of the site causes Ãlesund to have a broken up street pattern

* **AnnoRestaurant & Bar** is located in the center of town at Apotekergata #9 and open from early morning to mid evening, serving all three meals. For lunch they can get rather busy, but if you come in after 1 PM, it is quiet and the service is very friendly. They are known for their fresh seafood and also pizza, but with a Norwegian twist in that you can have a salmon pizza. The combination of good, fresh food and fast service enables you to still have plenty of time for sightseeing. They are open weekdays from 3 to 9 PM, Saturday from 2 to 9 PM and Sunday from 1 to 6 PM. Reservations are not necessary.

* **Fisketorget Delikatesse** – Located at Keiser Wilhelms gate # 25, this central delicatessen/restaurant serves a casual menu, but one heavily emphasizing fresh seafood served in Norwegian style along with a great selection of genuine Japanese sushi. The atmosphere is casual, but the quality of the menu is excellent. They open daily at 10 AM, closing at 6 PM Monday and Tuesday and 8 PM the rest of the week. Reservations are not necessary.

* **Lyst Cafe Bar & Food** is a very nice, traditional restaurant located in the city center on Kongens gate #12 and open from 11:30 AM to 5 PM Monday thru Thursday, remaining open until 10:30 PM Friday and Saturday. Sunday they serve from 2 to 8 PM. Reservations are not necessary. Again I recommend going later for lunch, as they do get rather busy. They offer a good selection of traditional and contemporary dishes with an emphasis on freshness, especially the seafood.

* **Sjobua** – One of the finer restaurants in Alesund that is within easy walking distance of the ship, located at Brunholmgata # 1-A, this is a delightful place for dinner if your ship is staying overnight. The décor is rather smart, the menu rich in choices, heavily weighted toward fresh seafood and the service is great. They serve Tuesday thru Friday from 5 to 10 PM, Saturday from Noon to 10 PM and Monday from Noon to Midnight.

* **Tante Bruun Cafe** - Located in the city at Grimmergata # 1, this is a popular local restaurant that specializes in traditional cuisine. Soups are a popular item on the menu, but they offer a wide variety of dishes to please any taste. The restaurant is open from 10 AM to 8 PM Monday thru Saturday. Reservations are not necessary.

Maritime antiques in a downtown store window

SHOPPING: There are several small souvenir stores, and also a few stores selling maritime antiques all located in the city center. There are two local shopping malls located in the downtown core, but they sell a variety of clothing, housewares, groceries and other items catering to the needs of local residents and not visitors. However, a look through these malls does give the discerning visitor a good look at the overall quality of life in this city, which is quite typical of Norway's smaller cities in general. But Ålesund is not a destination for any real high quality arts and crafts shopping. For that I do recommend the larger cities such as Bergen, Trondheim and Tromsø.

FINAL WORDS: I have personally always found Ålesund to be a refreshing stop. Simply wandering its streets and soaking in the unique Art Nouveau atmosphere is delightful. Local shops cater more to the needs of the residents, but there are two small shopping centers in the downtown that are interesting in that they give you a glimpse at what types of items the locals purchase. Remember that Norway has a very high living standard, but at the same time people are conservative and not motivated by conspicuous consumption. I also do recommend at least one half day tour to one of the outer islands if the weather is nice. And definitely drive or walk (if physically fit) to the top of Aksla for the incredible view, of course weather depending. You will find your stay in Ålesund to be quite memorable, and the city quite different from any other small city in Norway.

The city's main pedestrian shopping street

MAPS OF ÅLESUND

THE CITY OF ÅLESUND

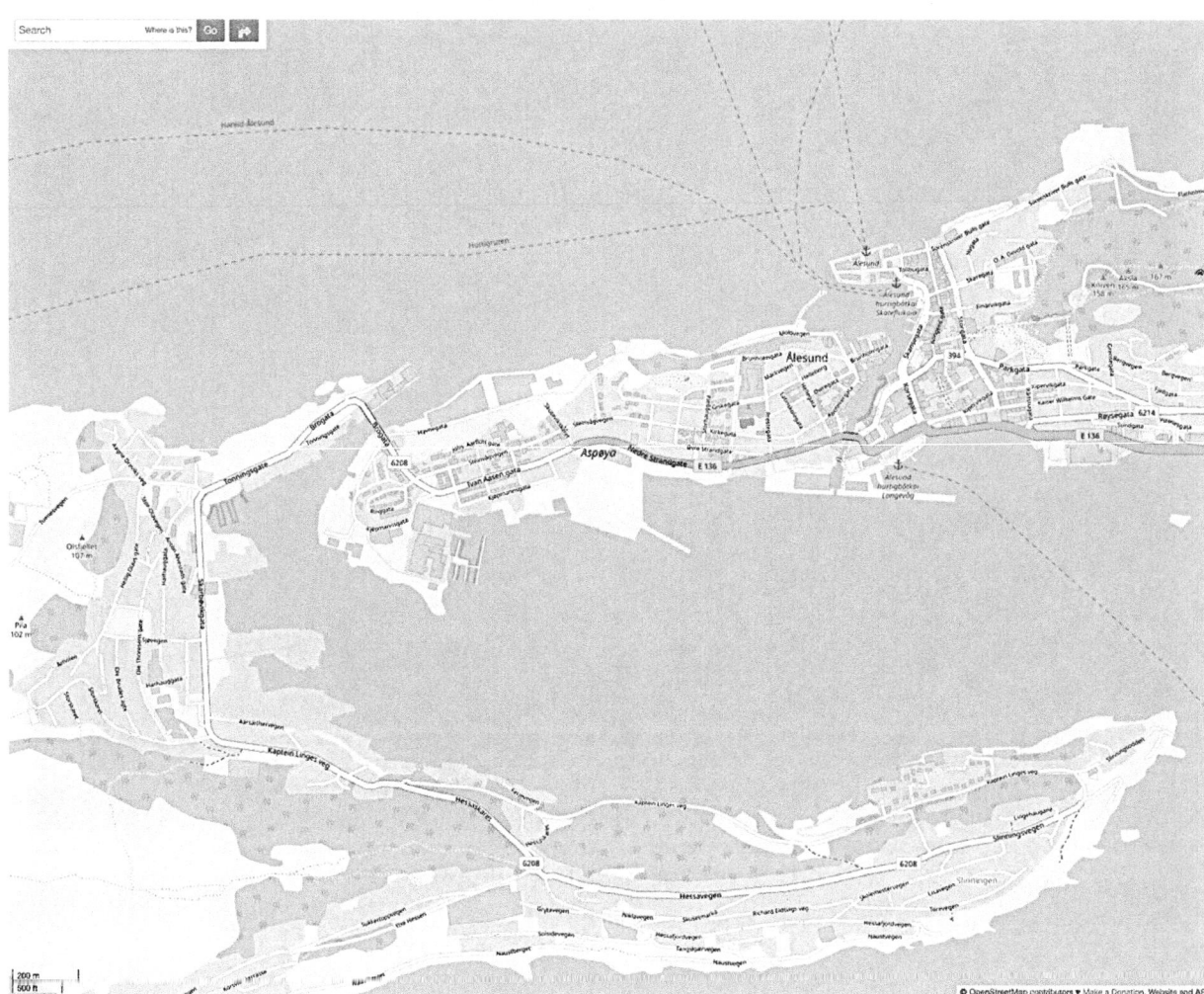

City of Ålesund

This map is best viewed directly from OpenStreetMap.com on your personal device where it can be expanded or one specific area can be enlarged. Given the format of this book, it is impossible to display maps with the level of detail you might wish to have while actually out exploring the city. But the OpenStreetMap maps used directly are the tool I always rely upon.

THE CENTER OF ÅLESUND

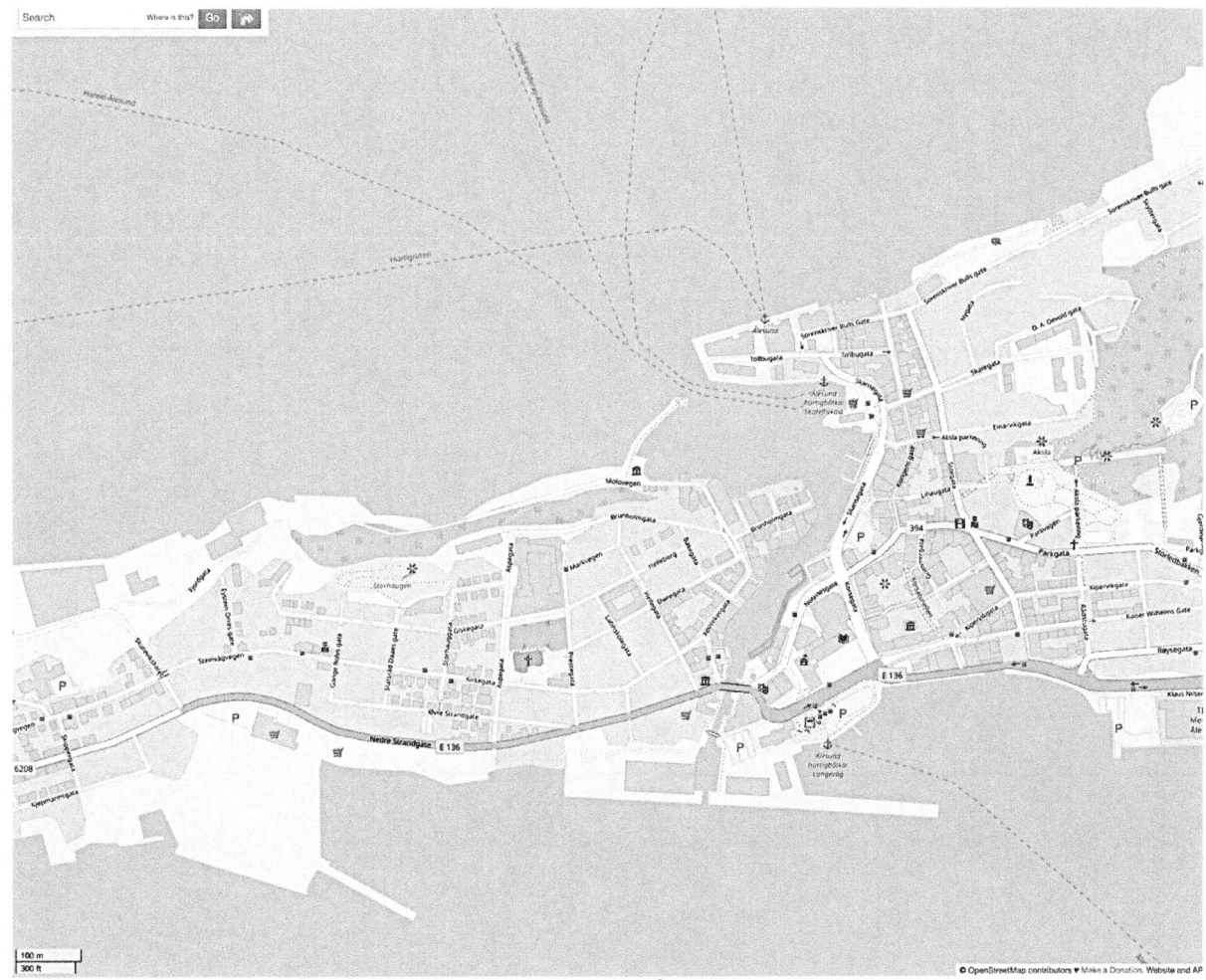

The center of Ålesund

This map is best viewed directly from OpenStreetMap.com on your personal device where it can be expanded or one specific area can be enlarged. Given the format of this book, it is impossible to display maps with the level of detail you might wish to have while actually out exploring the city. But the OpenStreetMap maps used directly are the tool I always rely upon.

MOLDE

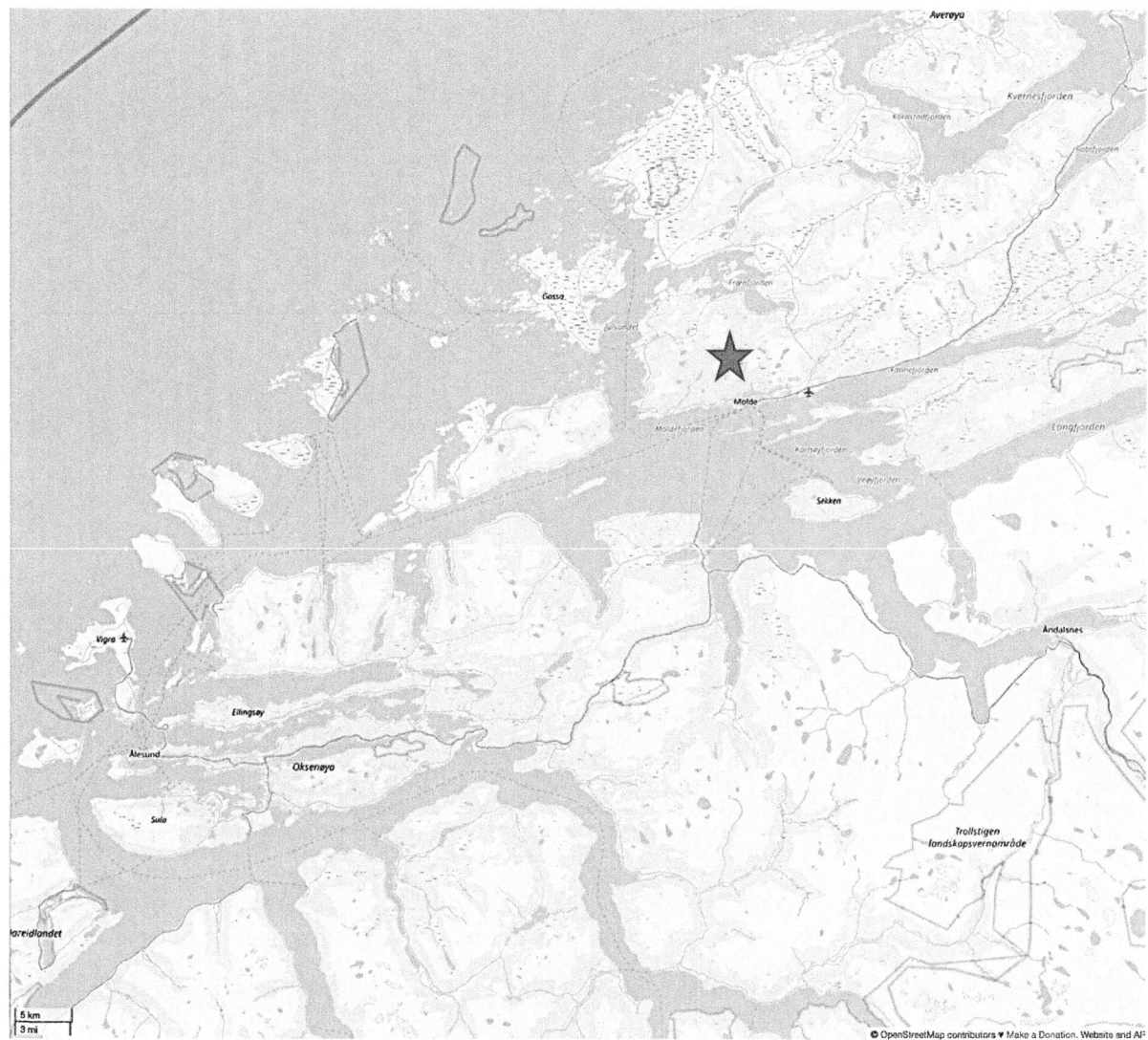

The Molde Area, (© OpenStreetMap contributors)

The Norwegian coast offers so many potential ports of call that for a single cruise to visit all the possibilities would require several weeks. Molde is one of those less visited ports because of its proximity to Ålesund, which is a much larger city with a very unique architectural history. For every ten cruise ships that cruise this far north, it is safe to say that eight would stop in Ålesund for those two that would visit Molde.

Molde is located 59 kilometers or 37 miles north of Ålesund by ship, which entails only a two to two and a half hours sailing. Thus in developing their itineraries, most cruise lines will consider one of the two ports and not both unless it is a longer 14-day cruise and one or the other of the two is visited on the southbound return leg. It lies on Moldefjorden, which extends inland marking the southern edge of the rugged Romsdal Peninsula. To the north is the Kvernesfjorden. Molde is the regional administrative and trade center, giving this small city a degree of local importance. Also during the summer months it is a popular tourist destination and has developed a good infrastructure of hotels, guest houses and restaurants.

Looking across Moldefjorden to the city

Molde clings to its hillside perch

THE NATURAL SETTING: Molde does not possess much level land, only a narrow fringe of flat land exists before the city rises abruptly into the hills. Moldeva Creek, which comes from the interior of the Romsdal Peninsula cascades through the city with a series of rapids and waterfalls, today a major attraction. Back in the 18th century there were lumber mills taking advantage of the water power and later a hydroelectric plant. Today the water flows essentially free of barriers and is exceptionally clean and pure. And the upper reaches of the city are afforded spectacular views across the fjord to snowcapped mountains and lush forests.

Molde's climate is typical of the mid coast of Norway, what is called a maritime or marine west coast regime. Winters are somewhat dark given the more northerly latitude and they are also quite rainy, as warmer moist air is swept in off the Atlantic by the Westerly winds and forced to rise by the mountains. Summer is cool with temperatures rarely exceeding the mid 20's Celsius or mid to upper 70's Fahrenheit.

A BRIEF HISTORY: The region surrounding Molde has a long history with mention in one of the sagas of where an important battle during Viking times took place in 1162. Molde has a long history that extends back to the Middle Ages when it officially became a designated trade center in 1614. And in 1742 Molde was granted a royal charter, making it one of the oldest recognized cities in the region. But it never grew to become the dominant city because of its proximity to Ålesund, which overshadowed it in size. Today Molde's metropolitan population is only 32,000 while Ålesund has a metropolitan population approaching 70,000.

During World War II when German forces were expanding across Norway from the south, Molde was temporarily the national capital, as the King, his family and many members of Parliament took up residence. It was their presence that prompted a series of air raids in 1940, causing a significant amount of property damage and loss of life.

Growth in Molde has been steady with somewhat of a surge following World War II, as Norway's textile and clothing industry expanded. Today light manufacturing is an important component of the local economy. The many beautiful old wood homes are considered to be local architectural treasures having survived a major fire in 1916 and German air raids in 1940.

SHIP DOCK IN MOLDE: The few cruise ships that do visit Molde dock along the edge of the city center, essentially in the very heart of town. There is no cruise terminal, however, tour busses, private cars and taxis are able to park adjacent to the ship. For those who choose to walk, stepping off the ship puts you in the center of Molde. The dock is just one block from the main street of the city, making it especially convenient for walking.

Docking in the heart of Molde

TOURING OPTIONS FOR MOLDE: There are fewer options open to visitors in Molde than in Ålesund because of its smaller population and the fact that fewer ships visit the port. These are the touring options open to ship passengers in Molde:

* **Ship sponsored tours** of Molde or full day tours outside of the city, either to drive the Atlantic Road or to drive the Trollstigen mountain road will be offered, variations depending upon the individual cruise line.

* **Private car and driver/guide** option is available in Molde through your ship's shore excursion desk.

In hopes of saving some money from what the cruise line will charge you may also wish to check *www.toursbylocals.com/PrivateTourAlesundGeiranger/Trollstigen* for their offerings.

* **Hop on hop off bus** service in Molde is not practical. The city is too small and does not have sufficient venues to operate such a service.

Molde homes cling to the hillside

* **Taxi Tours** - There may be some taxis waiting at the dock and it is often possible to negotiate a tour for part or all of the day. The main taxi company is Molde Taxientral and you can check their web page at *www.moldetaxi.no* to see if they can accept an advanced booking for tours.

* **Walking** will limit you to just the central part of Molde, which is quite interesting, but it limits your range and you do miss the fantastic surrounding countryside on those cruises that do offer tours into the fjord country around the city.

SIGHTS OF INTEREST TO VISITORS: Apart from being a beautiful small city, there are few specific sights in Molde that attract visitors. However, when used as a base for day tours into the interior mountains, Molde becomes a significant tourist destination. And cruise passengers can avail themselves of such tours since the majority of cruise lines will offer full day motor coach tours.

On the main street of Molde on a rather typical rainy day

The major sights worthy of note are shown here in alphabetical order, and they include those within the city of Molde combined with those in the surrounding countryside:

* **Atlantic Road** – This amazing piece of engineering consists of a series of bridges and viaducts that join together a string of small offshore islands linking the mainland north of the Romsdal Peninsula and the offshore coastal port of Kristiansund. This is a fascinating journey of 36 kilometers or 22 miles , starting 47 kilometers or 29 miles north of Molde and ending 30 kilometers or 19 miles southwest of Kristiansund with beautiful ocean views, quaint island villages and panoramas of the mainland mountains. If your ship stops in Kristiansund, this tour will also be offered, but in reverse order.

* **Bud** is a quaint fishing village, typical of the Norwegian coast, located west of Molde at the far end of the Romsdal Peninsula. It was once a major trading center. And during the Protestant Reformation it led a movement aimed at maintaining the old religious traditions.

* **Molde Cathedral** is a relatively new building completed in 1957. Its bell tower is the most dominant feature in the city center. Although rather simple in design, following

Lutheran tradition, there are beautiful stained glass windows. The cathedral is normally open to the public during daytime hours unless some specific service is being conducted.

* Molde & Romsdal Art Center – Located in the heart of the city at Goervellplassen #1, this is the city's fine art center and museum. The location is an easy walk from where the ship is docked alongside the downtown core. The art center features the local arts and handcrafts of the mid coastal region of Norway. The collection is essentially regional and does not include any major famous artists. But none the less the quality of the work is excellent. Hours are Tuesday thru Friday from 11 AM to 4 PM and closing Saturday at 3 PM.

* Moldeva Creek – This is a fast flowing mountain stream that cuts its way through the heart of Molde, having originated in the mountains above the city. With a series of white water rapids Moldeva Creek cuts a distinctive swath right through the city center just to the east of the main shopping district, an easy walk through the business district to the bridges over the fast flowing waters. Once this creek was harnessed for its energy, but today flows freely through town.

Moldeva Creek flows rapidly through town in a cascade of waterfalls

At the Romsdal Museum of Norwegian culture, (Work of Mænsard Vokser, CC BY SA 4.0, Wikimedia.org)

* **Romsdal Museum of Norwegian Culture** – This is a unique collection of old houses, shops and a church, representing the lifestyle of Norway in centuries past. You will gain an appreciation for what life was like in Norway before the 20th century brought such major changes. The museum is located at the edge of Molde at Per Amdams veg # 4 and it is open daily from 11 AM to 3 PM. It is a walkable distance from the ship if you are on your own, but a taxi is far quicker and easier to enable you to safe your energy for walking around the museum complex. .

* **Trollstigen** is one of those amazing feats of Norwegian engineering, as the road into the interior climbs to an elevation of 858 meters or 2,815 feet through 11 curves that are 180 degrees or more each, making this one of the most breathtaking drives in the country. Generally the drive is part of an all-day trip covering quite a bit of territory that will include a lunch at one of the mountain inns. Not all cruise lines will offer this more ambitious and expensive motor coach journeys, so if your itinerary includes Trollstigen, it should be a priority for anyone who wants to see incredible landscapes.

Trollstigen is an example of how Norwegians have managed to conquer their high mountains with an amazing system of roads, tunnels, bridges and intervening ferryboat links. However, if you are fearful of heights and steep drop-offs I would not recommend this drive, as it could be quite unnerving for anyone who has spent much of their life in flatlands.

The incredible Trollstigen Pass, (Work of Palickap, CC BY SA 4.0, Wikimedia.org)

DINING OUT IN MOLDE: If you are staying in the city and not participating in the all-day Trollstigen tour, there is not a great selection of restaurants from which to choose for lunch. Norwegian cuisine is heavily weighted toward fresh seafood, and during summer salmon is the most in demand catch. I have listed my two favorite restaurants where you can sample the delights of Norway in a pleasant atmosphere. There are others I could list, but unfortunately although I had a decent meal, their reviews are all over the chart. My two selections are:

* **Den Gode Smak AS** – This is a casual restaurant serving lighter meals and good sandwiches, open for both breakfast and lunch. The menu features a mix of Norwegian and continental menu items all sure to please. They are in the heart of town at Torget # 1, an easy walk from the ship. Their hours are Monday thru Friday from 10 AM to 8 PM and closing at 6 PM Saturday. Reservations are not necessary.

* **Kafe Kurt** – Located at Goervellplassen # 1 in the center of Molde, this is an excellent restaurant with its introduction to Norwegian cuisine. Seafood figures prominently and you can order from the menu or select from delicacies in what can be described as a Norwegian smorgasbord, which is a dining experience. Their hours are Tuesday and Wednesday from 10 AM to 5 PM, closing 6 PM Thursday, back to 5 PM for closing Friday and Saturday. Reservations can be made by calling +47 911 31 545.

Strawberry season is a major event in Molde during mid-summer and you will find stands in the city center where you can buy a box to enjoy now or take back on board ship

* **Restaurant Amalie** – This is an outstanding restaurant with a very beautiful and traditional Norwegian menu. Seafood figures prominently, but vegetarian dishes are also offered. They are located at Amtmann Krohgs gate # 5 a very short walk from the dock. Their serving hours are Monday through Wednesday and Friday from 4 to 10:30 PM, Thursday from 3 to 10:30 PM, Saturday from 2 to 10 PM and Sunday from 2 to 9 PM. This rather extensive schedule may or may not mesh with your ship's sailing time. Reservations are advised by calling +47 400 37 445.

* **Restaurant Fjordstuene** – Located at Julsundvegen #6 in the Hotel Molde Fjordstuer, this is a popular seafood restaurant serving in classic Norwegian style. The quality, service and atmosphere are all inviting and the menu offers vegetarian dishes as well as the seafood and meat selections. Their hours are Tuesday thru Friday from 6 to 9 PM and Saturday from 5 to 10 PM. To reserve a table call +47 71 20 10 60.

SHOPPING: The city center of Molde offers a variety of stores, but they tend to cater to the local populace. This is not a city where you will find specialty souvenir or handcraft stores since their tourist market is limited.

A clothing store featuring traditional Norwegian festival dress

FINAL WORDS: Most likely Molde will not be on your cruise itinerary unless you are on one of the specialized fjord cruises operated by such companies as Hertigruten or other highly specialized cruise lines.

If your ship visits Molde, I would highly suggest the Trollstigen mountain drive or the Atlantic Road. The city, although quite pleasant, offers so little to keep the visitor interested that your day could be rather long and boring. And the restaurant selection does leave much to be desired, as there are so few places open for lunch.

But again I offer the caution for anyone prone to travel sicknes brought on by twisting and winding roads.

THE CITY OF MOLDE

The center of Molde with the star showing where cruise ships dock

This map is best viewed directly from OpenStreetMap.com on your personal device where it can be expanded or one specific area can be enlarged. Given the format of this book, it is impossible to display maps with the level of detail you might wish to have while actually out exploring the city. But the OpenStreetMap maps used directly are the tool I always rely upon.

STORFJORDEN
VISITING HELLESYLT & GEIRANGER

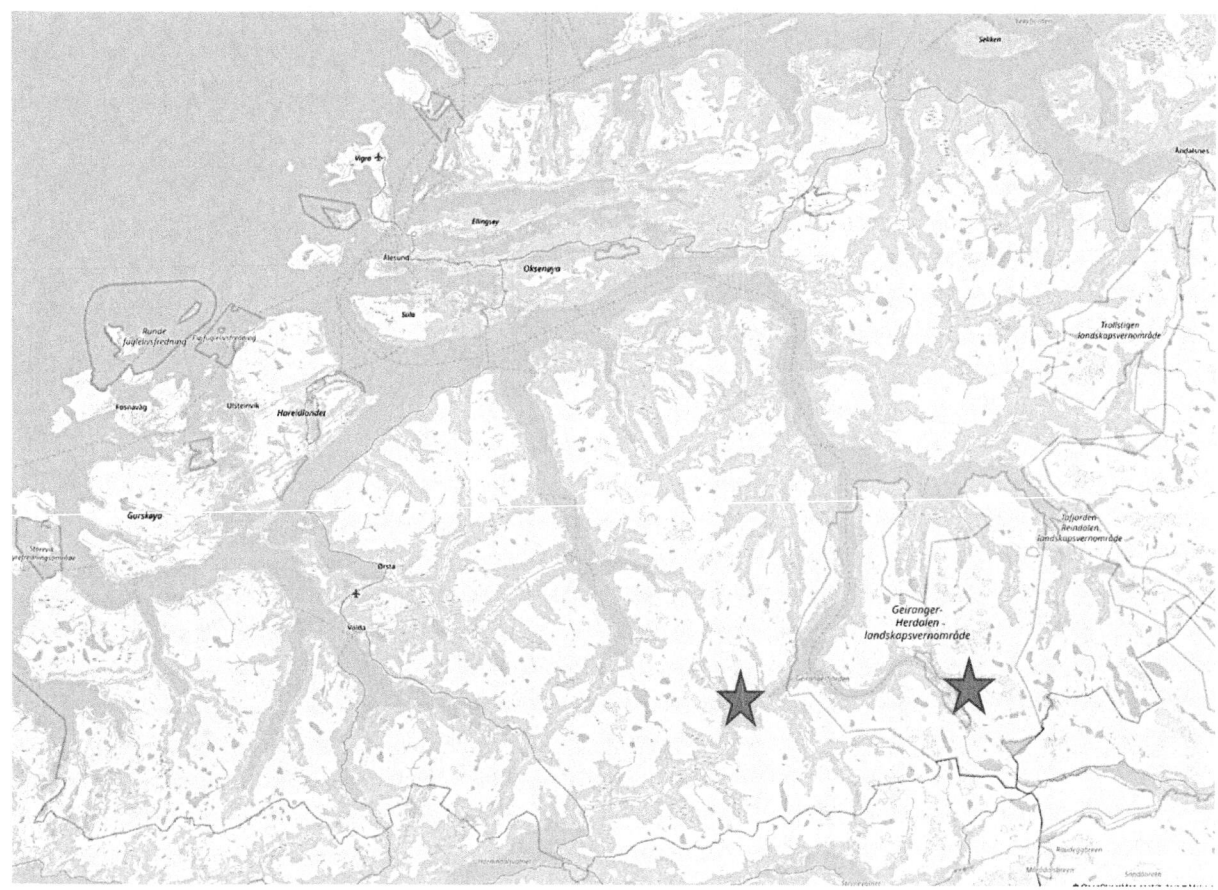

**Storfjorden showing Hellesylt (left star) and Geiranger (right star)
(© OpenStreetMap contributors)**

Every visitor to Norway comes away with his or her favorite fjord. As noted before, in reality it is difficult to say which is the more beautiful, as each has its own level of majesty and its own level of spectacular scenery. But there is a very strong favoritism shown to the Storfjorden system with its two beautiful tributary fjords of Sunnylvsfjorden (Hellesylt) and Geirangerfjorden leading off of Næyorfjorden. Many of the fjords see few if any cruise ships, but both the small ports of Hellesylt and Geiranger are especially popular destinations, and they appear on Norwegian calendars and travel posters quite regularly. It is difficult to say why these two have become the so called "poster children" for cruising the fjords of Norway other than the fact that they are the most spectacular of the southern fjord region that is reached easily on a seven-day cruise from Copenhagen or Oslo. I strongly believe this popularity developed out of proximity, as other fjords of equal or even greater magnificence lie much farther to the north of Storfjorden and thus require a longer cruise and not all are easily as accessible to the majority of large cruise ships. The port of Geiranger is possibly the most heavily visited of the deep fjords.

SAILING INTO STORFJORDEN: The distance to Hellesylt and Geiranger from the open sea requires several hours of sailing. Most cruise itineraries have the ship entering Storfjorden at around 6 AM in order to reach Hellesylt by 10 AM and Geiranger at around Noon or slightly earlier. I know most people like to sleep in during the early morning hours, especially if they attended a show or visited the casino the night before. But if you do so, you will miss some exceptionally spectacular scenery, especially if the weather is good. And in Norway that is always the big "if" factor. Even on days that do not exhibit a pure blue sky, this sail in can still be very spectacular, but in more of a moody way. Not every cruise can capture the rich blue skies of Norway because they are so fleeting. In any event, it pays to be up early to experience this sail in unless the weather is terrible. Then you can have no guilt about sleeping in that morning.

Entering Storfjorden in the early morning

Storfjorden initially begins with lower mountains closest to the sea and the shorelines are gentle with small villages and numerous farms. As your ship proceeds inward, the mountains progressively close in, at times framing the fjord with steep cliffs that are so close that the telltale scratches created by glacial scour are visible. Waterfalls are very numerous where streams plunge down into the fjord. Once the small streams that are now high above would have merged gently with the former river system now flooded by the sea after the glaciers scoured the valleys to such tremendous depths. These waterfalls are referred to as "hanging valleys." And even if you are not particularly interested in their geologic origin, their intense beauty will mesmerize you.

In the heart of Geirangerfjorden

HELLESYLT: By mid-morning, your ship may turn into Sunnylvsfjorden after your transit through Storfjorden and Næyorfjorden. This detour will only occur if your itinerary allows for a motor coach tour out of Hellesylt that will bring guests back to Geiranger just before late afternoon departure.

Sunnylvsfjorden is a short channel that ends at the tiny village of Hellesylt. Not all cruise ships will stop here, as there are no dock facilities and the village is too tiny to host large numbers of visitors. Only those cruise ships with itineraries that offer an all-day bus tour through the mountains to rejoin the ship at Geiranger will stop and tender those guests on shore to meet their coach.

For the majority of guests who are remaining on board, with binoculars you can take a visit to this tiny village and see its thundering whitewater river that empties into Sunnylvsfjorden.

It never hurts to ask your cabin attendant to check and see if you can possibly ride on the tender when it takes people ashore for their motor coach tour. Some cruise lines will allow a handful of guests to ride in and directly back without disembarking. The tender spends less than five minutes unloading those who are going on the all day tour, so the chances of you being allowed to ride in and back is strictly up to the discretion of the officer in charge.

Approaching Hellesyilt

The thundering whitewater of Helleysilt up close

GEIRANGERFJORDEN: Most ships will proceed to enter Geirangerfjorden directly from Storfjorden, with the day's destination being the resort village of Geiranger. It will take up to 90 minutes for your ship to sail the length of Geirangerfjorden, passing between towering cliffs where numerous waterfalls are plunging into the deep waters of the fjord.

The majesty of Geirangerfjorden

The most noted feature you will see on the port (left) side of the ship while sailing in will be the Seven Sisters Waterfall. This hanging valley feature results from a sizable river atop the cliffs that is clogged with numerous large boulders that braid the channel thus forcing the water to distribute itself into seven distinct channels before plunging down the face of the cliff, dropping a length of 410 meters or 1,350 feet. It is at its most spectacular flow in late spring and early summer, fed by the melting snow in the higher country above. The water splashes and dashes down the cliff face and when the sun is shining directly above, a beautiful rainbow is created.

According to Norse legend, these falls represent seven playful maidens who were once flirting with a handsome Viking suitor on the opposite shore. The handsome suitor was attempting to win their attention, but the primary Norse God turned him into a thundering waterfall to prevent him from crossing the fjord to try and win the affections of the maidens. And the maidens turned into delicate ribbons of water splashing down the cliff face. So now he is trapped opposite these water nymphs for all eternity. And their purity has been preserved as well. And between them is the depth of Geiranger Fjord that cannot be crossed.

The Seven Sisters Waterfall in Geirangerfjorden

The top of the Seven Sisters seen from the water.

GEIRANGER: After passing the Seven Sisters, the ship will round a bend in the fjord and there before you is the village of Geiranger clinging to the shore line. The town with only 300 full time residents is filled with numerous guesthouses, hotels and restaurants, as it is a major gathering place for visitors who are exploring the interior glaciers, lakes and meadows. Geiranger is one of Norway's major tourist destinations. And then entire fjord and surrounding mountain region has been given UNESCO World Heritage Site status.

SHIP TENDER AND TOURING OPTIONS IN GEIRANGE: There is only one small dock in Geiranger and thus most cruise ships will anchor in the fjord and tender guests on shore during their stay. But fortunately the waters are always calm and the distance from the ship to the shore is less than one kilometer. Once on shore, you will either join a motor coach for one of several tours into the high glacial valleys to both enjoy the scenery and the views down upon Geirangerfjorden. Or if you are not comfortable with winding roads and great heights, it is best to simply wander about Geiranger and enjoy the views from lower perspectives.

Looking down at Geiranger

Geiranger is such a small and isolated village that it offers few total options for touring. Here are your limited options:

* Ship sponsored motor coach tours provided by your cruise line are the most common option. These tours will take guests to different viewing locations, and the most popular tour is the one to the top of the mountains at the far end of the fjord above the village.

* Ordering a private car and driver guide through your cruise line may be difficult because of the extreme limitation of such a service. Most often you will be told it is impossible because this service would need to be provided by a limousine company either in Ålesund or Kristiansund, which is some distance.

* There is a hop on hop off bus in Geiranger that will meet guests at the dock where the ship tenders land. It will take you around to some of the most scenic spots through four different stops. For details visit *www.hop-on-hop-off-bus.com/geiranger/city-sighteeing-geiranger* to further explore this option.

* There is a local taxi service that will also offer individual touring by advanced arrangement. Visit their web page at *www.geirangertaxi.no/en-GB/hoyderpunkter* for more details. Unless you contact them well ahead of your visit, you will find that the service has already been booked.

SIGHTS IN GEIRANGER: As a small village devoted to servicing the needs of travelers, there are few specific designated sites in Geiranger. Walking around the village is a bit risky since there are no sidewalks and the one road that winds its way up through town is quite heavily travelled. There are so many panoramic vistas or trails, which I have listed below alphabetically:

* **Geiranger River** – One of the most exciting and beautiful sights in Geiranger is the cascading river that rushes down from the high glacier to the fjord. There is a massive stairway you can follow from the top end of the fjord that will take you along this thundering torrent all the way up to the high part of Geiranger where you can then follow the main Route 63 back into town, past the Grande Hotel. It is the highlight of walking around in Geiranger.

* **Glacial adventure** – Most cruise lines offer a motor coach tour or you can hire a local taxi to take you high up the valley into the upper reaches where once a mighty glacier carved its way down to where your ship docks today. This mountainous road with sharp curves and dynamic vistas will bring you high into the land above the tree line past a glacial lake and to a viewpoint that can only be described as absolutely astounding.

The present landscape has resulted from the prehistoric glacier having carved its way down to the fjord in a series of stages. Thus as you ascend to the highest viewpoint you actually pass through several level terraces that appear as hanging valleys, each higher than the last until you reach the summit where only a small remnant glacier still exists today. Each ascent is in itself quite spectacular, but for anyone afraid of heights I would offer this caution about going because once you are en route it is very difficult to retreat. The ultimate reward is a view all the way down to the present level of the fjord where you will see your ship.

The village of Geiranger from the plateau above

The beauty of the whitewater Geiranger River

At the top of the Geiranger River stairway where the water plunges over a cliff

Still higher above Geiranger en route to the glacier

A view of a portion of the Royal Farm used by King Haarald and family

* Royal Retreat – This royal farm perched high above the Geiranger River is a summer retreat for King Haarald and members of the Norwegian Royal Family. It can only be accessed coming up from the fjord by rather primitive means. His Majesty likes to get away from the pomp and ceremony of the Royal Palace in Oslo. This is a private retreat and the best us ordinary people can do is capture a telephoto image from the shoreline.

* Seven Sisters Waterfall – You will see this cascade along with The Suitor on the opposite wall of the fjord when your ship both arrives in Geiranger and then departs later in the day. The Seven Sisters Waterfall is actually one cascade, but at the very top where it plunges over the wall of the fjord a series of rocky outcrops breaks the flow into seven streams.

Depending upon the types of adventure tours your cruise line may offer, the one way to get up close to the Seven Sisters Waterfall is by kayak. There are cruise lines that make arrangements for their guests to visit the base of the Seven Sisters by kayak, a journey that is less than two kilometers each way. The fjord is especially deep, but the water is highly protected by steep cliffs and is therefore very calm. There are a few operators of motor launches that can take a handful of people to the base of the falls, but they do not contract out to the cruise lines.

Apart from a kayak adventure, there is no other way to enjoy the Seven Sisters Waterfall. No hiking trail or road tours will take you to either the base or very top of the falls. This is not saying that it is physically impossible, but rather that the local tour operators do not wish to assume the responsibility for safety of guests if such tours were offered. It is frankly too risky. For further details visit www.visitnorway.com'listings/the-seven-sisters for further explanations of possible hikes or tours.

The magnificent Seven Sisters

DINING IN GEIRANGER: While on shore, you can dine and sample local Norwegian cuisine. I recommend lunch at the following:

* Brasserie Posten - Located along the Stranda or waterfront, this restaurant is highly rated for its fish soups, fish cakes and fresh vegetables and salads. And of course no Norwegian meal is complete without delicate desserts. But keep in mind that this is a tourist destination and good food is expensive. The restaurant opens at 10:30 AM and remains open until 10 PM. Call +47 70 20 13 06 to reserve a table.

* Cafe Ole - In the heart of Geiranger's main shopping area and open from 10 AM to 5 PM. I would recommend this cafe for light fare, especially desserts and hot chocolate or excellent coffee. Reservations are not necessary.

* **Grande Fjord Hotel** - Located high above the waterfront on the main road, Route 53. It is one of the larger hotels and impossible to miss. They serve lunch from Noon onward in Restrant Hyskje. Their menu is extensive and of course fish soups, fresh fish, fish cakes and salads are very much a part of what is offered. There are also meat dishes for those wanting to indulge in a heavier meal. And adding to the delicious food is a spectacular view from their picture windows. Breakfast is served from 7:30 to 10 AM, lunch from 1:30 to 5:30 PM and dinner from 7 to 9 PM daily. Call +47 70 26 94 90 to reserve a table.

The top of the Seven Sisters

* **Westerås Gard** - Located high above Geiranger on a rather steep walking path that is not recommended for those unable to follow a steep grade. But if you are able to negotiate the path, the view is spectacular. And the food is also excellent, again serving a varied menu. However, roasted goat is considered to be a house specialty. For dessert, they do serve traditional waffles with ice cream and a rich sauce. The restaurant is open from Noon to 4 PM and 6 to 9 PM daily. Call +47 926 49 537 to reserve a table.

SHOPPING: Geiranger is very much a tourist resort. There are numerous shops selling souvenir arts and crafts, but for the most part the prices are higher than you would find in Bergen or other major cities. If your cruise will either begin or end in one of the major cities of Norway, Denmark or Sweden then I would recommend waiting to shop in those major cities.

The Geiranger Glacial Lake

The high mountain roads are not for the faint of heart

* **Westerås Gard** - Located high above Geiranger on a rather steep walking path that is not recommended for those unable to follow a steep grade. But if you are able to negotiate the path, the view is spectacular. And the food is also excellent, again serving a varied menu. However, roasted goat is considered to be a house specialty. For dessert, they do serve traditional waffles with ice cream and a rich sauce. The restaurant is open from Noon to 4 PM and 6 to 9 PM daily. Call +47 926 49 537 to reserve a table.

SHOPPING: Geiranger is very much a tourist resort. There are numerous shops selling souvenir arts and crafts, but for the most part the prices are higher than you would find in Bergen or other major cities. If your cruise will either begin or end in one of the major cities of Norway, Denmark or Sweden then I would recommend waiting to shop in those major cities.

SAILING OUT: If you still have not had enough scenery for one day, you might want to spend time out on deck or in your ship's forward observation lounge during the long sail out through Sognefjorden back to sea. From the time you leave Geiranger it will take about five hours to reach the open sea. And as the day progresses and the sun dips lower on the western horizon, the mountains and shoreline take on a very special glow. It is almost impossible to put into words the majestic aura that is created in the evening light. And few shipboard guests take the chance to enjoy the vistas. I have watched the entire sail out from Geiranger, even missing dinner, just to be able to absorb the changing moods. And clearly I will enjoy it again on future sailings out from Geiranger. It is easy to understand why this is such a popular destination. It is especially beautiful, filled with majestic views and it is in closer proximity to Copenhagen or Oslo to be accessible on shorter cruises.

Storfjorden in the late evening while sailing out toward the sea

Approaching the sea from Storfjorden at 11 PM

MAPS OF HELLESYLT AND GEIRANGER

THE VILLAGES OF HELLESYLT AND GEIRANGER

Hellesylt and Geiranger

This map is best viewed directly from OpenStreetMap.com on your personal device where it can be expanded or one specific area can be enlarged. Given the format of this book, it is impossible to display maps with the level of detail you might wish to have while actually out exploring the city. But the OpenStreetMap maps used directly are the tool I always rely upon.

THE CENTER OF GEIRANGER

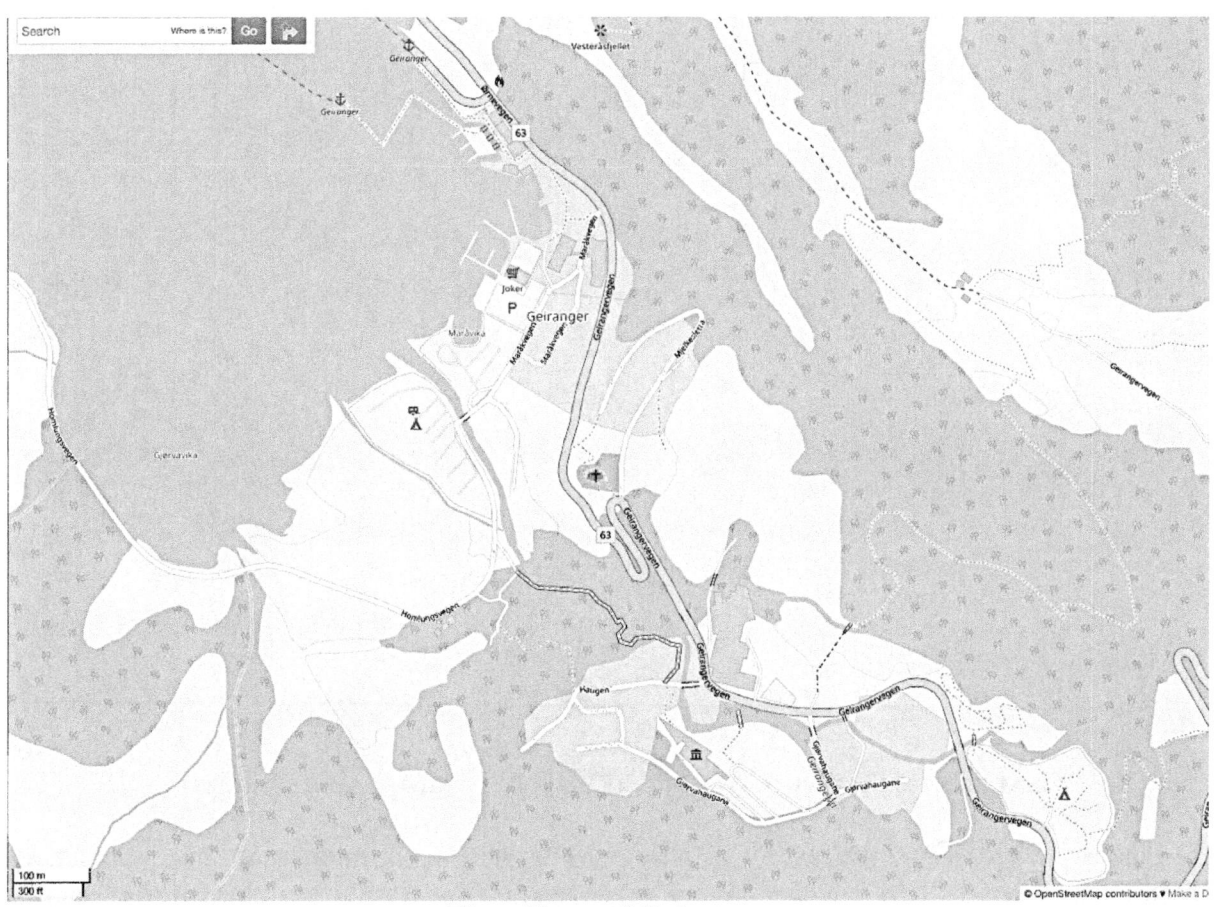

The village of Geiranger

This map is best viewed directly from OpenStreetMap.com on your personal device where it can be expanded or one specific area can be enlarged. Given the format of this book, it is impossible to display maps with the level of detail you might wish to have while actually out exploring the city. But the OpenStreetMap maps used directly are the tool I always rely upon.

ÅNDALSNES

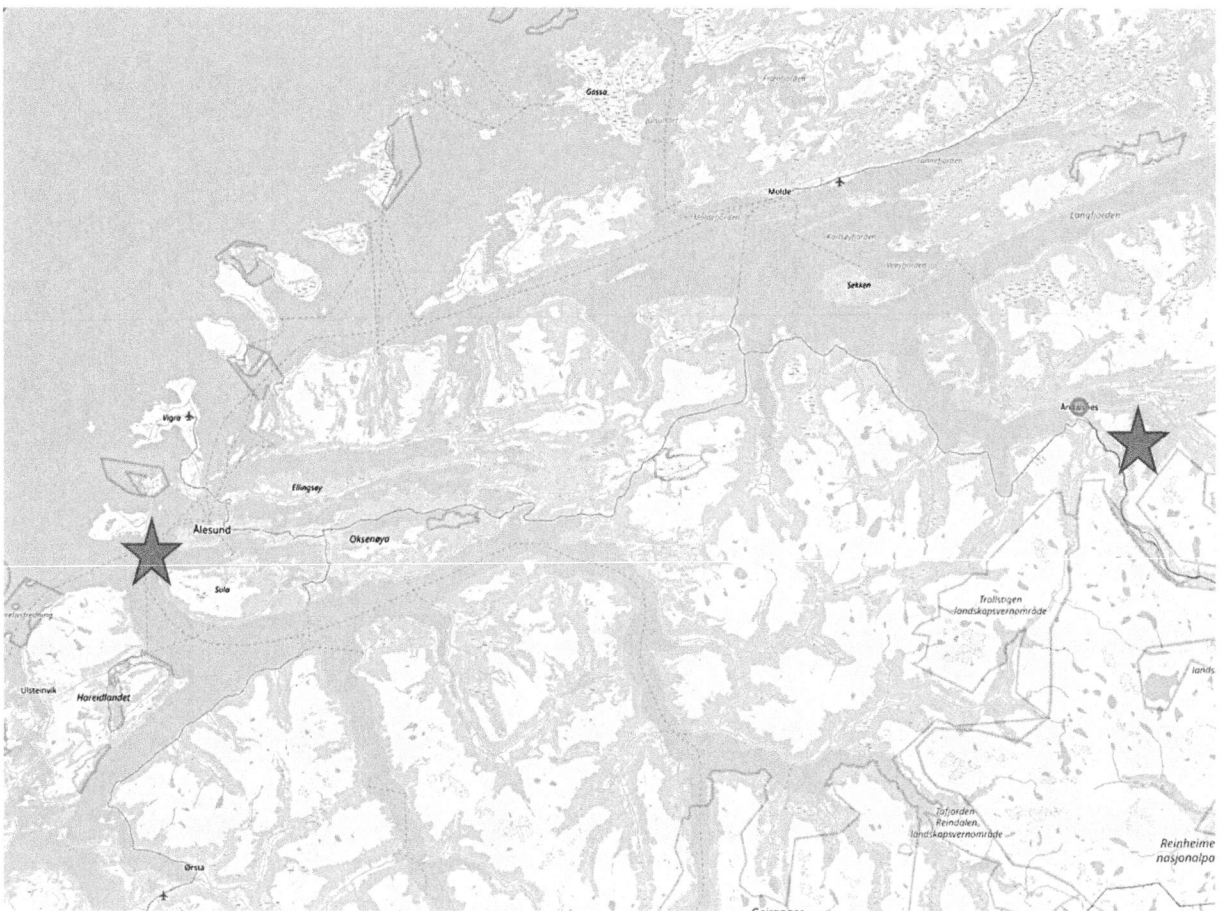
Åndalsnes relative to Ålesund, (© OpenStreetMap contributors)

Åndalsnes is located southeast of Molde and is not a common stop on most cruise itineraries because of its small size and more distant location from the country's outer coast. Molde takes about 1.5 hours to reach from the sea while Åndalsnes is more than three hours sailing time once coming into the fjord system north of Ålesund. Åndalsnes is located in the upper reaches of Isfjorden in an area rich in scenic beauty, but not easy to reach by road.

Åndalsnes has just over 2,400 residents, making it a moderate size town relative to the deeper fjords farther from the sea. It is surrounded by thick forests, rich, but small dairy farms and is a haven for fly fishermen and has been since the late 19th century. This is also one of the most dramatic regions in Norway with regard to spectacular scenery, especially the Trollstigen, a very incredible road journey, but most often undertaken by cruise passengers from Molde.

Tody apart from being a local administrative center Åndalsnes is quite a popular destination for those touring the fjords, but by automobile or motor coach and not by cruise ship. It cannot match Molde, Ålesund or Kristiansund with regard to the facilities and docking capabilities and therefore handles just a small number of cruise ships.

Andalsnes from high above the fjord, (Work of B Jonas, CC BY SA 4.0. Wikimedia.org)

The dramatic backdrop for Åndalsnes

A view looking at Åndalsnes, (Work of Alfred Diem, CC BY SA 2.0, Wikimedia.org)

The magnificent backdrop, (Work of Ludovic Péron, CC BY SA 2.0)

The early history of Åndalsnes is seldom noted in travel literature. The only event of any

historic note is the 1940 landing of British forces in Åndalsnes as part of an action to drive the German forces out of Trondheim. But even in this battle, Åndalsnes played little part.

SHIP DOCK IN ÅNDALSNES: The cruise ships visiting Åndalsnes dock in the very heart of this very small town and thus no shuttle bus is necessary. You literally disembark from the ship and are in town.

TOURING OPTIONS IN ÅNDALSNES: The town does limited options with regard to touring the local region. These are your options for touring:

* **Ship sponsored tours** – The most commonly offered tour is usually a walking tour around the town. And there is generally a longer tour by motor coach that takes passengers over the famous Trollstigen, a torturous mountain highway that is beyond breathtaking. But if your ship could also be offering this mountain tour out of Kristiansund or Molde if they are on your itinerary.

* **Private car and driver/guide option** – You can order a private car and driver through your cruise line, but personally I find it an extravagance that is not warranted given the small size of Åndalsnes unless you want to do the longer excursions privately. To date I have never found any private car and driver services advertised in Åndalsnes.

In the center of Åndalsnes, (Work of Vegard Gran, CC BY SA 4.0)

* **Hop on hop off bus** service in Åndalsnes is not available, as there is essentially no need for it.

* **Taxis are generally dockside** if they are not busy. There are very few and unless booked for private touring in advance, they will not be able to assist you. The main taxi service is Finn Ståle Unhjem and you would ned to call them at +47 71 22 24 26 in advance.

* **Walking** is definitely an option given that Åndalsnes is so small. If the weather cooperates, the cool air is refreshing, especially on a sunny day.

WHAT TO SEE AND DO: There are a few significant highlights in Åndalsnes that are worthy of your attention. Here are my recommendations shown alphabetically:

* **Rampestreken** – Here is a scenic hike that should only be undertaken by those in good physical condition. It is considered to be the number one attraction in Åndalsnes but please heed my warning if you are not up to hiking. It only takes about two and one half hours to accomplish the hike up and back for an incredible view out over Åndalsnes and the surrounding countryside, but it is indeed strenuous.

On the Raumabanen excursion, (Work of TomasEE, CC BY SA 3.0, Wikimedia.org)

* **Raumabanen** - Unlike the other two primary activities recommended for Åndalsnes, this is a local rail excursion through absolutely awesome countryside. Many cruise lines will organize this as a group excursion and given that the vast majority of people on this type of cruise are in mature years, this ends up being the perfect excursion because it does not require any physical exertion. And frankly the experience is equally as majestic as laboring up one of the hiking trails.

For more detailed background and vital information on this journey visit www.visitnorway.com/getting-around/raumabanen .

Early winter comes to Åndalsnes

* **Romsdalseggen** – This is another hike to achieve an incredible view. Once again the same warning applies as for Rampesstreken for those who are not physically able to hike a mountain trail. This hike is about three plus hours in length for the round trip and again the views are incomparable. Here you are high enough to have a 365 degree view of the surrounding countryside.

DINING: Most ship passengers return to the ship for lunch, but personally I believe strongly in sampling local cuisine, especially in a country like Norway where the health and sanitation standards are among the highest in the world. If you like fresh seafood you will always do well at any Norwegian restaurant. Given the small size of Åndalsnes, there are two spots for lunch that I recommend. They are:

* **Sodahlhuset** – This is a delightful café located in the heart of Åndalsnes at Gamle Romsdalsvegen # 8. The menu offers a mix of Norwegian dishes, sandwiches, pizza and other light items including vegan fare. Monday thru Saturday thy open at 11 AM, closing at 6 PM except Tuesday and Wednesday when they close at 3 PM. Sunday hours are from 1 to 6 PM. Reservations are unnecessary

* **Spiseriet Soltinn** – Located in Åndalsnes a short distance south of the town center but an easy walk for most. The menu is European but with a strong Norwegian influence. Both the quality and service are excellent and sure to please. They are open daily at 10 am,

closing at 6 PM with two exceptions.. Thursday they close at 7 PM and Saturday at 4 PM. Reservations are unnecessary. The atmosphere is casual, but welcoming and friendly

KRISTIANSUND

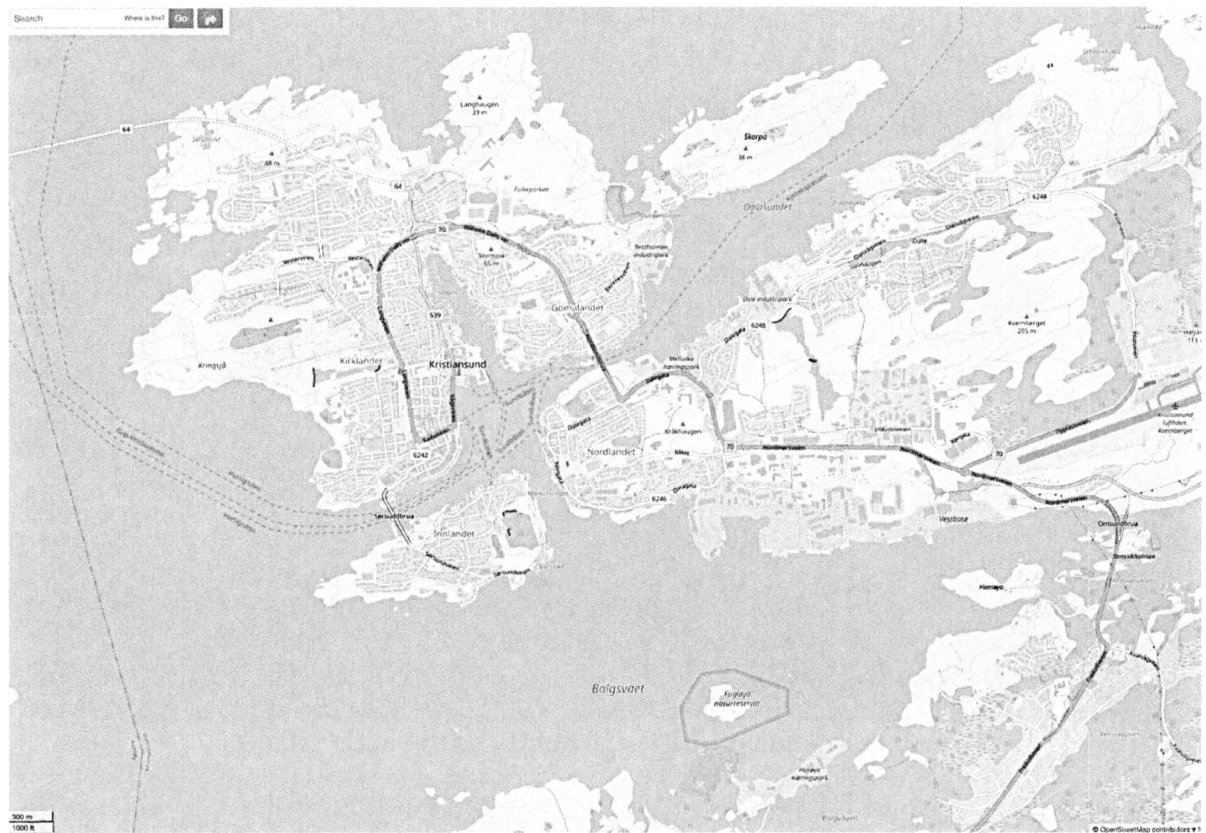

The coastal islands of Kristiansund (© OpenStreetMap contributors)

Kristiansund is the major city and administrative center in the Nordmøe region just north of Storfjorden. Not all cruise ships make a stop at this city whose history celebrates the one time importance of cod fishing. Today Kristiansund is very much a blue-collar city that supports various maintenance projects out on the North Sea oil drilling platforms. With a population of around 20,000, it is a substantial community, but one that many cruise passengers do not find as enjoyable because most of its historic architecture perished during World War II. Despite its lack of much historic architecture or monuments worthy of note, there is warm and welcoming environment in Kristiansund. I have always enjoyed spending a day in this unassuming but pleasant town. Here a visitor can obtain an appreciation for the basic everyday life of Norwegians living on the more northern shores of the sea.

THE GEOGRAPHIC SETTING: Kristiansund is a city by the sea, yet it turns its back to the harsh North Sea and faces inward, clustered on four islands around a sheltered central harbor. The city is quite densely populated, as its 20,000 residents occupy only 7.9 square kilometers, thus making it one of the country's most concentrated cities. Yet you will not feel a sense of crowding because of the fact that the city climbs steep hillsides on all four of its islands and the high ground is topped off by beautiful woodland. Facing out to sea on the backside of the northern and western islands, the land shows its rugged granite base, offering no beaches or safe anchorage. And in winter, it can be lashed by strong wind and surf.

The outer suburbs of Kristiansund on Innlandet Island

Docking in the town center of Kristiansund

Notwithstanding its island location, its proximity to the mainland has enabled Kristiansund to be connected by bridges and thus it does not quite feel like it is isolated from the rest of the nation. And it is also connected to a string of islands on which there are small fishing villages by a series of undersea tunnels and bridges known as the Great Atlantic Road. Apart from its very scenic potential and it being an architectural wonder, it is part of a very extensive system of roads that connect many of the near offshore islands to the mainland all along the Norwegian coast.

The country has invested heavily in its infrastructure. Despite its great oil wealth, Norway uses only monies raised through taxation for its superb infrastructure development. The entire earnings from the oil fields is placed in a superbly managed national pension fund. With its small population, everyone is able to retire and receive an annual pension essentially equal to their highest period of earning plus full medical coverage. The Norwegian people have the greatest degree of financial security of any nation in the world. Even with today's lower oil prices, Norway's pension fund continues to grow because of the high degree of management of the investment.

Kristiansund's climate is that of a temperate marine regime. Summers are relatively cool and sunny days are interspersed with cloudy periods that bring rain showers. When visiting in the summer, it is rather hit or miss as to having a bright sunny day, but Kristiansund does not have as high an incidence of gray or overcast days as does Bergen. Being closer to the Arctic Circle, Kristiansund has long winter nights with very short days, but its snowfall accumulation is far less than cities that are sheltered from the sea by way of being on the inner channels or deep into the fjords. But temperatures are still cold, hovering around the freezing mark. Winter days can be quite blustery and bone chilling. However, at this northern latitude, summer days are very long, almost reaching the 23 hour mark at the height of summer.

THE FASCINATING HISTORY: To appreciate your visit to Kristiansund it is important to have some understanding of the city's history. The first thing that will strike you when sailing into the harbor is the lack of a sense of history in its architecture. And this is part of the overall story of the city.

The Norwegian coast has a long history of settlement. There is archaeological evidence of pre Viking tribes having moved north along the edges of the retreating glacial ice as far back as 10,000 years ago. With the melt water mixing with seawater, high nutrient plankton provided a base for a rich and diverse marine population of shellfish and fish, and this encouraged human settlement along the coast.

Although during Viking times there were various battles fought in the immediate area, Kristiansund was never known to have been settled by the Norse warrior tribes, which is surprising given its sheltered waters.

During the Middle Ages, as Christianity was extending into Norway and the Norse tribes were settling down and developing more of a sedentary life, only the small island of Grip, off the coast from Kristiansund, saw any development as a fishing port. And it is assumed that the fishermen would have exploited the waters around what is now Kristiansund. An early Christian stave church is believed to have been built in 1470 in the village of Grip. The island continues to be inhabited to the present day, and it is connected during the summer by ferry to Kristiansund, a journey of approximately 30-minutes. But Grip does face the full fury of North Sea storms and the island has been swamped many times.

The main waterfront strand seen from onboard ship

Kristiansund only dates to the mid 1600's, when the first fishermen began to settle here. By the late 1600's, there was sufficient settlement based upon fishing and lumber to warrant the establishment of a government customs outpost.

It was in the waning years of the 17th century that Kristiansund's future was determined. Thanks to the introduction of the technique for drying cod, then a plentiful and bountiful species, exploitation began. And with a ready market in countries such as Portugal and Spain, Kristiansund became one of the most important fishing ports along the Norwegian coast. Known in the Norwegian language as "klippfisk," salted and dried cod was a basic staple to feed the hungry populations of the Iberian Peninsula and other parts of the western Mediterranean. Even today salted and dried cod is a very popular commodity on the Iberian Peninsula. Known as bacalao, it is reconstituted in water to soften and hydrate as well as remove the salt. Then it can be cooked with tomatoes, garlic or other seasonings into a very popular fish stew.

One of the oil platform service vessels docked in the city center

The importance of klippfisk is what put Kristiansund on the map, the town being given a city charter in 1742. The growth of Kristiansund was facilitated by the abundance of timber, and apart from the main church and the 19th century concert hall, the majority of buildings consisted of wood siding. There were occasional outbreaks of fire, but it was not until World War II and the Nazi occupation of Norway that Kristiansund would see a major conflagration. To exhort submission prior to occupying the port for military purposes, the German air force firebombed Kristiansund, destroying most of the community. Only the stone buildings survived to the present day. This is why Kristiansund lacks a distinctive architecture, as the majority of the city is of post-World War II origin, much of it hastily built to accommodate the need for housing without regard to style or decoration.

Kristiansund never had a large Jewish population, and the few who lived in the city were very much a part of community life. One of the most tragic moments of the Nazi occupation of the city was the rounding up of 18 Jewish citizens that ranged in age from five up into the 70's. They were shipped off to one of the concentration/death camps and nobody survived to return to Kristiansund. There is a small memorial in the park just up the hill from the city center and opposite the modern city church. The monument is small, but very poignant in its expression of loss. Their wartime sacrifice has become very much a part of the history of Kristiansund, and there were repeated stories in other Norwegian coastal communities.

The war memorial to the 18 Kristiansund Jews who were sent off to the Nazi death camps during World War II

With the discovery of oil in the North Sea, Kristiansund became one of the major service centers for the oil drilling and pumping platforms just over the horizon out at sea. The city also is home to the families of many of the oil workers who commute between the city and the platforms, living out at sea for periods of time before returning to the city. This has brought new life to Kristiansund since cod fishing has been greatly diminished by the declining numbers of fish and strict quotas as to their harvesting.

Tourism plays a small role in the city's economy because it is not located in one of the most scenic of areas, and it is not easy to reach in contrast to the many fjords where there is a strong tourist focus. Few cruise ships call in at Kristiansund, but for those that do, the people are quite welcoming.

SHIP DOCK IN KRISTIANSUND: The cruise ships visiting Kristiansund dock in the very heart of city, moored alongside the city's major shopping mall and just one block from the war memorial that marks the center of town. Thus a shuttle bus is totally unnecessary.

TOURING OPTIONS IN KRISTIANSUND: Kristiansund does offer the majority of touring services that are found in major cities, but not all of them at the same level of ease in booking since it is not that major a tourist destination. These are your options for touring:

* **Ship sponsored tours** – The most commonly offered tour is a four-hour guided tour by motor coach around the city of Kristiansund with a visit to the klippfisk museum where you learn the history of cod fishing, salting and drying and its impact upon the growth of the city. And there is generally a longer tour by motor coach along the Great Ocean Road, which can be quite spectacular on a nice sunny day. Some cruise lines offer more adventure oriented kayaking or sailing tours, and on occasion I have seen a tour to the historic island of Grip.

* **Private car and driver/guide option** – You can order a private car and driver through your cruise line, but personally I find it an extravagance that is not warranted given the small size of Kristiansund unless you want to do the longer excursions privately. To date I have never found any private car and driver services advertised in Kristiansund.

* **Hop on hop off bus** service in Kristiansund is not available, as there is essentially no need for it.

* **Ferryboat service** does exist with a circular route making three stops starting from the dock in front of the war memorial. This does give access to the different island sectors of the city. This yellow ferry is called the Sundbåten and runs all day. For more details visit on line at _www.sundbaten.no_ and click on English at the top right of the page.

* **Taxis are generally dockside** and will offer an hourly or daily rate for sightseeing in and around Kristiansund. To book in advance for sightseeing I advise you to check out the web pages for Kristiansund Taxi at *www.kristiansundtaxi.no* for further details.

* **Walking** is definitely an option and can be combined with the ferryboat to see much of the city. Be aware that Kristiansund is quite hilly and in walking you will get a good bit of exercise on the more strenuous side.

WHAT TO SEE AND DO: There are a few significant highlights in Kristiansund that are worthy of your attention. Here are my recommendations shown alphabetically:

* **Bautean** - This is the high hill where the canon is fired to welcome a cruise ship into port. It is a bit of a climb, but well worth the imposing view of the city and out to the surrounding islands. You can reach it by walking across the high bridge to Innlandet Island or by taking the ferryboat and getting off at the first stop. There are no given hours, but the trail has no lighting and if visiting in the spring or fall one should never walk the route after dark.

* **Holocaust Memorial** - Just down the hill from the church about one full block in the park is the memorial, which is somewhat hidden away. It is a very poignant reminder of the Holocaust and its impact upon Kristiansund. The memorial sits in the park and thus is always open to visitors. The fact that the town erected this memorial for only a handful of residents is a testament to the Norwegian people.

On the waterfront in the city center with its war monument

Flower beds in the heart of Kristiansund

The welcome cannon fired from Bauten

* **Kirkelandet Kirke** - This ultra-modern new church has replaced the old stone church across the harbor as the main Lutheran church for the city. It has beautiful stained glass windows and is worth a short visit. Its design is loved by some and despised by others because of its unique departure from tradition.

The church is open to visitors, but there may be special services when tourists are not permitted. No actual visitation hours are posted.

* **Mellemværftet Shipbuilding Museum** - Located down a steep hill from the main strand that runs along the harbor. This rather small museum is really for those who have a special interest in how the old fishing vessels were built back in the time period when Kristiansund was at the height of its cod fishing period. It is open daily from Noon to 5 PM, and very welcoming especially when a cruise ship is in port.

The old stone church survived the Nazi bombings in WWII

* **Nordlandet Kirke** - On the Nordlandet Island, which is the second ferry stop, you can see this old stone church up close. It is built of stone, but only dates back to 1914, and is one of the few buildings to survive the bombing of World War II. No specific visiting hours are posted, so you may find the church closed. Usually the doors are open on days when a ship is in port.

* **Norwegian Klippfisk Museum** - This is a major feature on the ship sponsored tour, but if you want to go on your own, you will need to take a taxi as it is too far to walk. You can take the ferryboat, getting off at the final stop, but it is a steep walk up to the museum. The guided tour is quite fascinating and it surprises you how much there is to learn. And you will get a taste of cod that has been dried and then reconstituted. The museum is open from Noon to 5 PM daily.

* **Sundbaten** - This yellow ferryboat that you will see at the World War II monument with the surrounding Norwegian flags is one quick way to spend time visiting all of the islands that make up the city. It travels in a counterclockwise direction, so you can either stay on for the entire ride or get off and catch some of the recommended sights. The ferry runs quite often and has its schedule posted.

* **Varden Tower** - This is the best way to get a visual overview of the city. It is a short distance from the city center, but it is not well marked. Stop at the local tourist office in the city center to ask specific directions. Essentially you start at the new church on the hill above the city center, follow the main street, which is Langveien for one long block to Vuggaveien and turn left, the right at the first cross street, which is Hagbart Brinchmanns vei and you will see the path to the tower on your left. The tower has a button at the door and when pressed, it triggers an automatic opener. No specific hours are posted, but it is generally open when ships are in port.

Summer is a time for fresh flowers in the homes of residents in Kristiansund

DINING OUT: Kristiansund has numerous restaurants, but you must remember that this is a blue collar community of fishermen and oil workers So do not expect gourmet quality or ambiance. I have eaten lunch in Kristiansund numerous times over the years, and these are my recommendations:

* **Bryggekanten Brasserie** - Located along the waterfront near to where cruise ships dock. It has a good reputation for quality cuisine and service. And it has great views of the harbor. Open from 11:30 AM to 10:30 PM, you will not go wrong dining here. They offer a variety of seafood and meat dishes, including burgers to satisfy those from North America. Reservations are not needed.

* **Dødeladen Cafe og Kultursted** - On the waterfront in the center of town very close to where cruise ships dock at Skippergata # 1a, this is a popular restaurant with a large outdoor deck overlooking the harbor. Again traditionally prepared seafood dishes dominate the menu, including the traditional baccalao, which had made Kristiansund famous. The restaurant is open Tuesday thru Thursday from 2 to 11 PM, Friday and Saturday from 2 Pm to Midnight and Sunday from 1 PM to Midnight. Reservations are not required.

* **Nordmorskafeen Homemade Food** - Located along the waterfront at Fosnagata #3 upstairs, and open from 9 AM to 6 PM, this is my favorite place for traditional, well-prepared Norwegian dishes. It is not fancy, and you order at the counter and then select your beverage and dessert. When the main course is ready, it is brought to your table. The staff is very friendly and will make substitutions to accommodate your tastes. Their menu is small, but changes daily. I have never had a bad lunch here.

* **Sjøstjerna** - Located in the city center on Skolegata. It is open from Noon to Midnight and serves genuine Norwegian cuisine, primarily specializing in fresh fish and seafood. But the food and service are good, and the atmosphere is typical of the cozy restaurants of the city. One of the specialties is bacalao, which is the Portuguese way of reconstituting dried and salted cod. It is very good and now accepted as a local delicacy. If fiskeboller are on the menu, it is my favorite. It is made from chopped fish that is formed into what would be like meatballs and then poached in a fish broth. You do not need to reserve a table. They are open Monday thru Saturday from 5 PM to Midlight, and some cruise ships do stay well into the evening.

* **Smia Fish Restauant** - Located along the downtown waterfront at Fosnagata #30b, this is a very traditional seafood restaurant in which authenticity rules. If you want to experience the best of Norwegian seafood preparation while in Kristiansund, this is the restaurant to try. It is open Monday thru Saturday 11 AM to 10 PM. Reservations are not necessary.

Fresh cut flowers for indoor enjoyment during the brief summer

SHOPPING: There are few shops that offer souvenirs or hand crafted items, as the tourist market is small. Opposite where the ship docks is the city's main indoor shopping arcade with dozens of shops on two levels. This mall serves local needs, but is interesting to visit. You will find quite a variety of merchandise, but it is oriented more toward the blue collar community, which is the nature of Kristiansund.

Across from the mall in the parking lot there are often vendors selling fresh fish and berries along with various pastries. If you are simply in the mood for dessert, the shopping mall across the street from where the ship docks has a very good pastry counter on the second floor. They offer sandwiches and pastries with coffee or tea, and it can sometimes be just the light snack you are looking for.

FINAL WORDS: Many of my fellow passengers have asked why the ship bothered to stop in Kristiansund, as they found it less interesting than other ports. But these people clearly had either not read up on the history of the town or attended my presentation. Kristiansund is not one of the more illustrious communities on the itinerary, but it is definitely interesting in giving you a look at a hard working blue-collar Norwegian coastal town. You develop more of a feeling from mingling with these hard working people from the oil rigs and fishing boats and can better understand the true nature of life in Norway. There is more to visiting a countryside than seeing its public monuments and museums.

MAPS OF KRISTIANSUND

THE MAIN ISLANDS OF KRISTIANSUND

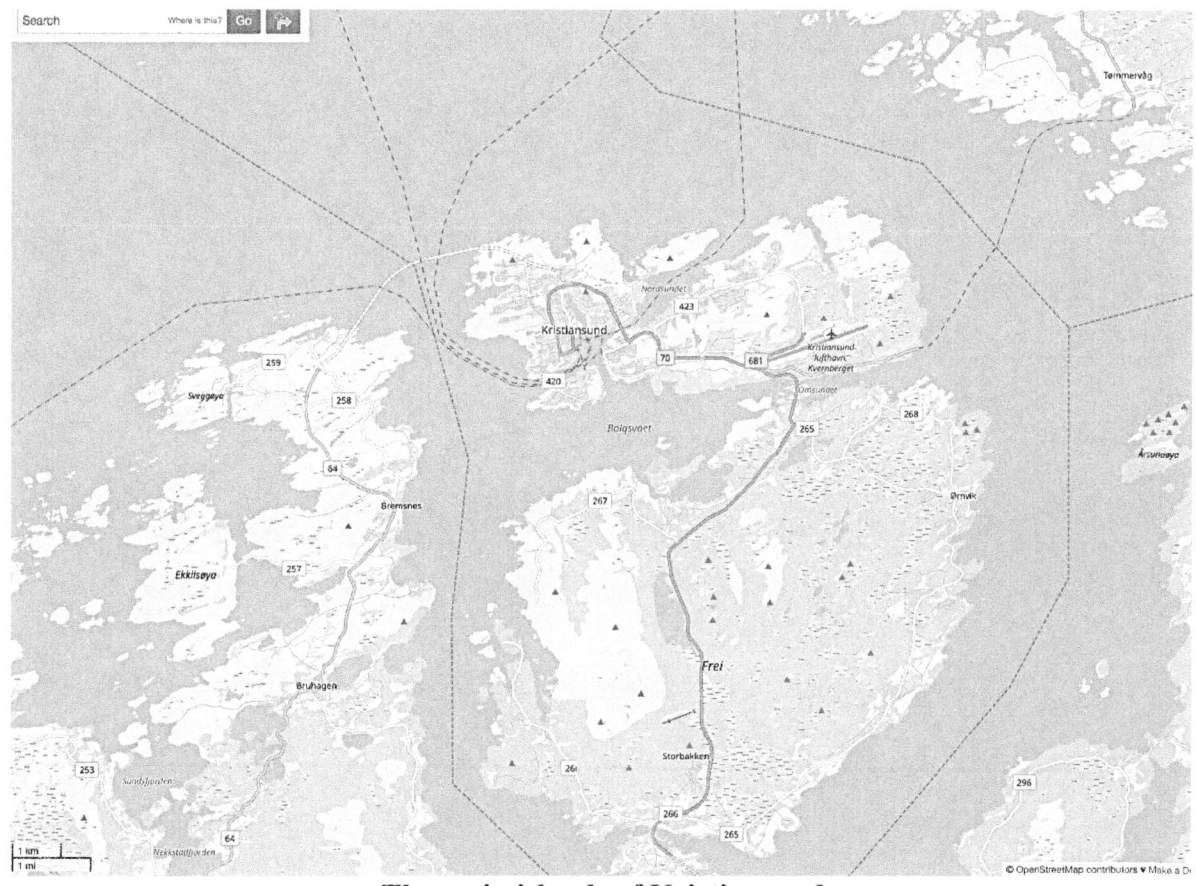

The main islands of Kristiansund

This map is best viewed directly from OpenStreetMap.com on your personal device where it can be expanded or one specific area can be enlarged. Given the format of this book, it is impossible to display maps with the level of detail you might wish to have while actually out exploring the city. But the OpenStreetMap maps used directly are the tool I always rely upon.

THE CITY OF KRISTIANSUND

The city of Kristiansund with the blue star showing where the cruise ship docks

This map is best viewed directly from OpenStreetMap.com on your personal device where it can be expanded or one specific area can be enlarged. Given the format of this book, it is impossible to display maps with the level of detail you might wish to have while actually out exploring the city. But the OpenStreetMap maps used directly are the tool I always rely upon.

THE CENTER OF KRISTIANSUND

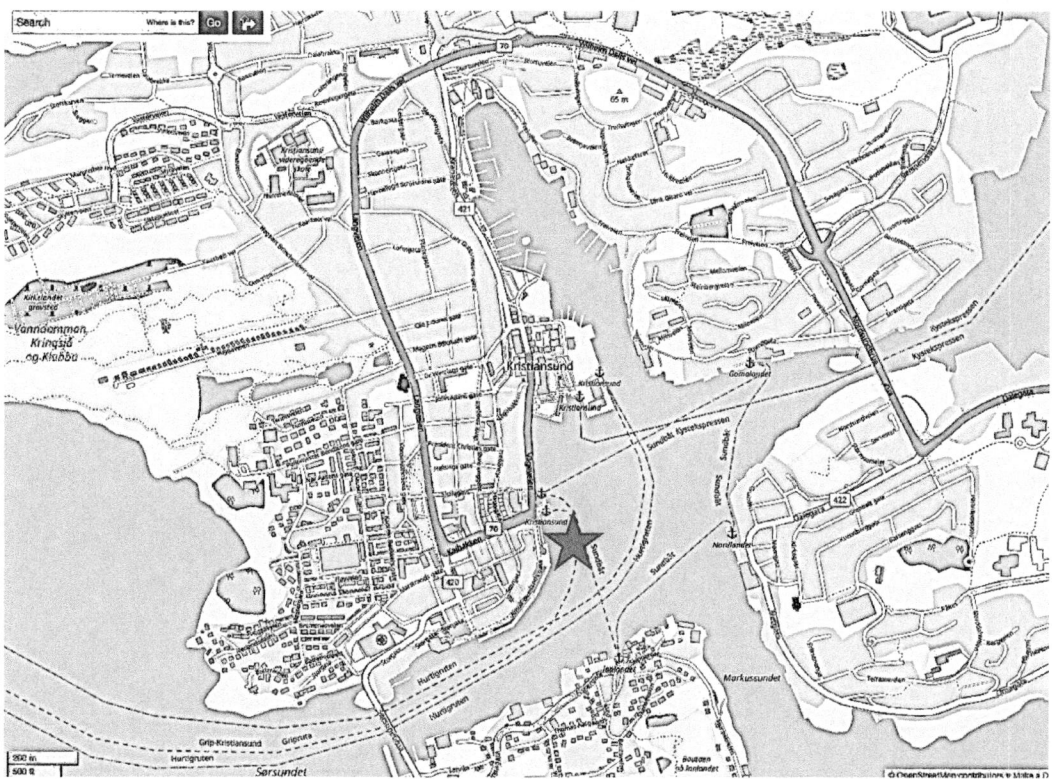

The center of Kristiansund with the blue star showing where the cruise ship docks

This map is best viewed directly from OpenStreetMap.com on your personal device where it can be expanded or one specific area can be enlarged. Given the format of this book, it is impossible to display maps with the level of detail you might wish to have while actually out exploring the city. But the OpenStreetMap maps used directly are the tool I always rely upon.

VISITING TRONDHEIM

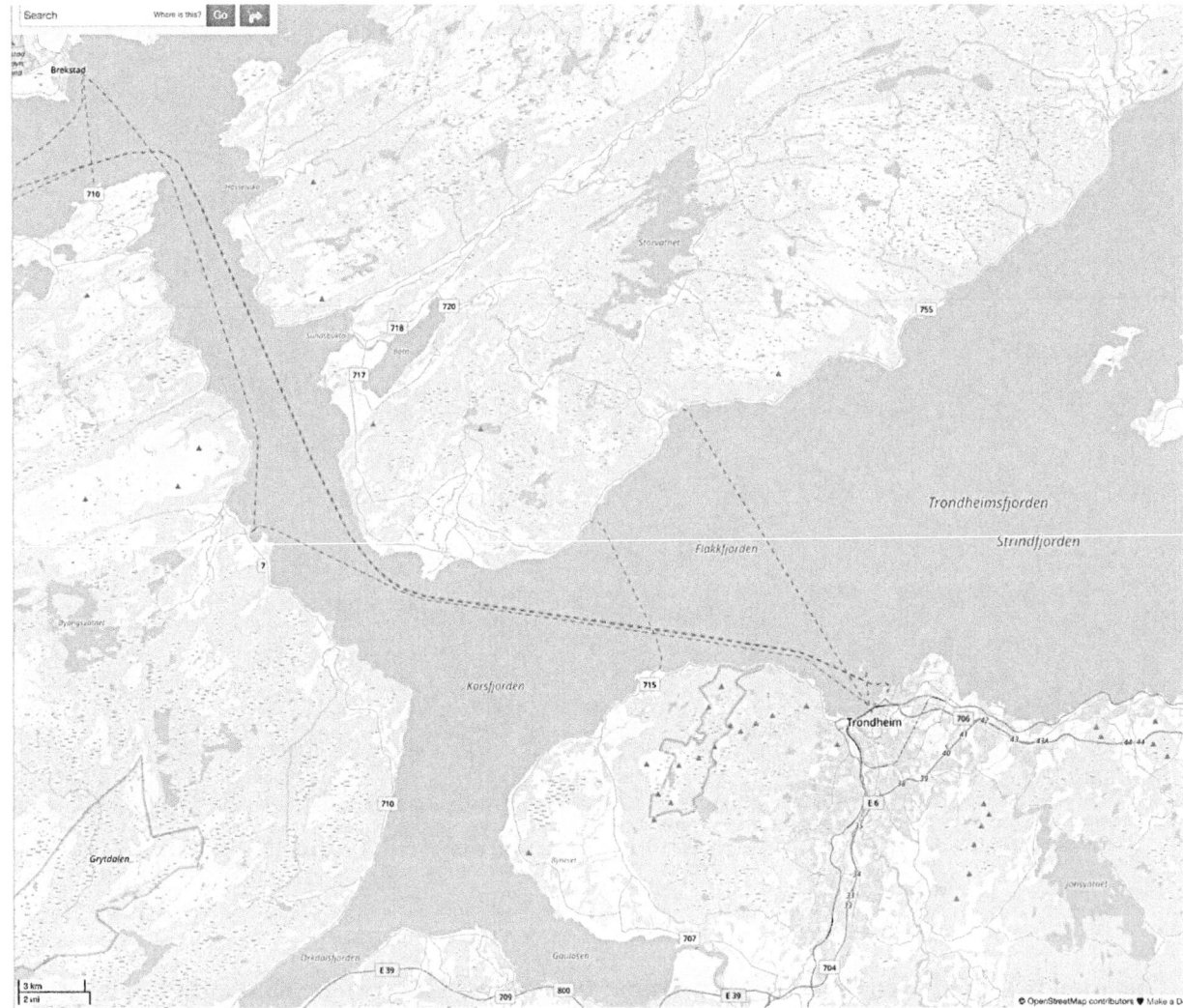

The surroundings of Trondheim (© OpenStreetMap contributors)

THE NATURAL LANDSCAPE: Trondheim is one of the four major cities of Norway, and it is the farthest north of the large cities. Oslo and Bergen are the number one and two cities with regard to size, but then there is a brewing argument between Stavanger and Trondheim as to which city is the third largest. Even at the time of writing this book, there is no agreement among various Norwegian or foreign sources as to giving a definitive answer. Essentially it is a matter of whether suburban areas are included and if so, how far out from the city center the source counts communities as suburbs. When I was last in Trondheim, everyone I spoke with was positive that their city is now Norway's third largest. The population of metropolitan Trondheim is around 200,000. Regardless of the ranking, Trondheim is one of the most beautiful cities in the country and also a very historic community. And it is the largest city in Norway located just ever so slightly south of the Arctic Circle by less than eight one hundredth of a degree of latitude. So officially the city is considered to be sub-Arctic. One degree of latitude is equal to approximately 111 kilometers or 69 miles. This means that Trondheim is less than five kilometers or three miles from the actual line that denotes the Arctic Circle.

Looking at the heart of Trondheim from Steinberget

GEOGRAPHIC SETTING: The city of Trondheim is located in the narrow valley of the Nidelva River at a point where the river empties into Trondheim Fjord. To the east and west of the city, the land rises abruptly into wooded hills that reach a maximum elevation of 565 meters or 1,854 feet. These hills provide a beautiful setting for the city, adding to its overall scenic quality. There are thick forests of spruce mixed with willow and birch giving the landscape a verdant appearance. At this far northern latitude, but close to the moderating influences of the sea, the temperatures on a year around basis are still significant enough to enable forests to grow.

Trondheim is the largest city in Norway at such far northerly latitude and is just shy of 24-hour daylight during several weeks of summer and then just shy of total darkness for the first few weeks of winter. The amount of difference between Trondheim and locations above the Arctic Circle are measured in mere seconds between full daylight or darkness.

Being close to the sea, but just enough inland has an impact upon the overall climate of Trondheim. It is essential a modified maritime climate with very cold winters and mild summers. The gale force winds that can blow off the North Sea do not quite reach Trondheim. At the same time the very heavy snows of the interior do not occur in the city. Its winters show a mix of rain and snow and are not as severe as the latitude would give one to believe. Summer days are mild, interspersed with fog, cloud and sunshine. By the standards of most visitors, Trondheim would appear to be very cold and definitely dark during the and after the winter solstice. And in summer with virtually 24-hours of daylight for several weeks, Trondheim is milder than one would expect. There are actually summer days when you would not need to wear a jacket.

Looking toward the cathedral in Trondheim from Steinberget

THE CITY'S LONG HISTORY: Trondheim has a history extending back to the year 997, founded during the reign of King Olav Tryggvason, one of the first two great Viking leaders to accept Christianity. Trondheim, then known as Nidaros, became the archdiocese in 1152, under the Catholic faith and it also served as the secular capital of Norway until 1217 when it was moved to Oslo.

The great Romanesque and gothic cathedral of Nidaros still stands as the cornerstone of the city center of Trondheim. Its construction dates to 1070 when it was built to honor King Olaf II who was canonized and became the patron of Norway. But it suffered three fires during its long history and the present edifice dates to the early 18th century and is of course the seat of the Lutheran bishop and has been since the reformation. When the cathedral was originally constructed, it was Roman Catholic. Even though the Lutheran faith does not believe in heavy ornamentation of its churches, Nidaros, even though reconstructed, does reflect its early Catholic heritage as a matter of historic importance.

As noted with reference to the cathedral experiencing several fires, this has been the fate of so many Norwegian cities in their early years because of the widespread use of wood for construction. Trondheim was no exception. The greatest fire occurred in 1651 when the major part of the city was destroyed. This did, however, lead to more careful rebuilding with the use of wider streets to prevent a block fire from easily spreading. But even today, the vast majority of homes in Trondheim and many business buildings are constructed of wood. But the city maintains a very modern fire brigade to meet the needs of today's reality.

The Nideros Cathedral's Romanesque facade

Norway and Sweden were drawn into the Danish dominated Kalmar Union in 1397, but Sweden withdrew in 1523, leaving Norway united with Denmark until 1814. However a brief war between Denmark and Sweden resulted in Trondheim briefly becoming Swedish territory from February 1658 until it was retaken less than a year later and validated by treaty in May 1660.

Norway was ceded to Sweden in 1814 through the Treaty of Kiel in which Denmark renounced all future claims. But in 1905, in an amicable arrangement Norway regained full independence. Trondheim never did, however, regain its political status, but the present king does enjoy frequent visits, staying it the small royal palace near the great cathedral. The king and his family do attempt to spend time in various parts of the country, and Trondheim is one of the most comfortable of locations. The old royal residence cannot be called palatial, but it is very comfortable.

A few high rise apartments given Trondheim is a major city

The city of Trondheim was occupied by Nazi forces in early April 1940 and remained under harsh rule until the German surrender in May 1945. Given the deep fjord and its sheltered interior location, but with easy access to the sea, Trondheim became a major submarine base, remnants still visible to the present day with large heavily constructed concrete buildings meant to withstand bombing raids. Citizens were under strict rules and regulations and penalties were harsh. However, the Norwegian resistance did inflict its share of retaliation all during the occupation. The German Navy had great plans to create a massive naval facility just outside of Trondheim, but fortunately they never realized their dream.

The modern history of Trondheim is still reflected in its old town district along the river where old wood warehouses, many now turned into fashionable lofts, recall the days when this was a major trade center. And overall there is a flavor of the city's Viking heritage seen in its architecture, and simply by the fact that such a major city exists this far north. And to reflect the city's early embrace of Christianity, the Nideros Cathedral stands as the most dominant downtown landmark. The city lays claim that it is the largest medieval building in all of Scandinavia, but I believe that the Lutheran cathedral in Uppsala, Sweden is every bit its equal in size.

View over the walls of Kristiansten Fortress

SHIP DOCK IN TRONDHEIM: Most cruise ships will dock at the cruise terminal, which is a modern structure just north of the city center, an easy walk of less than 15 minutes. But some of the more upmarket cruise lines will offer a shuttle bus generally to the Nideros Cathedral in the city center. An alternate dock used when more ships arrive than can be accommodated is located at Quay 68, which is just to the west of the city center, but a moderately long walk and thus most cruise lines will offer shuttle service. There are no terminal facilities at Quay 68 and it is essentially adjacent to a residential neighborhood, which is quite a pleasant area in which to walk after you have been out touring.

TOURING OPTIONS IN TRONDHEIM: As a major Norwegian city, Trondheim offers a variety of services making it easy for the visitor from a cruise ship to enjoy the sights. These options include:

* **Cruise sponsored tours** – All cruise lines will offer a variety of motor coach tours, but primarily oriented to the city and/or its offshore island fortress. There generally are no cruises offered into the interior regions, but rather all focus upon the city.

* **Private car and driver/guide** – All major cruise lines will be able to arrange for a private car and driver/guide in Trondheim. If you wish to arrange this service on your own in hopes of saving some money I recommend the following:

** Trondheim Limousine at www.trondheimlimousine.no/en is a very reliable company with excellent driver/guides.

** Also visit www.lonelyplanet.com/Europe/Norway/Activities and follow their prompts to car and driver services.

* **Hop on hop off bus** – There is no hop on hop off bus in Trondheim, as all the major sites that tourists wish to visit are close together in the city center and within easy walking distance of one another.

* **Taxi touring** – There are generally taxis waiting at the main cruise terminal, but seldom at Quay 68. You can arrange for a taxi to take you on a sightseeing tour by contacting Trønder Taxi AS through their web page at www.trondertaxi.no and first selecting English if Norwegian is not familiar to you.

* **Gråkallbanen** – This is the rather distinct white streetcar service in Trondheim that can be an enjoyable way to get around parts of the city. It operates on a route that is 8.8 kilometers long between Lian and St. Olasgate throughout the day. The one way journey takes 21 minutes on average and gives you a look at several parts of the city from commercial to residential. For more information email post@boreal.no.

* **Walking** is a very easy way to see the major sights of Trondheim, but if you are the type of visitor who wants to explore an entire city then you need to choose either the private car and driver/guide or taxi option.

SIGHTS TO SEE: There are few truly amazing sights to see in Trondheim, yet overall this is an interesting city because of the simple elegance of its old buildings and the stately character of the overall aura. My suggestions for the important highlights in Trondheim are as follows (listed alphabetically):

* **Kristiansten Fortress** - Standing on a prominent hill southeast of the city center, this fortress offers a total panorama of the city from a perspective that is well within the urbanized area. It was built in 1681 after a devastating fire swept the main town. The purpose was to offer protection from any landward invasion coming via Sweden. It did see some action during the Great Northern War in 1718 when Swedish forces laid siege, but were unable to take the fortress. Although not a major facility, it is of great historic

importance and also offers excellent views of the city. During the summer months, the fortress is open to the public from 9 AM to Midnight daily.

A detailed telephoto study of Trondheim architecture

* **Munkholmen** - This island fortress combined monastery is very interesting because of its unique history. It is located in the fjord a short ferry ride from the downtown waterfront. Initially built by Benedictine monks in the 11th century, it became a prison/fortress in 1658. During World War II, Nazi forces occupied it to help protect their submarine base from Allied invasion. During summer there is a small ferryboat that operates between the dock at Ravnkloa on the downtown waterfront and the island. Boat service is provided by Tripp's and you can check them out at *www.trippsbatservice.no* but their web page does not have English translation. No hours for the fortress or ferry are posted, but they do operate all day during summer.

* **Niderosdomen** - It is impossible to miss the imposing cathedral with its mix of gothic and Romanesque architectural styles. The cathedral of today represents a reconstruction of the original that was destroyed by fire. It is a massive structure sitting in a lush park and the most impressive building in the city. The cathedral is open daily from 9 AM to 2 PM The Visitor Center is open daily from 9 AM to 3 PM and tours of the cathedral in English are given daily at 10 AM.

Historic Old Town along the Nidelva River

* Old Town and Bridge - While in the city center, visit the preserved Old Town by walking across this beautiful bridge with its Viking carving, the original of which dated to **1681.** The view from both the bridge and the far bank of the river is worth the effort. The bridge is open 24 hours per day. It is located just a few short blocks south of the Cathedral and is very easy to reach. Then continue on into the Old Town.

* Ringve Museum - Located at Lade Alle #60 and open from 11 AM to 4 PM daily, this museum housed in a rather large, old building is devoted to traditional music and the instruments used to play. This is a museum for those who are truly interested in the history of music, as there are few such museums in the world, which makes this a must for anyone who has a passion for song, dance and the variety of musical instruments. And the surrounding gardens are also quite special. The museum is open Tuesday thru Sunday from 11 AM to 4 PM. For American visitors, the only such museum in the United States is the Musical Instrument Museum in Phoenix, Arizona.

* Rockheim Museum - Located on the waterfront at Brattoerkaia # 14 and open Tuesday, Wednesday and Friday from 10 AM to 4 PM, Thursday from 10 AM to 8 PM and Saturday and Sunday from 10 AM to 5 PM. This museum is devoted to popular Norwegian music. I only recommend it to those who are truly interested in contemporary music of the country you are visiting. Norwegian music is quite beautiful, but much of it has a somewhat somber quality, reflecting the hard lives of the vast majority of the people throughout so much of the history of Norway.

The Royal Palace known as Siftsgarden in the heart of the city

* **Stiftsgarden** – This is the old wooden royal palace in the city center. It was built in 1774 and is still used today by the Royal Family when they visit Trondheim. It is said to be the largest wooden royal residence in all of Scandinavia. Tours are given daily on the hour during summer, but the palace is closed to the public when the Royal Family is in residence. It is open Tuesday thru Saturday from 10 AM to 2 PM, Thursday Noon to 8 PM and Sunday from Noon to 4 PM.

* **Streets of the downtown and Olav Tryggvason Column** - Next you should stop in the downtown and simply spend an hour walking the pleasant streets, taking in the mix of architectural styles and the overall ambiance. The massive column dedicated to the first Norwegian king to have made Trondheim his capital dominates the main downtown square.

Much of central Trondheim has more of a small town feel than a major city

* Tyholttarnet – This is the observation tower overlooking the city. It is a long walk from the city center, and you will need a taxi to reach it at Otto Nielsens veg # 4. On a clear day it does provide a spectacular panoramic view of the entire city and its surroundings. It is open weekdays from 10 AM to 11 PM and on weekends from 11 AM to 10 PM.

* Viewpoint on the slopes of Steinberget - This viewpoint is just high enough to give you a sweeping panorama of the entire city and its surrounding hills. Yes there is an observation tower in the city that also contains a restaurant, but the viewpoint on Steinberget is quiet, out of the way, but close enough for a great first impression of Trondheim.

DINING OUT: Depending upon your itinerary, you may or may not be in Trondheim during lunch. Many ships arrive in the early afternoon, leaving just before dinner, thus spending about five or six hours in the city. If your ship does spend the entire day, then it is worth taking the time to have a traditional Norwegian lunch. This is what I am recommending in those instances, and I have chosen four restaurants where such an experience can be had.

* Antikavariatet – Located across the pedestrian bridge from the Old Town and facing the river with a nice view at Nedre Bakklander #4, this is a popular restaurant with locals and visitors alike. The menu is a mix of Norwegian and general European dishes, all served in a nice atmosphere. You will be surrounded by books in their back room where individuals can also perform at will. They are open from 3 PM to Midnight Tuesday thru Friday and Noon to midnight on weekends. Reserving a table is not necessary.

Sunday at Baklanded Skydsstation

*** Baklanded Skydsstation** - Located at Ovre Bakklandet #33, and open from 11 AM to 1 AM on weekdays and from Noon to 1 AM on weekends, this is one of the most popular restaurants for a traditional Norwegian menu. The restaurant sits along the east side of the Nidelva River, facing the large park housing the cathedral. You will find that if you check any restaurant source, there are no bad reviews for this establishment. They specialize in a variety of fresh fish and seafood dishes, and of course cod bacalao is one of the favorite entrees. And they also have traditional herring as an appetizer. If you are into sweet endings, there is a very rich hot chocolate along with a variety of Norwegian pastries. No need to reserve a table.

*** Kalas & Canasta** – Located at Nedra Baklanded # 5, which is across the river on the old pedestrian bridge. It is facing the Old Town. The restaurant serves lunch and dinner and the menu consists of many traditional Norwegian favorites plus many general European dishes. The cuisine and service are excellent and the atmosphere is casual. They are open Monday thru Thursday from 11 AM to Midnight, Friday from 11 AM to 1 AM, Saturday from Noon to 1 AM and Sunday from Noon to 9 PM. They will gladly take reservations by calling them at +47 928 52 527.

* **Ravnkloa Fish Market** - Located along the waterfront at Monkegata #70 and open Monday thru Saturday 10 AM to 5 PM. this is a combination fish market and restaurant. They specialize in incredibly fresh fish and shellfish, cooked to perfection. You cannot get anything fresher given that the restaurant is on the docks where the fishing boats tie up. Two specialties are traditional creamy fish soup and fiskeboller - the cooked fish balls that are a major Norwegian delicacy. Very casual and reservations are not necessary.

The beauty of Trondheim along the Nidelva River

FINAL WORDS: Trondheim is a delightful city to visit because of its long history, exceptionally beautiful parks and architecture, as well as its physical setting between forested hills and along the winding Nidelva River.

King Olav Tryggvason reminds everyone of Trondheim's long history

The city itself is relatively hilly, thickly wooded with tree-shaded streets and in essence more the atmosphere of a large town rather than one of the country's largest cities. It is an important regional center, also still has an active fishing fleet. Trondheim is essentially the cultural and educational center for northern Norway.

TRONDHEIM MAPS

GREATER TRONDHEIM

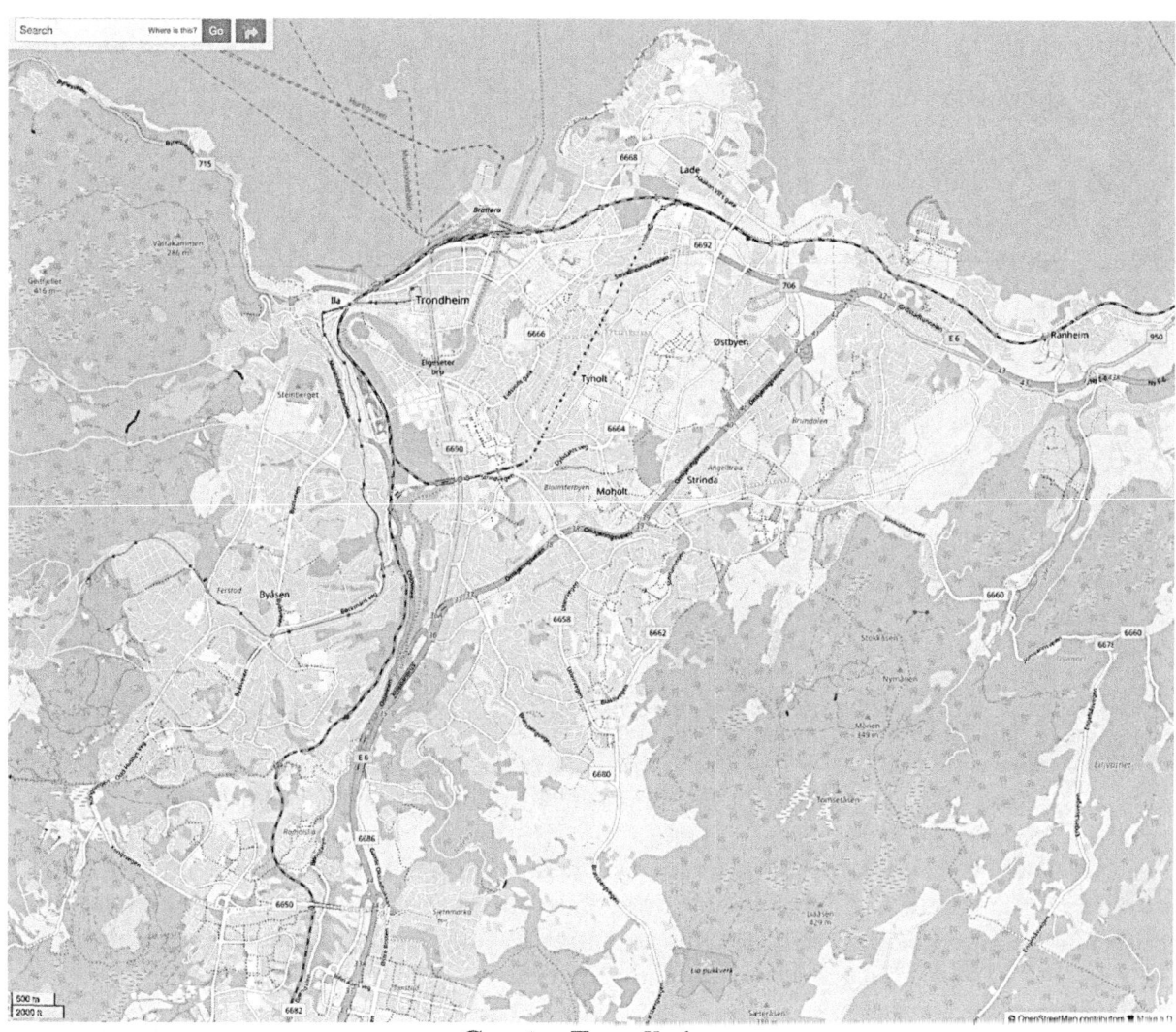

Greater Trondheim

This map is best viewed directly from OpenStreetMap.com on your personal device where it can be expanded or one specific area can be enlarged. Given the format of this book, it is impossible to display maps with the level of detail you might wish to have while actually out exploring the city. But the OpenStreetMap maps used directly are the tool I always rely upon.

CITY CENTER OF TRONDHEIM

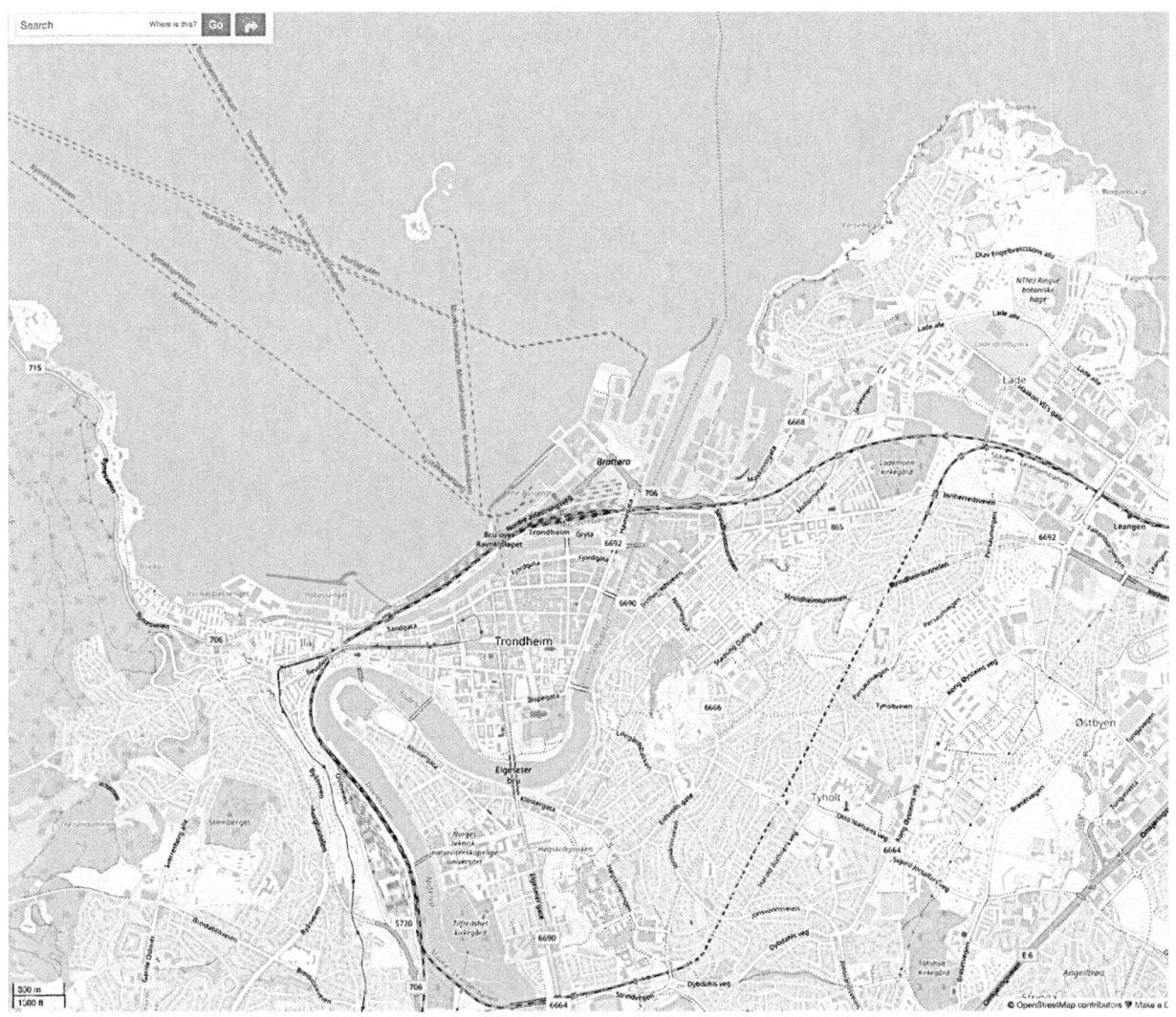

City of Trondheim

This map is best viewed directly from OpenStreetMap.com on your personal device where it can be expanded or one specific area can be enlarged. Given the format of this book, it is impossible to display maps with the level of detail you might wish to have while actually out exploring the city. But the OpenStreetMap maps used directly are the tool I always rely upon.

THE HEART OF TRONDHEIM

The heart of Trondheim

This map is best viewed directly from OpenStreetMap.com on your personal device where it can be expanded or one specific area can be enlarged. Given the format of this book, it is impossible to display maps with the level of detail you might wish to have while actually out exploring the city. But the OpenStreetMap maps used directly are the tool I always rely upon.

THE LOFOTEN ISLANDS
VISITING SVOLVÆR

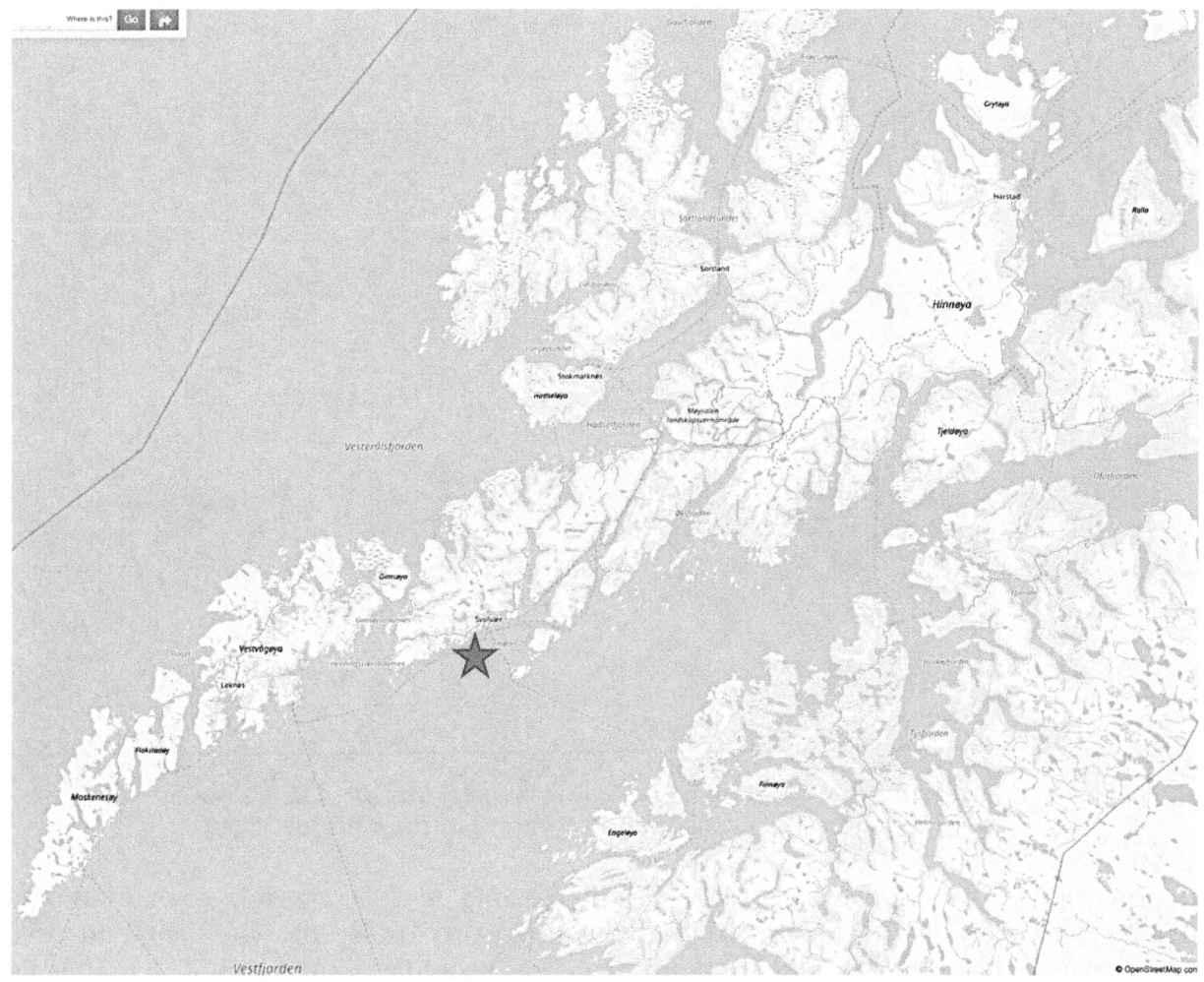
Map of the Lofoten Islands, (© OpenStreetMap contributors)

THE GEOGRAPHIC SEETTING: The Lofoten Islands are a group of heavily glaciated islands that extend away from the Norwegian coast into the North Sea, creating an ever-narrowing gulf between themselves and the mainland known as Vestfjorden traversed as one travels between Trondheim and Tromsø. But even these sheltered waters between the Lofoten Islands and the mainland can become quite choppy during moderate weather. Thus if your cruise itinerary does include a stop in Svolvær or farther north in Harstadt, there is a very strong chance that you will not be able to land in Svolvær, but a more than 60 percent chance of docking in Harstadt. Svolvær does not have docking space for very large cruise ships and the slightest chop in the water makes tendering ashore rather uncomfortable. But a breeze of 40 kilometers or 24 miles per hour is sufficient to make gaining access to the harbor difficult or at times impossible. Then there is fog to consider on days when it is very calm. During my most recent visit, the morning of the ship's visit to Svolvær turned out to have a combination of low fog and moderate wind. The local pilots absolutely refused to grant entry into the port, so the ship had to sail on to Tromsø since Harstadt was not on that particular itinerary.

Along the shoreline of Austvågøya Island in the Lofoten group

In spite of the difficulty often associated with landing in Svolvær, this is an especially striking part of Norway with regard to the beauty of its landscape. The mountains rise quite abruptly from the sea, and there are numerous small bays and coves. The islands lie just north of the Arctic Circle, but given the proximity of the Gulf Stream, they have a more moderate climate than interior locations at their latitude. Water temperatures are kept above freezing throughout the winter by the passing Gulf Stream that continues on into the Arctic Ocean all the way to Murmansk, Russia. On the leeward sides of the islands where temperatures drop below freezing, heavy snows can fall whereas on the windward side the snow level is far higher and rain predominates along the coast along with gale force winds. Summers are very mild and during spring there is actually a pronounced drier period with little to no rain and clear sunny days.

The island geography is very distinct, characterized by tall peaks that rise dramatically, the highest being 1,252 meters or 4,140 feet high. The lower slopes show a mix of lush grassland and wooded areas whereas the peaks are essentially barren. At these far northern latitudes with the long period of winter darkness the overall temperature at altitudes only a few hundred meters above sea level are cold enough to keep tree growth to the lowest reaches of the slopes. The softer nature of the rock layers, dating back to over 60,000,000 years, made them very susceptible to being eroded into their present form during the great ice age.

The high mountains of Austvågøya Island

This is a region very rich in sea life, which has encouraged much fishing. On land there are many species of sea birds, otter and moose. Today only smaller minke whales frequent these islands because whaling is still practiced along the Norwegian coast, an economic activity controversial in the eyes of the world. Norwegians still consider whale meat a delicacy and it will be found in fish markets across the country even though it is a warm blooded mammal. Over hunting has decimated the once more plentiful species. Whether you taste whale while dining out is a personal matter, but please remember that they are highly intelligent mammals and not fish.

LOFOTEN ISLAND HISTORY: Despite their blustery climate, settlement in the Lofoten islands can be traced back for over 10,000 years, long before the Vikings sailed these waters. The earliest inhabitants practiced farming on the lowland shores, supplemented by limited fishing.

By the 10th century there is evidence of early Viking communities in the islands south of the present day location of Svolvær. From here they were able to range up and down the coast and spread their influence. By the middle ages, commercial fishing began to play a major role, as trade increased. What the history books call stockfish is primarily dried and salted cod, known in Norwegian as klipfisk. It could be packed into barrels and easily exported, especially to Spain and Portugal where it became a major food source.

Not only did Norwegian fishermen congregate in these waters, but fishermen from as far away as southern Europe also began to arrive and exploit these waters by the 10th century. Local residents would build and then rent out small cabins for the migratory fishermen to spend their time ashore, especially during stormy weather. Some of these cabins today can still be seen and are now historic treasures. Because of strong government controls, the dried fish had to be sent to Bergen before it could be exported abroad. Much of the profit gained by the export of klipfisk advanced the Hanseatic League merchants of Bergen.

The peaceful beauty of the Lofoten Islands

Today the islands still engage in fishing, but more for local consumption since cod stocks have been greatly diminished by overfishing during the past centuries.

During World War II, the islands did see some military action, especially in March, 1941 when a British Commando raid occurred primarily to divert Nazi attention away from action on the mainland.

The primary focus of attention in the Lofoten Islands today is tourism. With many of the islands interconnected by bridges and with one bridge to the mainland, campers and other tourists do motor through to enjoy the fantastic scenery and the various pleasures of hiking and mountain climbing, as well as kayaking.

The harbor at Svolvær (Work of Vincent van Zeijst, CC BY SDA 3.0, Wikimedia.org)

VISITING SVOLVÆR: If your ship visits the port of Svolvær you can consider yourself fortunate since this is a very picturesque small town set amid towering mountain peaks. There are several smaller fishing villages along the coast and depending upon what activities are planned by your cruise line, there may be small boat or land tours along the shoreline of the island of Austvågøya. Svolvær is a small town with only 4,500 permanent residents, yet its waterfront gives the illusion of this being a much larger community.

This area has a long history of settlement dating back to the early Viking era. The village of Vågar west of Svolvær can be dated back to approximately the year 800. Fishing and limited farming, especially the raising of dairy cattle have always been the main economic activities. Today with depleted cod stocks, many fishermen have turned to aquaculture, the farming of fish, especially of Atlantic salmon since there is a great market across Scandinavia for both fresh, smoked or cured salmon.

The magnificent scenery combined with a series of bridges linking the islands and one major bridge connecting to the mainland, this has become an important vacation spot for

Norwegian and other Scandinavian visitors. Foreign tourism apart from cruise passengers is far outweighed by those from Scandinavia.

CRUISE SHIP DOCK/TENDER: Small to medium size vessels under 200 meters or 656 feet in length can dock to the west of the city center, but within walking distance. There is no terminal or service facilities at this dock. Vessels larger than 200 meters must anchor and tender their guests to the shore at the same location as docked vessels. There is plenty of room for tour coaches, private cars and taxis to meet guests.

TOURING OPTIONS IN SVOLVÆR: Surprisingly there are several interesting things for visitors to do in Svolvær if they decide to explore on their own. These are your options for touring:

* Cruise sponsored tours – Cruise ship companies offer different local tours and visits to nearby fishing villages, and your own offering will depend upon which line you are with. If you are on your own, the transport services are especially limited. The more upmarket cruise lines are more likely to be the ones offering these tours outside of the port.

The beautiful waters of Vaterfjord in the surroundings of Svolvær

* Having a private car and driver is quite difficult, as these services are just not available locally in sufficient quantity for the cruise ships to be able to book such service.

Most often the car will have to come from Tromsø, which adds greatly to the cost of your day. You can check on line at *www.lofoten.info* to see what might be available and at what rate.

The beauty of Austnestfjord outside of Svolvær, (Work of Hesse 1309, GNU 1.2, Wikimedia.org)

* Hop on hop off bus service – There is no hop on hop off bus because Svolvær is simply too small to offer such a service. The town is easy to walk on one's own.

* Local taxis are few in number, but they do make themselves available for sightseeing on an hourly or flat fee basis. Check on line with Svolvar and Kabelvåg Taxi at *www.lofotentaxi.no* for details. Be sure to check your language preference at the top right of the page.

* Walking – The town is very small, and unless you wish to visit outlying areas, it is very easy to walk around and see all of the major sights.

WHAT TO SEE AND DO: For those who will be sightseeing on their own, here are my recommendations (shown alphabetically:

* Artist galleries and craft shops - Located in the town center, there are a few very good galleries selling the work of local painters and photographers who are very good at capturing the distinct light that is a major draw in the Lofoten Islands. Visitors often ask if it is acceptable to bargain in an art gallery. It is not considered to be rude if done in a respectful manner. Many gallery owners are prepared to negotiate a price on a piece of art, but not to any extreme degree.

* **Lofoten Explorer** is a company on the waterfront that offers a variety of rib boat excursions into the surrounding waters. There are those tours that focus upon having a wildlife and landscape experience while others are oriented toward fishing. In either case, you will find their tours or fishing trips to be a great way to explore the immediate island vicinity. For more details or booking, contact them at *www.lofoten-explorer.no/en*.

* **Lofoten Krigsminnemuseum** - Located along the main waterfront quay at Fiskergata # 3 in Svolvær, this museum does provide a rather graphic picture of life in this remote coastal location during World War II and the Nazi occupation. The collection of artifacts and the displays are both outstanding and offer a reminder of what Norwegians experienced during the long occupation. It is a highlight not to be missed. Hours are Monday thru Friday from 10 AM to 4 PM and from 6:30 to 10 PM, Saturday from 11 AM to 3 PM and 6:30 to 10 PM and on Sunday from Noon to 3 PM and 6:30 to 10 PM.

The Torget or main square of Svolvær on a bright winter day

* **Lofoten Torget** – This is the main square in the heart of Svolvær where you will find most of the shops, galleries and restaurants.

* **Tjeldbergtind Hike** - This is an interesting, but moderately steep hiking trail leading out of the town from the intersection of the main highway (E10) and Kongsvatnveien that will take you up to a panoramic overview point where you can grasp the total surrounding of Svolvær. The smaller and more adventure oriented cruise lines may sometimes offer this hike as a guided tour.

DINING OUT: There are only a handful of restaurants in Svolvær that are open during the lunch period, but most open at 4 PM, which may provide you with an early dinner if your ship is staying into the early evening, as many do. The majority of ship passengers always seem to prefer to return to the ship to dine, which I personally believe is a mistake. The seafood is so good in Norway, as are the desserts, so those who do not sample local cuisine are missing one of the pleasures of the cruise. Here are my recommendations for a good Norwegian lunch in Svolvær:

* **Bacalao** - Located right on the main waterfront and it name is boldly written so you cannot miss it. The restaurant is open from 10:30 AM to 1 AM daily but on Sunday opening is delayed until 11 AM. Lunch is often busy, but if you go around 2 PM, it is quieter. Fresh fish and seafood along with traditional reconstituted dried cod known as bacalao are featured. And a more commonplace English fish and chips dish is also available. And as is true in Norway, dessert is also worth looking into. You can make a reservation at the height of lunch hour. Call them at +47 76 07 94 00.

* **Du Verden** is located at Torget 15 on the waterfront. It offers a more diverse menu apart from just fish and seafood. And it also provides a good dessert selection. Service can sometimes be a bit slow, especially when busy. but it is best to go for lunch around 2 PM. Call to see if they take bookings at +47 412 92 000. They serve from 3 to 10 PM Monday thru Thursday, and between 11 AM and Midnight on Friday and Saturday.

* **Paleo Arctic** – Located on the Torget, or main square, this is a superb restaurant that meets Michelin Star criteria. It is considered to be the best restaurant in the town, featuring a wide array of seafood dishes prepared to perfection. The atmosphere, cuisine and service all meet top standards. They serve between 7 and 9 AM and 6 and 10 PM on weekdays only between 8 and 11 AM on Sunday. A reservation is essential, as this is a more high end restaurant. Call +47 76 04 90 00.

* **Restaurant Kjøkkenet** is located at Lamholmen on the waterfront. It provides a diverse lunch menu that of course features the sea, but also offers meat entrees. Their soups are thick and creamy, they often have crab cakes as an appetizer and of course serve the freshest of fish. Service is generally excellent. Some guests complain that prices are relatively high, but the old expression saying you get what you pay for does hold true. In true Norwegian tradition, butter and cream are widely used so if you are watching cholesterol, you need to pick less traditional items. Open from 4 to 11 PM Monday thru Saturday. Call to reserve a table if it is necessary when you plan to visit. Their number is +47 76 06 64 80.

FINAL WORDS: If your itinerary includes Svolvær the old Norse gods will be kind an enable your visit by keeping the sea nice and calm. This is a very special town set amid towering jagged peaks that give it a dramatic setting.

The charm of Svolvær (Work of Paul Berzinn, CC BY SA 3.0, Wikimedia.org)

SVOLVÆR MAPS

THE INNER LOFOTEN ISLANDS

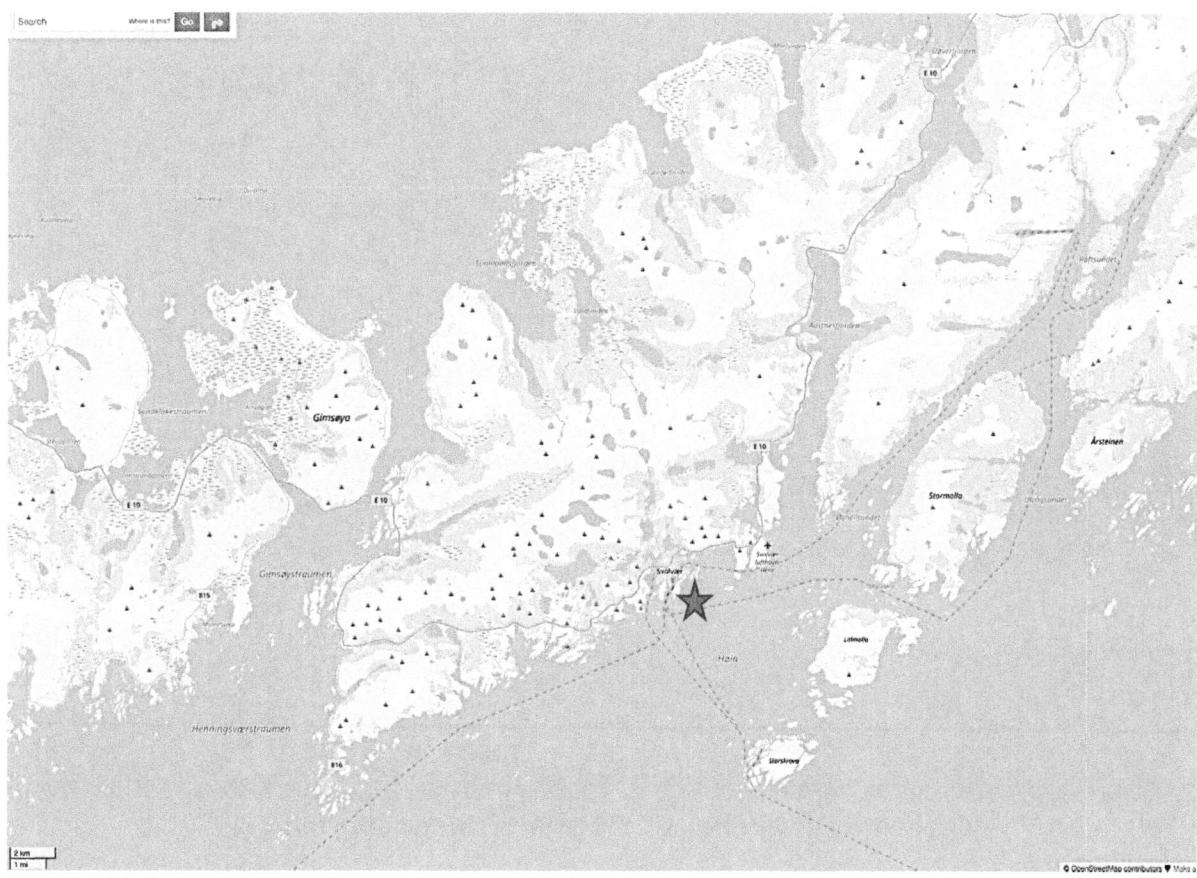

Inner Lofoten Islands with the star showing Svolvær, (© OpenStreetMap contributors)

This map is best viewed directly from OpenStreetMap.com on your personal device where it can be expanded or one specific area can be enlarged. Given the format of this book, it is impossible to display maps with the level of detail you might wish to have while actually out exploring the city. But the OpenStreetMap maps used directly are the tool I always rely upon.

GREATER SVOLVÆR AREA

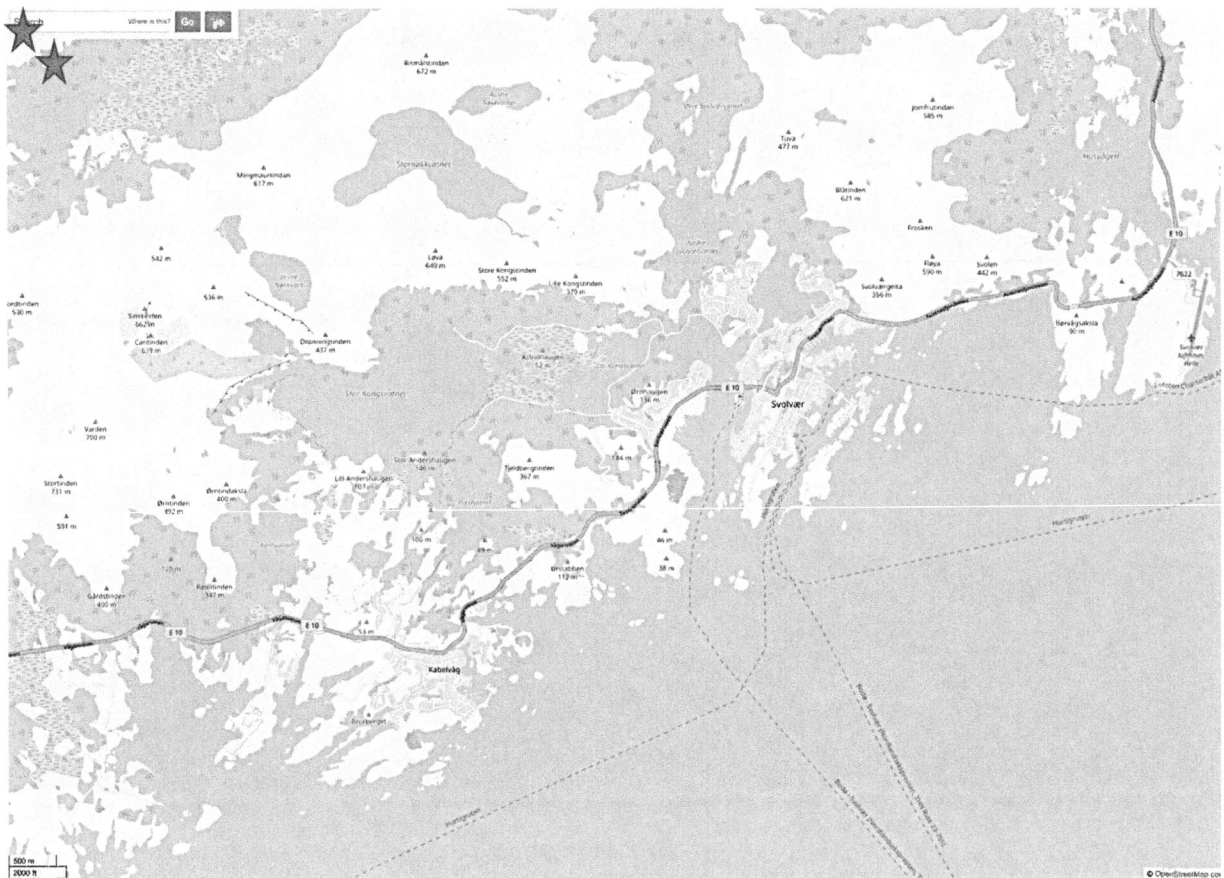

Greater Svolvær area, (© OpenStreetMap contributors)

This map is best viewed directly from OpenStreetMap.com on your personal device where it can be expanded or one specific area can be enlarged. Given the format of this book, it is impossible to display maps with the level of detail you might wish to have while actually out exploring the city. But the OpenStreetMap maps used directly are the tool I always rely upon.

TOWN OF SVOLVÆR

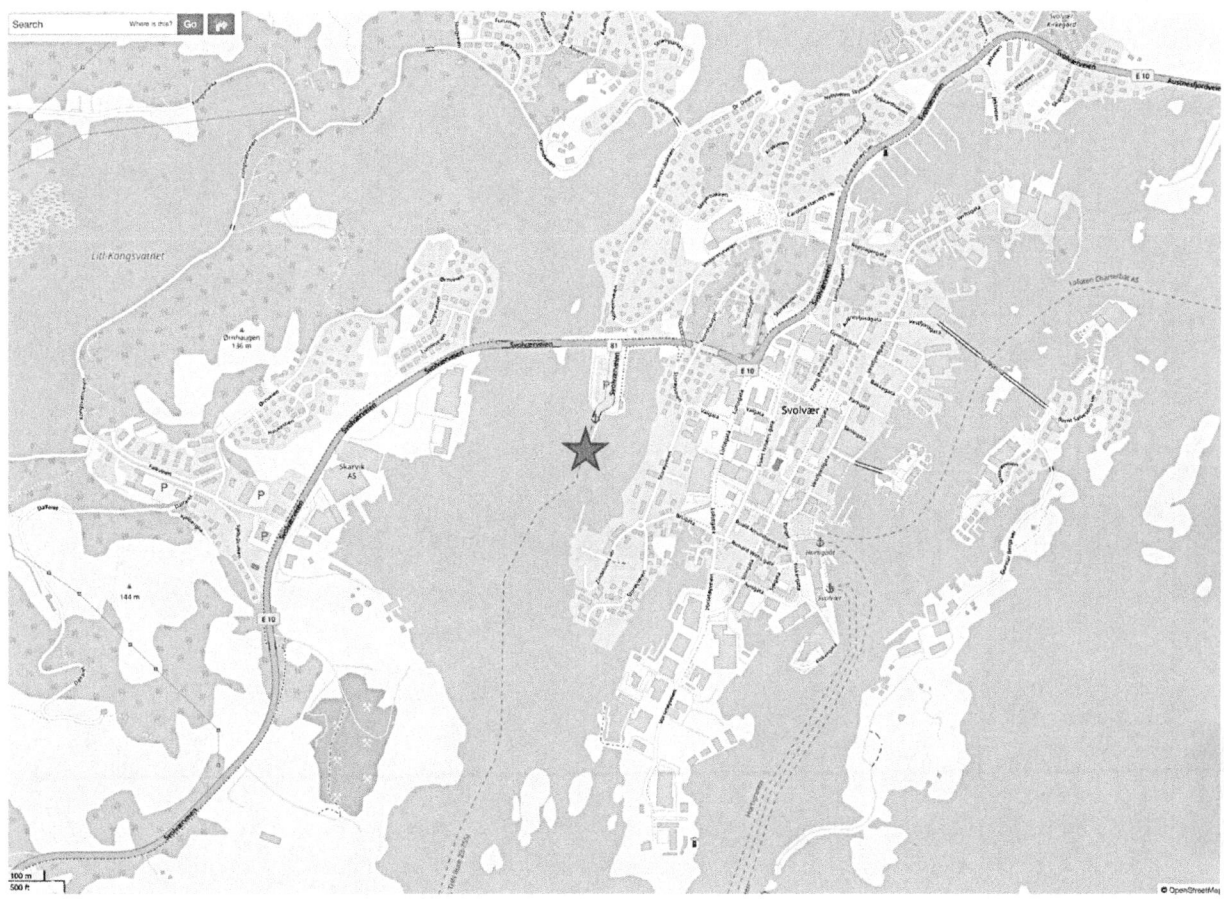
Town of Svolvær with star showing cruise dock, (© OpenStreetMap contributors)

This map is best viewed directly from OpenStreetMap.com on your personal device where it can be expanded or one specific area can be enlarged. Given the format of this book, it is impossible to display maps with the level of detail you might wish to have while actually out exploring the city. But the OpenStreetMap maps used directly are the tool I always rely upon.

HARSTAD

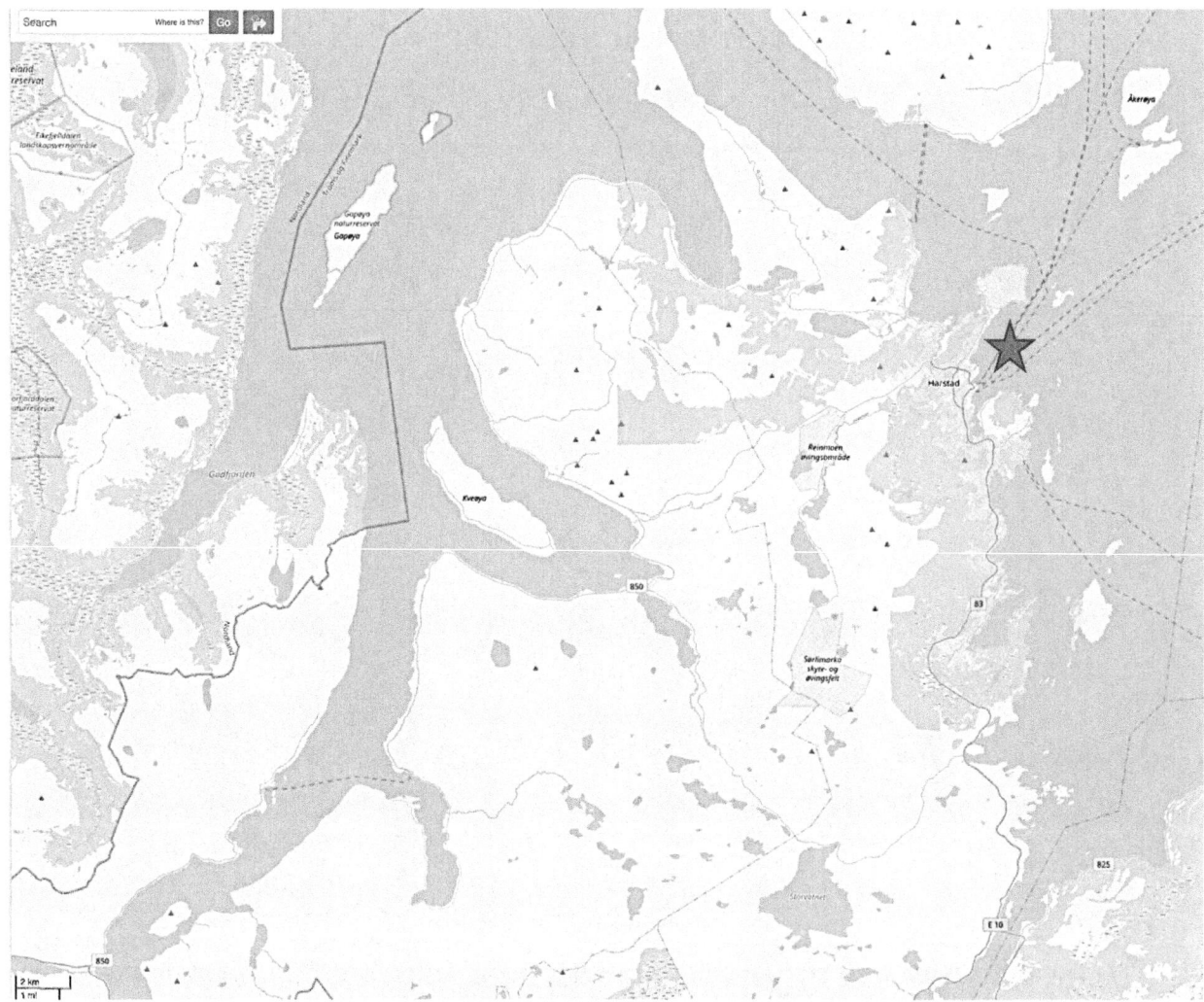

Map of the greater Harstad area (© OpenStreetMap contributors)

THE HARSTAD ENVIRONMENT: Harstad is the largest and most important town in the northern Lofoten Islands, situated on the island of Hinnøya. It is a major port and fishing oriented community with a population of nearly 24,000, making it a significant stop for cruise ships traveling into the far northern fjord region.

Harstad is located on the eastern side of Hinnøya Island, facing what has now become a narrow channel known as the Tjeldsundet, between the mainland and the Lofoten Islands. Thus it is in a very sheltered location with regard to the blustery storms that blow in from the North Sea. The city is connected to the mainland by way of the Tjeldsund Bridge that is located just southeast of the city center.

The climatic patterns show a relative mildness despite Harstad being above the Arctic Circle, this being the result of the Gulf Stream that moderates the coastal environments while   inland

winters are quite severe. And during summer there is a period of over six weeks when there are 24 hours of perpetual daylight. However, in winter the same amount of permanent darkness makes up for the summer sun.

Hinnøya Island is quite mountainous and the highest peak in the immediate vicinity of the city center is 1,095 meters or 3,593 feet above sea level. The surrounding forests are quite thick and provide a beautiful backdrop for the city, offering its residents and visitors a variety of recreational activities.

The beauty of Hinnøya Island, (Work of Asbjørn, CC BY SA 4.0, Wikimedia.org)

HARSTAD HISTORY: The Harstad area has a long history of settlement that dates back over 3,000 years, well before the rise of the Vikings. By the time of the Viking golden age, Harstad was an important community and in the 15th century it was the seat of the most northern extent of Christian teaching, as its small church at Trondenes was at the outer limit of the Christian world.

Throughout its long history, Harstad was oriented both toward fishing and also as the trade center for the northern end of the Lofoten Islands and the adjacent mainland. There is also a significant amount of agriculture practiced in the vicinity of Harstad, as the climate is excellent for raising root crops, hearty grains and dairy cattle. Local craftsmen have developed a reputation for building small fishing and transport vessels, adding to the overall economic picture. Today Harstad, like many other small cities along the Norwegian coast, participates in the servicing of oil drilling platforms as well as maintenance and repair of vessels servicing the industry. And it is headquarters for new exploration by Statoil, Norway's government controlled oil company.

A view of central Harstad from the deck of the ship

Tourism is limited, as few foreign tourists other than cruise passengers add to the overall economic market. However, with the bridge connecting Harstad to the mainland, more people are likely to venture out to the Lofoten Islands given their magnificent scenery and summertime recreational potential, but these are mainly Scandinavian visitors who enjoy the rugged out of doors lifestyle.

As a cruise passenger you will find the people of Harstad very welcoming, and a high percentage do speak English. Depending upon what activities your cruise line plans if stopping here, the day can be quite memorable. But as in all far northern ports, the weather is always unpredictable. You can have a beautiful day of sunshine and mild temperatures or it could feel like a winter day where many of you no doubt live.

CRUISE SHIP DOCK IN HARSTAD: Your cruise ship will dock in the very heart of the city only a few steps from the center. There is no cruise terminal and no shuttle bus is needed because of the proximity to the center of Harstad. You step off the ship and just one block away is the center of this small city.

A Hertigruten ship also stops in Harstad at the same time

SIGHTSEEING OPTIONS IN HARSTAD: The options for touring Harstad are not as extensive as in the major ports of call. Here are the options open to you:

* **Cruise sponsored tours** – Most cruise lines that stop in Harstad will offer a minimum of a half day tour around the city to show you the major sights. I highly recommend this tour because the various venues are spread out over several kilometers, and walking as a means of covering all the basics is rather intensive.
d
* **Private car and driver/guide** – If you wish to have a private car and driver, your cruise line may be able to organize it. Most likely the car will need to come from Tromsø, which would add to the overall cost. But you can independently check out Visit Tromsø on line for information regarding what they have in Harstad. Their web address is www.visittromso.no.

* **Hop on hop off bus or trolley** service does not exist in Harstad, as the city is too small and the sights to be shared with visitors are too few in number.

* **Taxi touring** – There may be one or two taxis waiting on the dock for anyone who wants to have a city excursion for a few hours. But rather than anticipate there being one, you can contact Harstad Taxisentral at *www.harstadtaxi.no* for information or booking in advance.

Harstad is a very walkable city

* **Walking** – If just seeing the town center is all you wish to do, the ship docks just steps away from the main commercial area. If the weather is favorable, walking is quite enjoyable, but keep in mind that apart from the immediate waterfront, Harstad is quite hilly and some streets will present you will a physical workout.

MAJOR SITES TO VISIT IN HARSTAD: The primary highlights that make Harstad interesting include (shown alphabetically):

* **Meløyvær Fortress** – Just outside of Harstad, this fortress was built by NATO to protect the coastal waters during the Cold War when the Soviet Union was thought to have designs upon Norway because of its many harbors and warm water access. The fortress has 120 mm Bofors guns, which would have been a major deterrent. No specific hours are posted, so if you wish to visit, make certain your driver has the opening and closing times.

* **Trondenes Church** – This medieval church dating back as early as the 15th century is just a few kilometers from the town center on the northern margins, but a bit far to walk. The church is a stunning example of early medieval architecture with both the interior and exterior offering excellent photo opportunities. Services and weddings still take place and perhaps you will be there when an event is taking place. If this is the case, please be respectful and you will be welcomed. There are no specific hours posted for the church. However, guided tours are offered daily at Noon, 1:30 and 4:30 PM.

Historic Trondenes Church, (Work of ADSUBIA, CC BY SA 3.0, Wikimedia.org)

* **Trondenes Fort and Adlof Guns** sitting above the city of Harstad is a must see for anyone who has an interest in local World War II history. The guns, which were a threat to any navigation of the inside passage, were quite massive and show you the power that Nazi forces brought to protect their interests while holding Norway.

* **Trondenes Historical Center** is located adjacent to the church and is also a must see venue. It is adjacent to the church and will provide you with a good historical overview of the city and its surroundings. It is open daily so you should plan to visit before or after touring the church. Hours are weekdays between 10 AM and 2 PM, Sunday between 11 AM and 4 PM.

Surviving Nazi gun is now a historic relic, (Work of Calvin, CC BY SA 3.0, Wikimedia.org)

Inside the Trondenes Historical Center, (Work of Larry Lamds, CC BY SA 2.0, Wikimedia.org)

These are the major venues that should be seen while visiting Harstad. Depending upon the offerings of your cruise line, there could be more outdoor activities offered such as a mountain hike or drives to view the countryside and the interior passage.

DINING OUT: If your port call is sufficiently long or stays into the evening hours, I would strongly urge you to partake of lunch or dinner. Harstad may be a very small city, but its few excellent restaurants do offer outstanding examples of traditional Norwegian cuisine, especially fresh fish and seafood.

There are few upmarket restaurants in Harstad, most catering to the local population. They are unpretentious, but do provide good food. Here are my few recommendations (listed alphabetically):

* **Bakerinnen** – Located in the heart of town at Storgata #17, this bakery and café is ideal for a light lunch. Their sandwiches, salads and traditional Norwegian pastries and desserts make for a very good lunch. Their hours of service are from 8 AM to 4:30 PM Monday thru Friday and from 10 AM to 3 PM on Saturday. No reservations are necessary.

* **Bark Spiseri Og Bar** As is a very excellent restaurant for lunch or dinner. It is located at Rikard Kaarboes Gate #6 on the waterfront and open from 3 to 11 PM Monday thru Saturday with closing extended to Midnight Friday and Saturday. The only complaint is that this is not a cozy restaurant. It is often quite crowded and can be a bit loud, but that does not take away much from its very fine traditional Norwegian cuisine at reasonable prices. Their fish and fresh halibut are among the most favored specialties during summer. Reservations are not generally necessary.

The small, but colorful flower market

In the Storget, which is somewhat a marketplace

* **De 4 Roser** is said by many to be the finest restaurant in northern Norway. I do not know if I would go that far, but it does offer delicious food and very friendly service that is truly hard to beat. Located at Torvey # 7A and open from 110 AM to 5 PM you will not go wrong with its fresh fish, cold salads and other local delicacies such as elk or duck. Reservations are not necessary.

* **Umami** is another highly rated and popular restaurant serving outstandingly prepared food in a very comfortable atmosphere with excellent service. It is open only for dinner from 6 PM to Midnight Tuesday thru Saturday and it will only be possible for you to dine here if your ship is leaving in the later evening. It is located at Havnegata #23A on the waterfront. They serve daily from 5 PM to Midnight. Call +47 950 90 911 to reserve a table if your ship is staying into the evening hours.

SHOPPING: There many nice stores in the city center, but they primarily sell basic needs and cater to the local community. There are often small stands set up in the main square selling flowers, plants and locally made food items. There are so few cruise ships that stop and thus the souvenir and handcraft market is limited.

The Strandgate is the main shopping street of Harstad

Harstad is enveloped in late afternoon mist

Spring brings regeneration to Harstad, (Work of Simo Räsänen, CC BY SA 4.0, Wikimedia.org)

Along the shoreline north of Harstad< (Work of Simo Räsänen, CC BY SA 4.0, Wikimedia.org)

FINAL WORDS: Harstad may not be the highlight of your cruise into northern Norway. But the town is rather typical of the offerings available for foreign visitors. This part of the country is still developing its tourist infrastructure, as more foreign visitors want to experience Arctic life.

HARSTAD MAPS

THE GREATER HARSTAD AREA

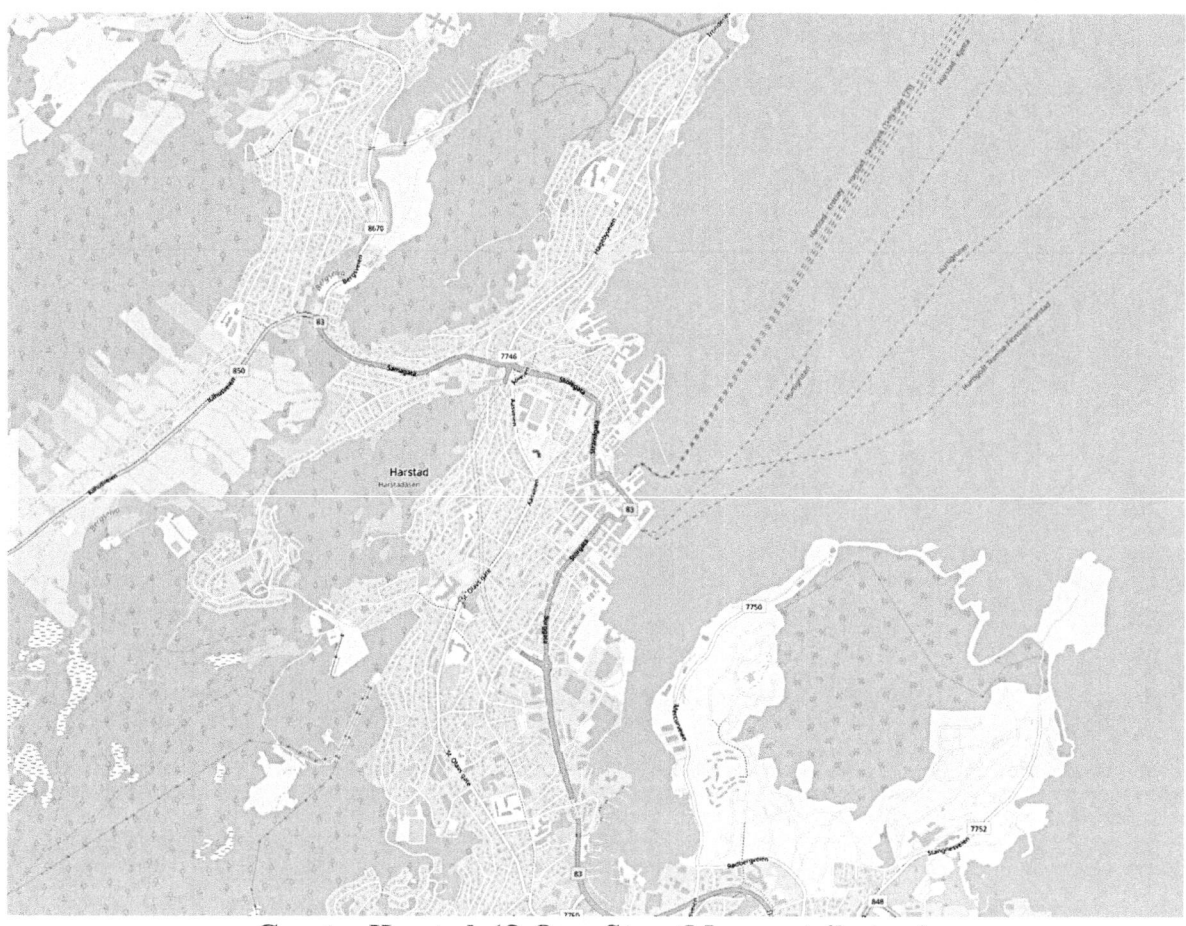

Greater Harstad, (© OpenStreetMap contributors)

This map is best viewed directly from OpenStreetMap.com on your personal device where it can be expanded or one specific area can be enlarged. Given the format of this book, it is impossible to display maps with the level of detail you might wish to have while actually out exploring the city. But the OpenStreetMap maps used directly are the tool I always rely upon.

THE CENTER OF HARSTAD

The center of Harstad, (© OpenStreetMap contributors)

This map is best viewed directly from OpenStreetMap.com on your personal device where it can be expanded or one specific area can be enlarged. Given the format of this book, it is impossible to display maps with the level of detail you might wish to have while actually out exploring the city. But the OpenStreetMap maps used directly are the tool I always rely upon.

TROMSØ

A map of greater Tromsø (© OpenStreetMap contributors)

THE LOCAL ENVIRONMENT: Tromsø is the largest city in Arctic Norway. Geographically it is farther north in latitude than Murmansk, Russia, thus making Tromsø one of the three largest cities in the world at such a northerly latitude. The metro population is just under 100,000 with around 75,000 within the city proper. There are no cities as large in the same latitudinal zone of North America.

The geographic setting for Tromsø is in itself rather unique in that the bulk of the city occupies an elongated and rugged island known as Tromsøya in the middle of the inside passage. Its suburbs spill over onto the narrow shorelines to both the mainland side on the east and to Kvaløya Island side on the west, connected to each by a graceful suspension bridge. There is also a tunnel connecting the city to the mainland side.

Not only is Tromsø the region's largest city, but it is also rather sophisticated in that the performing arts are very well integrated into the social life and during the summer days

there are numerous important musical and artistic events. The city also presents a rather urban face that visitors are surprised to see. Modern buildings, including a few moderate size high-rises vie with two to three hundred year old wood houses that date back to when all of northern Norway was still considered to be quite provincial and isolated. Thus the mix
of modernity and traditional Norwegian design intermingles as if the styles were mated, giving Tromsø a very distinct architectural matrix.

Aerial view of Tromsø, (Work of Municipality of Tromsø, CC BY SA 2.0, Wikimedia.org)

Although sheltered from the gale force winds of the North Atlantic, Tromsø does have relatively cold winters with most of the precipitation falling as snow. With mountains on both sides, the island essentially wedged in between, temperatures have a more continental rather than maritime regime. And being above the Arctic Circle there is a period during winter of at least six or more weeks of total darkness. On either end the days are still exceptionally short from the middle of November to early March, graduating from approximately six hours to zero and then back again to six hours.

Summer in Tromsø is very mild with daytime temperatures generally below 20 degrees Celsius or 68 degrees Fahrenheit. There are occasional days when a jacket would not be necessary. In contrast to the depths of winter, Tromsø is located within the zone of 24-hour daylight for approximately six weeks starting in late June. And like the winter counterpart, from the middle of May until the early part of September nights go from being 17 hours in length to zero and back to 17 hours.

The dramatic beauty of Tromsøfjorden on a late summer afternoon

HISTORIC SKETCH: Tromsø is an old city, and its surroundings are even older with evidence from archaeological sites showing it had pre Norse settlers at the time of the last glacial retreat, which is around 10,000 years ago.

By the 9th century, the Tromsø area was a meeting zone between the northern most Norse tribes and the southernmost Sámi, those we often call the Lapplanders. The actual town of Tromsø dates back to the construction of the first Christian church between 1240 and 1250, believed to have been the first church built in such far northern latitudes. The city was more of a frontier outpost rather than much of a settled community. But it served as a military and diplomatic buffer between Norway, mainly to the south and Russia primarily to the East. As Norwegian power in the region increased, Russian influence waned and by the year 1794 Tromsø received its charter as a city. It became an important trade center with the crown's permission for cod fishing to develop, and also it served as the gateway for explorations and hunting parties traveling farther north and east into the interior. Yet it was a cultural outpost of Norwegian and Germanic civilization.

By the early 1800's, hunting for whales and seals in the Arctic Ocean was a major activity, exploiting them for oil, meat and hides, Tromsø became a very significant port and also a center for shipbuilding. This enabled Tromsø to develop the amenities of a real city with proper schools, churches, shops and restaurants. By 1850, it was the largest city anywhere

in the Arctic. Today its population has been exceeded by Murmansk and Norilsk in Russia as the largest cities above the Arctic Circle.

Most housing in Tromsø is beautifully crafted out of wood

The arrival of the 20th century saw the city replete with its own museum, a small college, several hotels and even its own brewery. The city prospered and grew in the early 20th century.

In 1940, Norway was invaded by Nazi troops. At first Tromsø was far enough north to have not been under occupation and even briefly served as the center of the free Norwegian government in exile. And it also became the command center for Norwegian General Carl Gustav who attempted to mount a counter offensive against the German advance, but German forces proved to be too strong and eventually conquered the entire country. Tromsø was ultimately under occupation, but the city was not bombed even though the great German battleship Tirpitz was attacked and ultimately sunk by allied aircraft south of the urban area.

The lighting and mood around Tromsø changes every few minutes, seen here in the late evening hours

The early 19th century wood domkyrka, which is highly decorated in the old style

Tromsø celebrates the life of Roald Amundsen

After Norwegian liberation, there was a major migration of people into Tromsø from the far north where the Germans had devastated the countryside because of their fear that Red Army forces would advance across from Murmansk and drive them out. Eventually the population of the north stabilized.

Tromsø has continued to prosper through the late 20th century and into the first decades of the 21st century based upon the combination of oil exploration and development, fishing and timber. As the largest city of the far north, it has developed as the major center for commerce, banking, medical services and higher education. It is the only city in northern Norway to be home to a major university, which serves all of the northern districts. The city is also now an important research center with the Norwegian Polar Institute and the Northern Lights Observatory. Thus despite its far northern location and less than hospitable climate, Tromsø has managed to attract skilled workers and professionals. It essentially offers its residents all of the basic services as larger cities to the south.

CRUISE SHIP DOCK IN TROMSO: Cruise ships conveniently dock in the city center just immediately to the east of the historic Tromsø Domkyrka. There is no terminal building, but the tourist information center is adjacent to the dock. There is no need for a shuttle bus since the dock is so convenient to the city center, which favors walking to many of the important sites. And for those going on tours, there is plenty of room for motor coaches, private vehicles and taxis.

The modern side of Tromsø is reflected in parts of its downtown core

During the brief spring and summer blooms appear

c **SIGHTSEEING OPTIONS IN TROMO:** There are several interesting sights to see in and around the city of Tromsø, and each cruise line develops its own shore excursions. Most cruise lines do not stop for a lengthy visit, thus few if any offer tours out away from the immediate city area. Here are the options available to visitors:c

* **Ship sponsored tours** – Most cruise lines offer a coach tour of the city. The more upmarket lines with smaller ships also offer various tours into the immediate countryside for such activities as visiting a dog sled training facility. But there are so few roads or sites of interest outside of the city.

* **Private car and driver/guide** – Tromsø is large enough to have many private cars replete with guides so that the cruise lines can arrange for private sightseeing. I do, however, recommend that if this is your wish, contact the following companies for rate comparison:

** Orange Smile is a major operator so check their rates and services. Their web page is *www.orangesmile.com.*

** You may also wish to check *www.limousine-center.com* to see what they can offer.

* **There is no hop on hop off bus service** in Tromsø except during the mid-winter northern lights season. It does not operate in summer. However, the Tromsø Tourist Information Office is adjacent to the cruise ship dock. They can provide information regarding use of the city bus service, which is actually quite good for getting around Tromsø.

* **Taxi touring** – There are many taxis in Tromso and often a few are waiting at the dock. You can sightsee on an hourly basis. The major taxi service is Tromsø Taxi, which can be viewed on line at *www.tromso-taxi.no* for rates and booking.

* **The city center is very walkable** and you can see numerous interesting venues on your own. However, beyond the immediate downtown you need to be in good shape to walk, as most of the island on which the city is built is very hilly and the majority of streets ascend very steep inclines.

MAJOR SITES TO VISIT IN TROMSØ: My recommendations for what to see in Tromsø, either on your own, or through one or more tours, includes the following (shown alphabetically):

The dramatic Arctic Cathedral across the harbor from the city center

* **Arctic Cathedral** is the city's signature building, sitting across the fjord on a hill opposite the city center. The large "A" frame shape and beautiful stained glass windows make this an architectural gem that is worthy of a visit. And it is easy to reach across the main bridge from the city center if you are walking, taking a taxi or using the local city bus # 26 , which you can board in the city center. No specific hours are posted, but the cathedral is open daily unless special services are being held.

When your ship docks in Tromsø the Arctic Cathedral will be visible off the starboard side of the ship and it makes quite a visual statement, so totally different from the normal style of church architecture in Norway.

* **Northern Lights** - If you happen to be doing one of the winter cruises on the Hurtigruten Line, Norway's main passenger ship line that plies the coast year around, you will find that the number one attraction in Tromsø and all along the coast is an evening viewing of the Northern Lights. Also if you are doing a late summer early fall cruise where there are at least eight hours of darkness in September, you will have a chance to witness this great spectacle. The sky is illuminated for anywhere from a few minutes to a couple of hours with a variety of filmy or wispy strands of light, mainly green, that are the result of particles of energy from the solar wind becoming caught in the earth's magnetic field. Once

you have seen the Northern Lights, you will carry that memory with you. But if you come during summer, as most cruisers do, there is insufficient darkness to enable you to see the lights. The earliest you may see them will be in mid-September.

The Northern Lights seen in Tromsø in November

The Polar Museum

* **Polar Museum** sits on the shore not far from where cruise ships dock. The building resembles a small barn and does not initially look inviting. Open daily between 10 AM and 6 PM, this museum tells the story of Tromsø and of various northern expeditions, including the famous Roald Amundsen. Do not let the outside dissuade you from touring this very fascinating museum.

Most of the city motor coach tours will include the Polar Museum as part of their itinerary.

* **Polaria** is a unique museum located on the waterfront not far from where cruise ships dock. It is open daily from 10 AM to 7 PM and worthy of a visit. From its name you can deduce that the featured exhibits relate to the high Arctic, both natural and historic. And the building itself is unique, looking like a series of concrete boxes collapsing down toward the water.

Most of the city motor coach tours will also include Polaria along with the Polar Museum as part of the half day itinerary.

The very unique architecture of Polaria

Strandvagen is the principal commercial street of the city

Old classic Norwegian architecture on Strandvagen

* **Strandvagen** – The city has a quite large central business area being that this is the major city of the far north of Norway. The principal commercial street is Strandvagen, which runs parallel to the waterfront but just to the west. It is a long pedestrian street lined with a great variety of shops, boutiques, cafes and public buildings. Any of the buildings are constructed of wood and date back to the mid 19th century. The architectural style is very similar to the older buildings seen in Russian arctic cities.

The banking and finance sector is one to two blocks farther west and this section is dominated over by modern buildings some of which are eight to 10 stories in height. The central business district, including Clarion Hotel, which tops out at 14 stories. is quite impressive. Shops in the downtown core are well-stocked with varied merchandise items, mainly for the northern climate.

* **Tromsø Domkyrka** is the main city church located on the Storgata # 25. It is a traditional wood church and reflects the 19th century era when everything in Tromsø was constructed of wood and lavishly decorated and painted. It is very easy to spot with its almost pink walls and spire trimmed in gray. No specific hours are posted, but you can visit during the day except when special services are held.

* **Tromsø Museum** is located a bit out of town on Lars Thoringsvei #10, but worth the effort to visit. You can get there by taxi or city bus # 37 from the city center. There are excellent exhibits on the local region, the Northern Lights and the Sámi people. The

museum is open weekdays between 10 AM and 4:30 PM and between Noon and 3 PM Saturday and from 11 AM to 4 PM on Sunday.

The dramatic Tromsø Public Library

*** Tromsø Public Library and City Archives** occupy a very modern building just off of the Storgata with a commanding view across to the Arctic Church. This is a nice place to just sit and relax during your walking explorations of the city center, and you will be surprised at both the architectural design and size of this building for a city of under 100,000. The library is open weekdays between 9 AM and 7 PM and Saturday between 11 AM and 3 PM and on Sunday between Noon and 4 PM.

There are many adventure tours offered locally in Tromsø that vary from hiking, sailing the beautiful fjords, visiting a sled dog kennel to fishing. But these tours may or may not be included in your ship's itinerary and are too numerous and season to mention here. If adventure tours are of interest to you, I would strongly recommend you visit the Tromsø Tourist Information Office on the waterfront near the cruise dock, or visit them on line at: visittromso.no

Modern apartments appear along the shoreline

DINING OUT: Depending upon your ship's schedule you will either have time for lunch or dinner in Tromsø. Some cruise ships arrive in the early evening and stay overnight so in that case you may be able to enjoy two meals in the city. I am listing several restaurants below, but I have limited the category to those serving traditional Norwegian cuisine, as I strongly urge my readers to choose local cuisine for the gastronomic experience.
 (shown alphabetically):

* **Art Cafe** is located in the city center at Richard Withs Plass # 2 and open from 11 AM to 9 PM Tuesday thru Friday, remaining open until 10 PM Saturday. Reservations are unnecessary. It is a very beautiful restaurant with an artistic atmosphere as the name implies. In traditional Norwegian style, you get the feel you are eating in someone's home. Their soups, main dishes and desserts are all excellent.

* **Bardus Bistro** is located at Cora Sandeisgate # 4 in the city center and an easy walk from the ship. It is open from Noon to 9PM Tuesday thru Thursday and remains open until 10 PM Friday and Saturday with continuous service. Once again the theme is traditional Norwegian cuisine with outstanding fish soups, fresh cod and salmon and reindeer stew. The atmosphere has a bit of a pub like flavor, but the food is very traditional and outstandingly prepared. Reservations are not necessary.

* **Emma's Drommenkjokken** is located at Kirkengata # 8 in the city center and open Monday thru Saturday from Noon to 10:30 PM. Call +47 77 63 77 30 to reserve a table. This traditional Norwegian restaurant has a very extensive menu with dishes served in a very pleasing manner. Fish and seafood clearly dominate, but whale and other meat dishes are also part of the menu. As starters there are herring dishes and wonderful soups, especially fish soups. And of course this being Norway you must save room for dessert.

Tromsø is surrounded by snow covered mountains

* **Fiskekompaniet** – Located on the waterfront at Killens gate, this restaurant definitely offers the best in local seafood dishes. Fish is a major staple in Norway, and this restaurant offers quite a variety of whatever is in season at the time. Two of my personal favorites are the rich fish soups and fiskeballer, a type of meatball, but made with fish. It is a popular dish. The menu does include a holiday favorite called Lutefisk, which is an acquired taste. But they also do serve reindeer, which is the most common land animal protein this far north. The cuisine, atmosphere and service are all excellent. The restaurant hours are from 5 to 10 PM Tuesday thru Saturday. Call +47 77 68 76 00 to see if you need to reserve a table.

* **Mathallen** is one of the city's best-known restaurants located at Gronnegata # 58/60 in the city center. It is open from 10 AM to 11 PM with continuous service. They do offer a tasting menu that gives you samples of a variety of dishes. Specialties include fish, seafood, reindeer and even unique dishes such as a fish burger. You will not be disappointed. Call them at +47 77 68 01 00 to see if you need a reservation.

With Tromsø being quite a significant city there are dozens more restaurants in the city center with easy access to and from the ship. I have only chosen those that I thought best represented the Norwegian tradition. But for anyone longing for a burger and fries, pizza or other more non-traditional foods, you will find Tromsø sure to please.

FINAL WORDS: I have been to Tromsø on numerous occasions and have always enjoyed the city and its surroundings. Although the urban landscape mirrors that of the other major Norwegian cities, the snow covered mountains that totally surround the city offer an ever changing panorama. And this far north, the weather patterns change almost hourly and offer up some dramatic skies.

Tromsø is a very interesting city architecturally because much of it dates to the 19th century with its quaint wood houses, yet there are many very modern 21st century buildings that reflect the progress this city is making as a major trade, financial and educational center for the Arctic regions.

The sail in and also the departure can be very spectacular and often quite dramatic. So I advise being out on deck for both. Normally the northbound sail out is just before midnight so you can enjoy the far northern evening.

The drama of sailing from Tromsø at Midnight

TROMSØ MAPS

THE GREATER TROMSØ AREA

Greater Tromsø

This map is best viewed directly from OpenStreetMap.com on your personal device where it can be expanded or one specific area can be enlarged. Given the format of this book, it is impossible to display maps with the level of detail you might wish to have while actually out exploring the city. But the OpenStreetMap maps used directly are the tool I always rely upon.

THE CITY OF TROMSØ

The city of Tromsø with star showing cruise ship dock

This map is best viewed directly from OpenStreetMap.com on your personal device where it can be expanded or one specific area can be enlarged. Given the format of this book, it is impossible to display maps with the level of detail you might wish to have while actually out exploring the city. But the OpenStreetMap maps used directly are the tool I always rely upon.

THE HEART OF TROMSØ

The heart of Tromsø with star showing cruise ship dock

This map is best viewed directly from OpenStreetMap.com on your personal device where it can be expanded or one specific area can be enlarged. Given the format of this book, it is impossible to display maps with the level of detail you might wish to have while actually out exploring the city. But the OpenStreetMap maps used directly are the tool I always rely upon.

ALTA

The surroundings of Alta, Norway (© OpenStreetMap contributors)

THE LOCAL LANDSCAPE: Alta is one of those lesser ports that in all likelihood you will not visit. Only a few of the more upmarket cruise lines along with the local Hurtigruten ships call in at Alta. The surrounding fjord country is noted for its magnificent scenery, but the town is quite small and does not really offer any significant tourist services, especially for the larger cruise vessels. Alta has less than 7,000 permanent residents and it is located away from the open sea on a very protected fjord.

Because the town is sheltered, the winter climate is not as harsh as locations closer to the open sea. Although well into the high Arctic, the sheltered location means that around Alta and in the valley to the south there is little or no permafrost. And rather than being in a bare tundra environment the hillsides around Alta are covered with groves of birch trees. Winters are cold and bleak, but the short three month summer is somewhat mild with temperatures around 10 degrees Celsius, which is approximately 52 degrees Fahrenheit. Because of the sheltering effect of the fjord, Alta does not receive heavy snowfall, but there is a moderate permanent snow cover for about five to six months.

With the air being relatively clear and there being a lower frequency of storms or cloud cover, Alta has become one of the prime viewing sites in which to enjoy the spectacular displays of the Northern Lights. Hurtigruten, Norway's prime mail and passenger carrier that plies between almost every small port along the coast, does offer special Northern Lights cruises. And in recent years, a few of the upmarket cruise lines have begun to promote this rather unique sight. Alta therefore does benefit from such promotion.

The Altaleva Valley south of the town of Alta, (Work of Simo Rasanen, CC BY SA 4.0),Wikimedia.org

The Altaelva River flows through a rather peaceful and beautiful valley before emptying into the Altafjorden. Farther up river from Alta is Sautso Canyon, a rather magnificent gorge carved through soft rock by the river. It is said to be one of the deepest canyons in Europe. Again some cruise lines may offer a short motor coach tour to visit the river and its spectacular gorge. If you happen to be on such a cruise, I would strongly recommend this coach tour, as it is outstanding.

There was a major controversy that brewed up in 1979 when the government wanted to build a hydroelectric dam and power plant south of the town. Locals fought the move, but the government ultimately prevailed. The argument was that the building of the dam would curtail the spawning of salmon, which are a big part of the local economy. But fortunately measures were taken to mitigate the impact and this is still considered to be a prime salmon fishing location.

The Altaleva River has carved Sautso Canyon, one of Europe's deepest canyons (Work of Sami Keinanen, CC BY SA 2.0, Wikimedia.org)

The prehistoric rock art of Alta (Work of Vulcano, CC BY SA 4.0, Wikimedia.org)

A BRIEF LOCAL HISTORY: The earliest inhabitants in the Alta region can be dated back over 6,200 years. Little is known about how they lived other than that they were primarily hunters living at the edge of the last of the glacial ice. They did leave an artistic record in the form of some carvings on the exposed rock that are today protected as a UNESCO World Heritage Site. This site at Hjemmeluft is easily visited from the town of Alta and some cruise itineraries do offer a tour.

Until the start of the 20th century, tensions existed between the local Sámi tribe and the Norwegian settlers, the origins going back to mistrust since the earliest settlement. Today the migratory Sámi with their reindeer herds are more readily accepted and there is little to no visible hostility between the two ethnic groups.

Fall colors come early to Alta, Work of Simo Rasanen, CC BY SA 4.0),Wikimedia.org

Today's town of Alta has the appearance of a modern, well-planned community and bears little resemblance to the earlier village. This is because the town suffered a catastrophic fire at the close of World War II. What keeps such an isolate town functioning? That is a fair question that people often ask when they see where Alta is located. It is the major trade center for the northern region of Finnmark. And it also is home to Finnmark University College, the most northerly institution of higher learning in the country. During winter, an ice hotel offering luxurious accommodation is created for those few winter visitors that come primarily for the Northern Lights.

Over the rooftops of the modern town center of Alta

CRUISE SHIP DOCK: The port for Alta is too far from the town center for guests to walk. Most cruise lines will offer shuttle service into the town center. At the port there are no facilities for guests.

TOURING OPTIONS AND SIGHTS TO SEE: There are only a handful of specific sites or activities in Alta worthy of note. Local services for private sightseeing are exceptionally limited. The majority of cruise ships that do stop either offer a brief tour of the town along with the Hjemmeluft rock carvings. But few, if any, will take guests into Sautso Canyon.

*Below are listed the limited touring options for Alta:

** **Ship sponsored tours** are the primary option given that Alta has so few services available, not being a major destination for cruise ships.

** **Private car and driver** option is difficult to fill. If you wish to try on your own, I recommend Holtens Limousine Service. It is listed as being in Alta, but it presently does not have a web page. The only way to reach them, if they are still operating is by telephone. To check on availability for private sightseeing and fares, telephone +47 78 43 57 90.

In the center of Alta (Work of Andreas Haldorsen, CC BY SA 3.0, Wikimedia.org)

** **Alta Taxi** is the small taxi company in the town. They may be able to offer hourly rates for sightseeing in and around the town. Their web page is *www.altataxi.no.*

* The major sights to see if you are on your own are as follows (shown alphabetically):

** **Alta Museum** located at Altaveien # 19 on the edge of town is open from 11 AM to 4 PM daily. Its primary feature is the collection of rock carvings that have been given UNESCO World Heritage Site status. You will either need to come by taxi or take the tour from your ship if it is offered.

** **Northern Lights Cathedral** is the grandest building in Alta. Its bold spiral design is unique and has no rival in Scandinavia. It sits on a rise above the city and is a must see venue. You can visit the cathedral during daylight hours except when special services are being conducted.

Alta's grand cathedral, (Work of Lars Palczak, CC BY SA 4.0, Wikimedia.org)

** Northern Lights Observatory for those who will brave the cold and dark of winter to come and see this spectacular sight. For those of you coming in the very late summer or early fall on the few remaining cruises, you may have a chance to observe the Northern Lights, but it is essentially a mid-winter experience.

** Seiland National Park – This beautiful park south of Alta with its whitewater river, green woodlands and rugged hills is a perfect example of the raw wilderness that Arctic Norway has to offer. The coastal margins contain deep water fjords and show signs of active glaciation with two small glaciers. However, unless your cruise line has organized an excursion by motor launch, there is no other way to reach the park since it occupies an island with no road access. I only mention it here in the event your cruise line does offer you the chance to visit. It is a memorable experience in the wildness of the high Arctic.

** Tirpitz Museum is located along Kafjord about a 40 minute drive outside of Alta. It is open from10 AM to 9 PM and is worth visiting if you have a tour offered or can find or have pre booked a local taxi. This small museum is filled with Tirpitz memorabilia and is located not far from where the great battleship was attacked.

DINING OUT: There are a few restaurants in the main town of Alta that offer lunch with a Norwegian flair. In the event you have time for lunch and do not wish to return to the ship, here are my few suggestions:

* **Du Verden Matbar** is located at Markedsgata #21-25 and is open from 11 AM to 11:30 PM. This is a good restaurant for lunch or dinner and is very popular with locals. Stockfish and reindeer are of course house specialties, but they also offer vegetarian dishes. You will find the food and service comparable to what you would expect in a major city. They are open Monday thru Saturday from 10 AM to 11 PM , Sunday from 1 to 10PM. Reservations can be made by calling +47 459 08 213.

* **Restaurant Haldde** in the Thon Hotel Vica at Fogdebakkan #6 is open for lunch and dinner. It is a good restaurant by Alta standards, but a bit over priced for what it offers. Lunch and dinner hours can be rather busy, but if you are patient you will find that their lunch selection will include a variety of fish and seafood dishes, and this far north, reindeer meat is the main red meat you will find. Good desserts are a part of the restaurant's offerings. They are open from Noon to 11 PM daily. Reservations are a must by calling them to book at +47 78 48 22 22.

* **Sorrisniva** – Located about 20 kilometers south of the town, necessitating a taxi, this is a very fine local restaurant featuring locally sourced foods prepared according to local traditions. Reindeer meat and fresh seafood are prime on their menu. The restaurant is located amid beautiful natural woodland so that you can appreciate the countryside from which so many of the ingredients come. Lunch is served daily from Noon to 3 PM. Your taxi will know how to find this out of the way, but special restaurant, so highly acclaimed by the local populace. If you happen to be there for the Northern Lights in the middle of winter, the restaurant also features a traditional ice house known as an igloo. Call ahead to reserve a table at +47 48 43 33 78.

* **Trasti & Trine** – This very traditional restaurant is located about half an hour drive south of Alta at Gariaveien # 29, so you would need to have a private car or taxi at your disposal to visit. The restaurant is part of a lodge and husky dog complex where you can also witness dog training. The cuisine is that of the high Arctic, featuring fresh salmon, char, reindeer and such delicacies as local wild berries. The whole ambiance is rustic, but superbly presented and gives you a glimpse into the world of the northland. Before going, you should contact them for reservations. The restaurant serves daily from 9 AM to 9 PM. Phone them at +47 78 30 40.

FINAL WORDS: Alta is small, remote and does not have many cruise ship visitors. The venues within the town are few, but the surrounding countryside offers up the wilds of the northland, providing you are able to get out of town on a ship sponsored tour or with a private car or tax. Remember that Alta is a small community and choices for restaurants at lunch are rather limited when it comes to good, traditional cuisine. But you should try to at least get some taste of this off the beaten path community.

The cold waters of the Altaleva River south of Alta

THE CITY OF ALTA

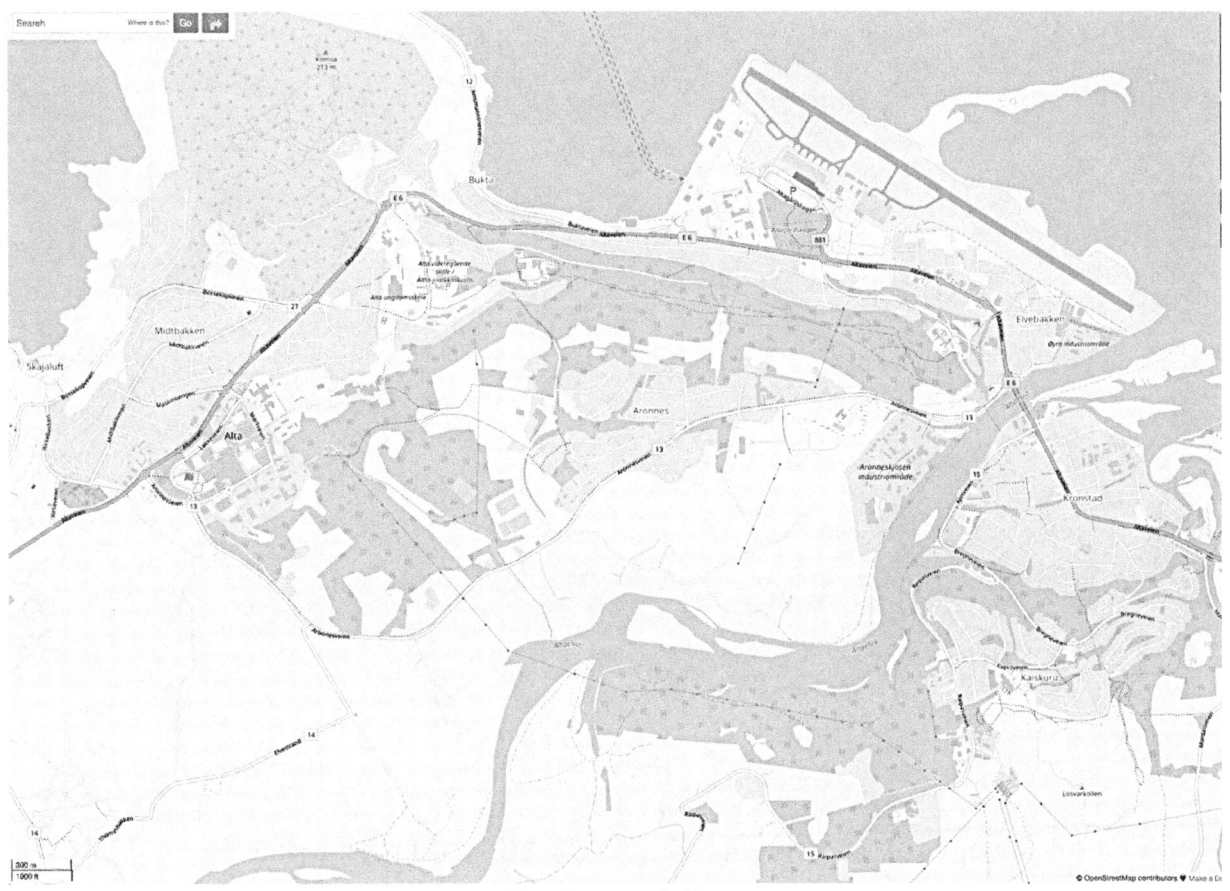

The heart of Alta

This map is best viewed directly from OpenStreetMap.com on your personal device where it can be expanded or one specific area can be enlarged. Given the format of this book, it is impossible to display maps with the level of detail you might wish to have while actually out exploring the city. But the OpenStreetMap maps used directly are the tool I always rely upon.

HAMMERFEST

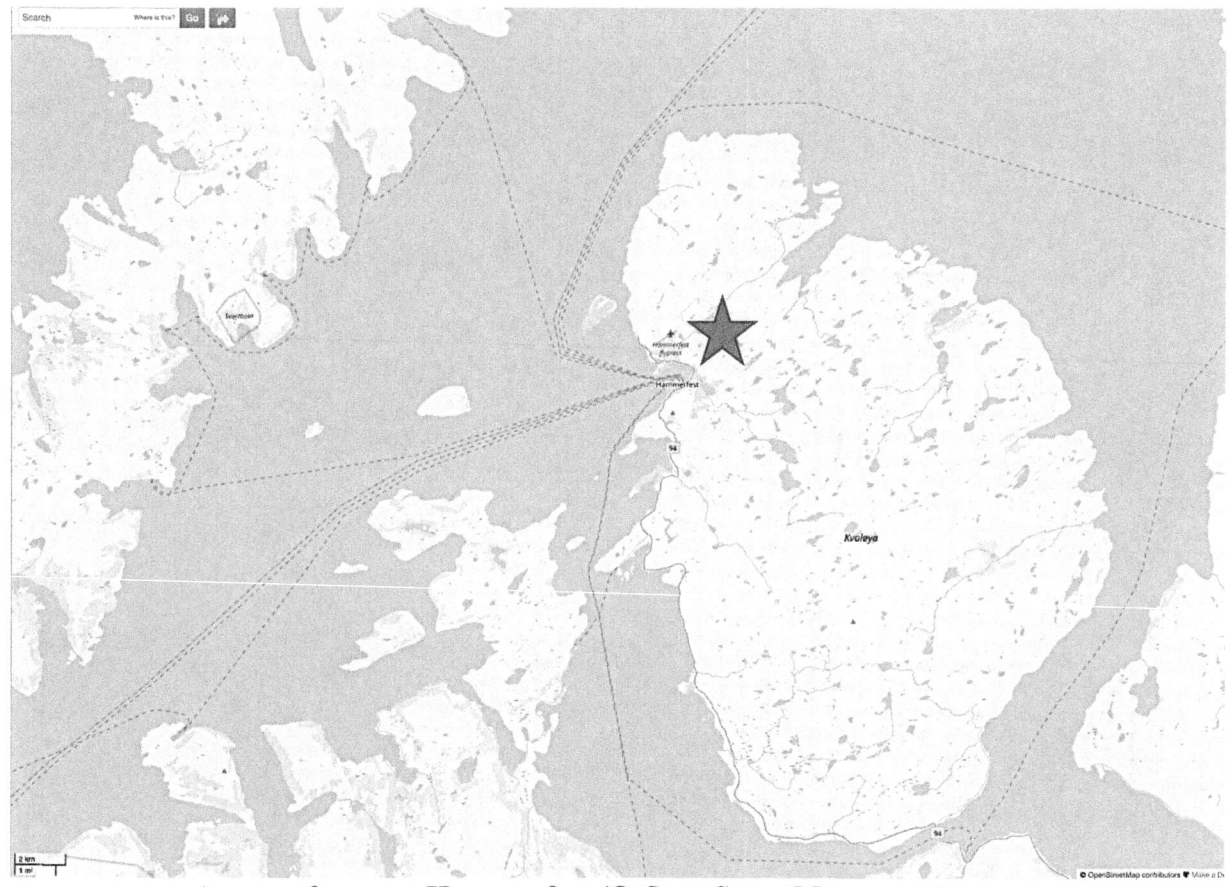

A map of greater Hammerfest (© OpenStreetMap contributors)

NORTHERN LANDSCAPE: Hammerfest is located in the very far northern reaches of Norway, a short distance south of where the Arctic and North Atlantic Oceans meet. The city occupies the northern end of the island of Kvaløya, which is connected to the mainland by a bridge. The city is built around a deep water harbor and has unrestricted access to the open ocean and the main shipping routes between the Russian Arctic and the rest of Europe. The island is protected from the brunt of winter storms off the ocean by the mountainous island of Sørøya, but this island does not block access to the northwest opening into the ocean.

This far north one would expect a brutally cold winter climate, but surprisingly because of the Gulf Stream, Hammerfest receives a mix of rain, sleet and snow with temperatures not drastically below freezing. However, when it snows, the amounts at times can be exceptionally heavy and this poses an avalanche danger since the surrounding rocky hillsides are bare of trees. The weather is essentially harsh, but not as brutal as it would be inland. Summers are cool, damp and often cloudy or foggy. Remember that Hammerfest is well above the Arctic Circle, and therefore there are swings between having approximately six weeks of total daylight in summer and then the reverse in winter, with days on either end of the daylight or darkness where only a few minutes to a couple of hours of daylight or darkness occur. This far north in latitude gives the people of Hammerfest a much stronger view of the Northern Lights, and this is now considered to be a tourist selling point for those who want to witness this spectacle.

Hammerfest residentialarea, (Work of Udovic Perón, CC BY SA 3.0, Wikimedia.org)

New and modern waterfront residences, (Work of Virtual Pano, CC BY SA 4.0, Wikimedia.org)

Hammerfest overview, (Work of Clemensfranz, (CC BY SA 3.0, Wikimedia.org)

The landscape at this latitude and with the exposure to winds from the open sea is definitely described as tundra. There are very few trees capable of growing under such conditions. The combination of strong winds and overall low temperatures are what inhibit the growth of trees. Permafrost is also a factor in inland areas where there is little time during the year when the temperatures are above freezing. But in Hammerfest, given its maritime influences, this is not a factor in preventing tree growth. Wind is the prime factor.

A FASCINATING HISTORY: Hammerfest as a town only dates back to 1789 when it was granted trade rights in the far north by King Christian VII or Denmark. Prior to being given those rights, the harbor was used for fishing boats to take shelter. It was also used as a base for high Arctic expeditions to hunt for fur bearing seals and for whaling. It officially became a town in 1838 with regard to establishing its charter.

One would not have expected the Napoleonic Wars to have an impact upon Norway, especially not a town as far north as Hammerfest, but surprisingly it did. Norway was under Danish rule and Denmark did participate in the war on the side of Napoleon. Because Hammerfest was the major trade center for the rich fishing and Arctic hunting waters of the high Arctic, the British blockaded the coast and it was only a matter of time before their ships would attack the town. In July 1809, two British warships attacked

Hammerfest, which was defended by two cannons. The battle lasted for over one hour, but ended when the Hammerfest batteries depleted their ammunition. The British proceeded to loot what the Hammerfest locals had not been able to cart away before the British came ashore. Following the British departure, Hammerfest was established as a garrison, as prior to being attacked and looted, it was locals that had manned the batteries, and they were not either well equipped or trained, but yet they had been able to inflict some casualties upon the British. To this day, the story of the role of Hammerfest in the Napoleonic Wars is still taught with great pride, as Norwegian school children develop their sense of national identity and loyalty.

A busy far northern harbor (Work of Simo Räsänen, CC BY SA 4.0, Wikimedia.org)

Hammerfest had to be partially rebuilt after the great 1890 fire that had destroyed much of the community, which like most Norwegian towns, was built primarily of wood. But in the case of the reconstruction, a good portion of the funds raised came from Kaiser Wilhelm II of Germany because of his prior visits on his royal yacht and his affection for the town and its people.

During World War II, Hammerfest became a major Nazi base because it was very close to the Allied shipping lanes where supplies were being convoyed to Murmansk to help the Soviet Union in fighting the German invasion. Unlike the defenses the Norwegians had in place after the Napoleonic Wars, the Nazi made Hammerfest almost impregnable with the coastal and inland batteries they established. To attempt to hamper Allied shipping, the German U-boat was the main weapon of choice, and given its proximity to the shipping lanes, Hammerfest became a very strategic submarine base. Hammerfest paid a terrible price because it had become such an important German base of operations. The Soviet Air

Force bombed Hammerfest in early 1944 and again in late summer of the same year. Although this did significant damage, the Germans evacuated all of the local residents when the Red Army began to press its invasion into the eastern margins of Finnmark. To hamper the Russian onslaught, the Germans systematically looted and burned all of the towns and villages, including Hammerfest. The destruction to the community and local infrastructure was essentially total, unlike any other damage inflicted either by the retreating Germans or allied forces anywhere else in Norway.

Following the war, the entire community of Hammerfest and all of the surrounding villages had to be totally rebuilt. But the Norwegians were determined to remove the battle damage, which they did. Today there is the Reconstruction Museum in Hammerfest, which tells the story of the destruction and resurrection of the town, and it is a major attraction.

Today Hammerfest is profiting from the new liquefied natural gas plant at Snøhvit, which will stimulate the economy with the addition of many well-paying jobs. Tourism is a growing part of the economic scene because of the increased interest in recreational fishing. There is also a daily tour boat that takes visitors around Nordkapp, known in English as North Cape, the northernmost point of land in Europe. There is also a significant glacier close by on the mainland that is the most northerly such feature on the continent. The town also serves as a local trade center, especially for the Sámi who keep significant herds of reindeer on Mageroya and Kvaløya Island for the summer. The reindeer have the run of both islands, and in Hammerfest they often come right into the town to graze on people's flowerbeds or vegetable gardens. It may sound charming, but the local residents find it disruptive as well as unsanitary having so many animals wandering through their yards and gardens.

Mageroya being also the home to North Cape, which is visited during summer by numerous cruise ships. Many cruise liners now do stop in Hammerfest for a few hours, but often not long enough for any tours into the more rugged interior.

The city's reindeer problem (Work of Manxruler, CC BY SA 3.0, Wikimedia.org)

CRUISE SHIP DOCK: Most cruise ships visiting Hammerfest will dock at Quay # 1 or # 2, which is right in the city center, so no shuttle bus is needed for people who just wish to walk around the urban area. If there is an overload of ships, which is not likely, then Quay # 9 located on the opposite side of the small bay will be used. This may necessitate a shuttle bus given the distance of 1.5 kilometers or approximately one mile. Neither location offers any terminal facilities. Some cruise lines prefer to drop anchor in the bay and tender guests to the center of town rather than using Quay # 9.

TOURING OPTIONS & LOCAL SIGHTS TO SEE: There are few venues of any great significance in Hammerfest. The overall flavor of the town, which encircles the bay is interesting because of its colorful houses that seem to take the place of having lush vegetation. Just seeing a significant town of around 10,000 in a bleak tundra environment is in itself interesting.

* There are very few options open for touring Hammerfest:

** **Motor coach tours** – A few cruise ships stay long enough to offer their own motor coach tours of this small city and its surroundings.

** **Private touring** – If you wish to have a private car and driver, the cruise concierge can attempt to make arrangements, but the supply of cars and drivers is limited. If you wish to try and arrange this on your own, I suggest you check with Mozio, as they appear to be the only company offering shuttle or limousine service. Their web page is *www.mozio.com.* They will be able to advise if they even offer sightseeing service.

** **Taxi services** in Hammerfest are limited. Depending upon their traffic, one or two may be waiting at the cruise dock to offer their services. However, you can check on line at *www.hammerfesttaxi.no* to see if it is possible to book in advance.

** **Walking** – Hammerfest is very spread out. Cruise ships can dock alongside the small city center or across the harbor, the larger ships being on the opposite shore from the city center. In such cases, a shuttle bus is provided to bring guests to the city center. From the dock, you can explore much of the city center on foot. But if you happen to have an interest in the residential areas most are quite scattered amid the barren hills.
* There are just a few sites of any importance or of interest to visitors. The major sights in Hammerfest include (shown in alphabetical order):

** **Hammerfest Church** located on Kirkegata # 21 is a new post World War II construct, but built in the delightful manner of local wood churches around the country. It is quite tastefully decorated and reflects true Norwegian sensibilities regarding decorum. No specific hours for visits to the church are posted, but on days when a ship is in port the church is generally open..

The attractive Hammerfest church (Work of Balou46, CC BY SA 4.0, Wikimedia.org)

The Hammerfest Museum of Reconstruction

** **Hammerfest Town Center** with its mother and child fountain is a pleasant place to sit for a while and simply watch the people about their daily activities. The fountain is quite charming and is the focus of the town center. Hammerfest is considered to be the most northern city in Norway and some say in all of Europe, but it is essentially a large town and lacks the urban ambiance of a city. None the less, it is a community with a distinct charm and atmosphere given its northerly location.

** **Museum of Reconstruction for Finnmark and Northern Troms** is located at Kirkegata #21 adjacent to the town's main church. It is open daily and is considered the major attraction. The exhibits and artifacts tell of the Nazi forced evacuation and subsequent destruction of the towns in the region. And it portrays the heroism of the people and their determination to rebuild.

Hammerfest was heavily destroyed during World War II

** Polar Bear Society is located on Hamnegata # 3, which is on the waterfront. The museum is only open from 10 AM to 2 PM, but it is a must see venue. Although there are no polar bears in Norway proper, they are major on Svalbard Island off the north coast, west from Hammerfest. And they have figured greatly into Norwegian explorations of the far north. The museum is always a big hit with visitors because of all the mystique surrounding the Polar Bear.

Residential Hammerfest, (Work of Banja-Frans Mulder, CC BY SA 3.0, Wikimedia.org)

** Struve Geodetic Arc is a monument located around the harbor from the town center, but often cruise ships dock on this side of the harbor making the monument a short walk away. Over 100 years ago a Russian scientist named Friedrich Struve led a team that measured an arc of longitude from Hammerfest south to the Black Sea in an attempt to better calculate the earth's radius and determine its overall size. This project was accomplished long before computers or scientific equipment and is an amazing feat, which has earned the site UNESCO World Heritage Site status.

DINING OUT: There are few restaurants overall in Hammerfest and depending upon your itinerary, thus you may not have time for lunch. However, if you are fortunate enough to stay for a few hours and would like to sample some traditional cuisine, I have the following two recommendations, as the majority of Hammerfest restaurants feature more North American style food such as hamburgers and pizza. And the quality of these other restaurants is not up to the standards I set for recommendation. My choices are:

* **Brygga Mathus** – Located at Strandgata # 16 in the heart of town, this delightful restaurant serves lighter fare, but in the Norwegian tradition. Soups, sandwiches and salads are a major part of the lunch offering. The atmosphere is quaint and the service is excellent. Their menu also is vegetarian friendly. Hours of service are between 11 AM and 5 PM weekdays only. Reservations are not necessary.

* **Qa spiseri** is in the center of town at Sjogata #8 and open daily for lunch and dinner. It is far from elegant, simply a rather ordinary restaurant serving basic local fare. It is popular with the local community and I have never heard any serious complaints from returning guests once onboard ship. As is expected, fish soup, fish and reindeer are on the menu, all nicely prepared. They are open from 10 AM to Midnight on weekdays. Saturday hours are from 11 to 1 AM. Sunday hours are from 1 to 8 PM. Reservations are not necessary.

Large cruise ships do call in at Hammerfest, (Work of Balou46, CC BY SA 3.0, Wikimedia.org)

HAMMERFEST MAPS

GREATER HAMMERFEST

Greater Hammerfest

This map is best viewed directly from OpenStreetMap.com on your personal device where it can be expanded or one specific area can be enlarged. Given the format of this book, it is impossible to display maps with the level of detail you might wish to have while actually out exploring the city. But the OpenStreetMap maps used directly are the tool I always rely upon.

THE CENTER OF HAMMERFEST

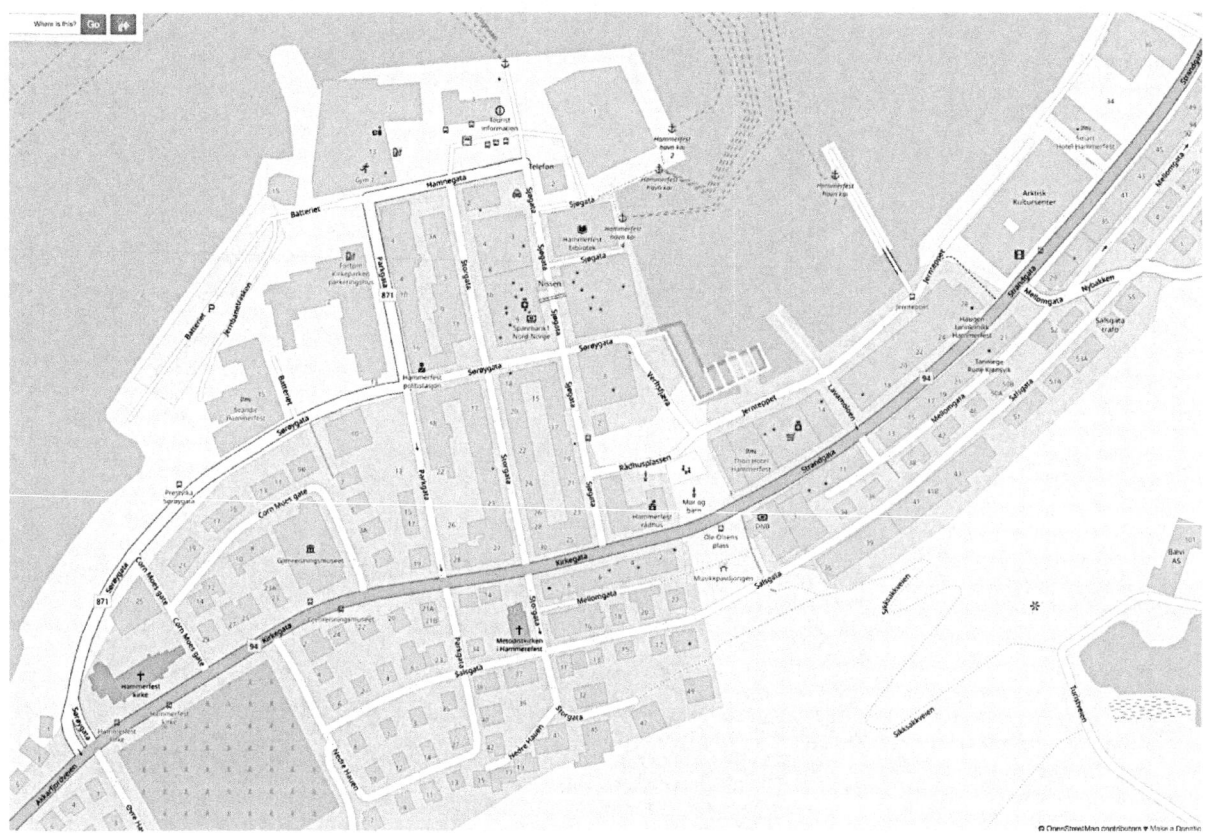

The heart of Hammerfest

This map is best viewed directly from OpenStreetMap.com on your personal device where it can be expanded or one specific area can be enlarged. Given the format of this book, it is impossible to display maps with the level of detail you might wish to have while actually out exploring the city. But the OpenStreetMap maps used directly are the tool I always rely upon.

HONNINGSVÅG AND NORDKAPP

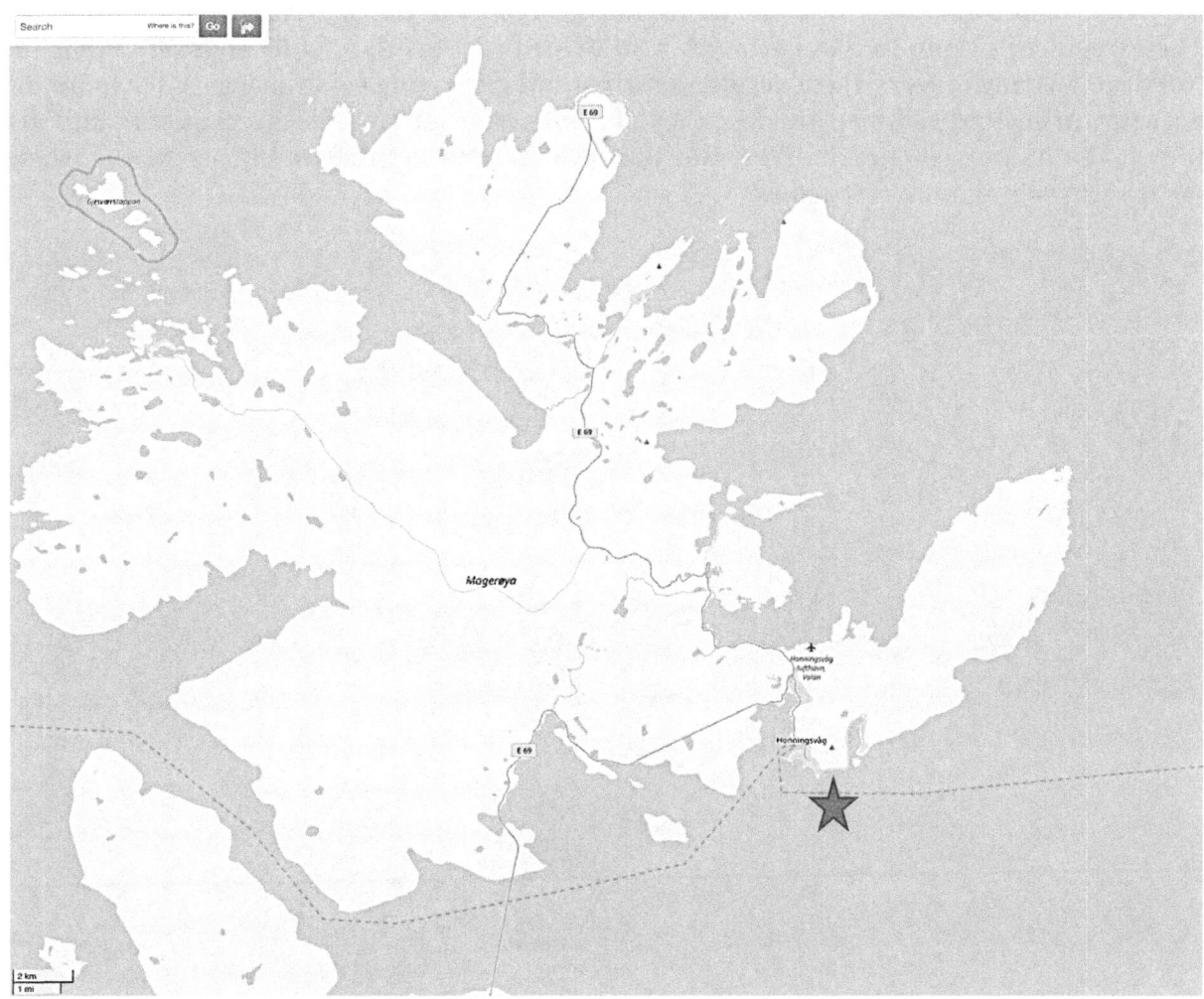

Map of Magerøya Island and Honningsvåg, (© OpenStreetMap contributors)

Magerøya Island is the most northerly island in Norway, facing out onto the Barents Sea, which is part of the Arctic Ocean. The only significant town on this large island, which is connected by tunnel to the mainland, is Honningsvåg, the port of call for visits to Nordkapp, known in English as North Cape, the very northernmost tip of Europe. Honningsvåg has the distinction of being the most northerly city in Norway, but only by a bit of political sleight of hand. The Norwegian government legislated that to have the designation of being a city, the population must be over 5,000. Honningsvåg only has about 2,400 residents, but it received its city status one year before the new legislation went into effect in 1997. A special waiver was given so that it would not lose its recognition as the most northerly "city" in the country. Yet Hammerfest, which is larger, attempts to call itself the largest city in Europe based upon its population.

A TUNDRA LANDSCAPE: Honningsvåg is located on a deep water bay that is quite sheltered from storms, situated on the island's south coast, just across a relatively narrow channel from the mainland. North Cape, which is the object of the port call is located atop a high set of cliffs facing the stormy waters of the Arctic Ocean, a drive of approximately one hour across the island. But it gives visitors an opportunity to see a true tundra landscape and also catch sight of thousands of reindeer during their summer grazing. These reindeer belong to Sámi families who drive them overland and then rely upon the Norwegian Army to ferry them across to their summer grazing each spring. After fattening up with spring and summer grazing, they are able to swim back to the mainland and are then taken to more sheltered areas. But they are allowed to graze freely across the island for the warmer months of summer.

The tundra landscape of Magerøya with its summer reindeer herds

The climate of the island is heavily influenced by strong gale force winds that blow off the Arctic Ocean. Magerøya Island is brutally cold in winter and even though it is alongside the Gulf Stream waters, it does receive large quantities of inter snow. But it is not as bitterly cold temperature wise as places to the south that are farther inland. Summers are mild, but very short. If you visit in June, you will still see large areas in the island's interior partially covered in snow. And by September, it is possible for a new snow cover to begin returning.

HONNINGSVÅG HISTORY: Settlement by early people who depended upon fishing dates back to prehistoric times, but not much is known about their culture or lifestyle. By the Viking Era, there was very little interest shown in these far northern latitudes because there were few resources to exploit and no communities worthy of pillage.

There are a few Sámi camps on Magerøya you can visit en route to North Cape

By the latter part of the 16th century, there were a handful of fishing settlements scattered around the shores of Magerøya Island, and by 1589 there were at least six small churches known to have existed. But by the start of the 19th century, population had greatly decreased and only one church was known to have existed.

After a devastating storm, which some scientists believe may have been a true hurricane, struck the island in 1882, even the sole church in the village of Kjelvik was destroyed. It is doubtful if the storm was a true hurricane given the extreme northerly latitude, but did have gale force winds. Because of its sheltered harbor on the southern side of the island, Honningsvåg ultimately became the most logical place to live and in 1885, a church was consecrated there. Today it is the only major settlement on the island.

During World War II, Nazi forces occupied the few communities of the far north, fearful that the Red Army in Murmansk may take control of the area and hinder German harassment of allied shipping. When the war was nearing its end, the German forces retreated but left in their wake a scorched earth by burning every farm, town or village to hinder the Russians when they advanced.

An attempt to grow some trees in Honningsvåg is not easy

Today Honningsvåg is primarily a fishing center, and it offers training, repair and supply services to the fishing fleets. Added to this primary role is tourism, as many cruise ships do make it this far north so that their guests can say they have been to the Arctic shores.

SHIP DOCK IN HONNIGSVÅG: There is a significant size pier in Honnigsvåg capable of accommodating cruise ships. There are no terminal facilities, but it is a very short walk from the ship to the center of the town.

Docking in Honningsvåg

TOURING OPTIONS & THINGS TO DO IN HONNINGSVÅG: There is little for the visitor to see in Honningsvåg, as it is strictly a fishing and local service center. But either before or after taking a tour to North Cape, a walk through town does give you a chance to capture the flavor of living on the tundra in such a northerly location. Winter would be quite extreme, both cold and continuously dark for over six or seven weeks. This is the quiet time when little happens in Honningsvåg, but they do receive Hurtigruten ships that bring passengers who want to come and experience the Northern Lights.

* **Cruise sponsored tour** – If your ship is coming to Honningsvåg, the main purpose will be to offer guests a motor coach tour to North Cape where several monuments, a museum and restaurant enable visitors to enjoy being at the top end of Europe.

* **Touring by taxi** is the only other option in Honningsvåg other than the tours offered by your cruise line. This is such a remote community that it cannot support private car and driver/guide options but the local taxi service can accommodate a mere handful of people who want to visit North Cape. You must email taxi@nordkapptaxi.no as soon as possible to try and be successful in booking a tour. You may try calling then at +47 78 47 22 34 if you are not successful on line.

The colorful harbor of Honningsvåg

* **Local van service** – There is a local van service that provides airport transfers, but they may be able to cobble together a private tour. You can check the Mozio Honningsvåg web page at <u>www.mozio.com</u> or to VIP Transportation at <u>www.assist-ant.com</u> to see what services they offer.

* **Walking** is an option only if you plan to remain in town. A visit to North Cape does require transport, as it is quite a distance from where the ship docks. The journey takes around 90 minutes by motor coach.

The major sights to see in town are limited to two, which are:

* **Nordkappmusset** is located on the waterfront at Holmen #1 and is open only from Noon to 4 PM. It does offer various exhibits on the importance of North Cape, the fishing industry of Honningsvåg and the Nazi occupation of the town during World War II. Although small, the museum is well organized and worth your effort to visit.

Honningsvåg is rather a quiet town

* **Perloportenkulturhus** located in town at Storgata # 19 is an interesting place to see a short live presentation called "Our Northernmost Life." This show with local talent gives you a feel for the culture of the region and a taste of what life is like in Europe's most northerly city. Upon arrival, you can check with the visitor's center or ask anyone in town what time the show will be put on.

VISITING NORDKAPP: Most visitors will book their ship's motor coach tour to Nordkapp (North Cape,) as this is the major highlight of visiting Honningsvåg. The drive will take about an hour to 90 minutes during which time you will see both the rugged nature of the island of Magerøya and the importance of its tundra vegetation as food for thousands of reindeer. During early summer there will still be snow on the ground in partial cover

The Visitor's Center at Nordkapp is an impressive multi-level building that extends down the cliff face. It contains a restaurant, cafe, gift shop and theater where special presentations are shown. And the windows present panoramic sweeping views out over the cape and the Arctic Ocean. There is an outdoor promenade leading right to the cliff's edge, but protected by guardrails. If the weather is tolerable, you can enjoy the impact of the cape while being out of doors.

Actually Nordkapp is not the most northerly point, as guides will note. There is one cape to the west that is just a few meters farther north, but because of the broken topography it is inaccessible by road or even on foot and thus Nordkapp became officially recognized as the most northerly point in Europe. Since Europe is in reality a portion of the greater Eurasian Continent, the Russians therefore claim that there are numerous peninsulas and islands in their vast region of Siberia that extend much farther toward the North Pole. Among geographers and world travelers the debate has never been settled as to whether Europe is a continent or not. This author prefers the concept of Eurasia since there is no natural boundary that makes Europe a separate landmass.

The visitor's center and museum at Nordkapp are most interesting, and there is a small restaurant and a snack bar where you can get snacks, hot drinks or light lunches. Visitors generally rate the restaurant as being of fair to good quality. Generally after standing out along the railing looking into the Arctic Ocean, you will want to spend the rest of the time viewing the landscape from inside through the large picture windows. At this far northern latitude and being atop a high cliff the breeze to often fierce wind blowing across the cape makes it quite uncomfortable even in summertime. Some cruise lines will offer a cruise around the entire island before continuing on their journey, so you then get to see North Cape from out at sea.

Looking up at North Cape from the ocean

The Nordkapp Visitor's Center

The outdoor Nordcaoo Monument

At the northern tip of Europe

DINING OUT: Dining in Honningsvåg is exceptionally limited at lunchtime. But if you are going on the tour to Nordkapp, the visitor's center there does have both a restaurant and snack bar where you can have anything from a full meal to something light to satisfy until you return to your ship. In Honningsvåg I do recommend:

* **Corner Spiceri** located on Fiskeriveien # 2A and open from 11 AM to 8 PM Monday thru Saturday and from 1 to 8 PM on Sunday. The menu includes fish, especially cod, shellfish such as crab and also a selection of burgers. The quality is very good and the service is friendly, but often a bit slow if the restaurant is crowded. You will be surprised by such a nice restaurant in this small of a community. Reservations are not necessary.

* **Havly** – In the center of town at Storgata 12 B, this small restaurant has a fine reputation for traditional Norwegian cuisine served in a warm atmosphere. Seafood dishes are the specialty, but you can also find meat items on the menu, and of course that includes reindeer. They do receive very high reviews by the majority of their ship visitors. Their hours are Tuesday thru Thursday from 4 to 10 PM, Friday and Saturday from 4 PM to Midnight. Reservations are not necessary.

* **Honnis Bakis** – Located on the waterfront at Storgata 18, this café features a mix of Norwegian and French dishes. It is essentially a bakery and café and the menu is somewhat limited, but the quality is good. And the service is friendly and efficient. They are open Tuesday thru Saturday from 11 AM to 4 PM and reservations are not needed.

* **King Crab House Brasserie and Bar** – On the waterfront at Sjogata # 6, this restaurant does offer good meals in a friendly atmosphere. The overall ratings from guests I have spoken with say it is adequate to good, but not exceptional. They do feature fresh fish, crab and also rich fish soups. They are open Wednesday and Thursday from 3 to 10 PM, Friday and Saturday from Noon to Midnight and Sunday from Noon to 7 PM. Call them at +47 901 21 133 to see if you need to reserve a table.

FINAL WORDS: Honningsvåg is a rather small town that can be walked in an hour. I highly recommend taking the tour to North Cape. Upon return you will have time to walk in Honningsvåg. The harbor with its wood fishing boats is quite colorful and worthy of photographing providing the weather is nice. A lunch in Honningsvåg is one way to sample some fresh seafood. I would say that even though most of the restaurants are not gourmet oriented, it is an opportunity to sample really fresh seafood in the high Arctic. If the restaurants feature Arctic char, that is one fish you are not likely to be served on board ship. It is a fish lover's treasure.

THE CENTER OF HONNINGSVÅG

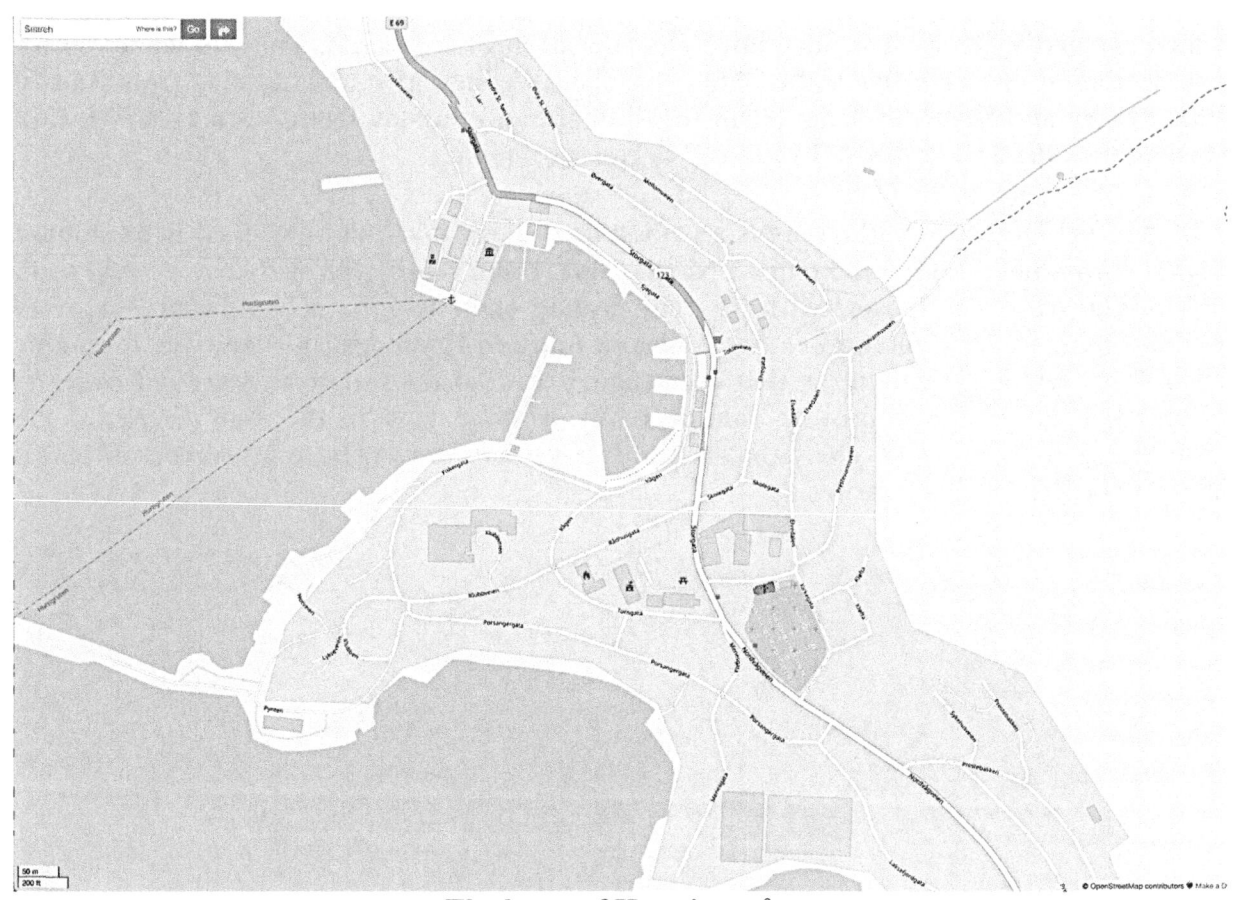

The heart of Honningsvåg

This map is best viewed directly from OpenStreetMap.com on your personal device where it can be expanded or one specific area can be enlarged. Given the format of this book, it is impossible to display maps with the level of detail you might wish to have while actually out exploring the city. But the OpenStreetMap maps used directly are the tool I always rely upon.

CRUISING TO MURMANSK AND ARKHANGELSK, RUSSIA

МУРМАНСК И АРХАНГЕЛСК, РОССИЯ

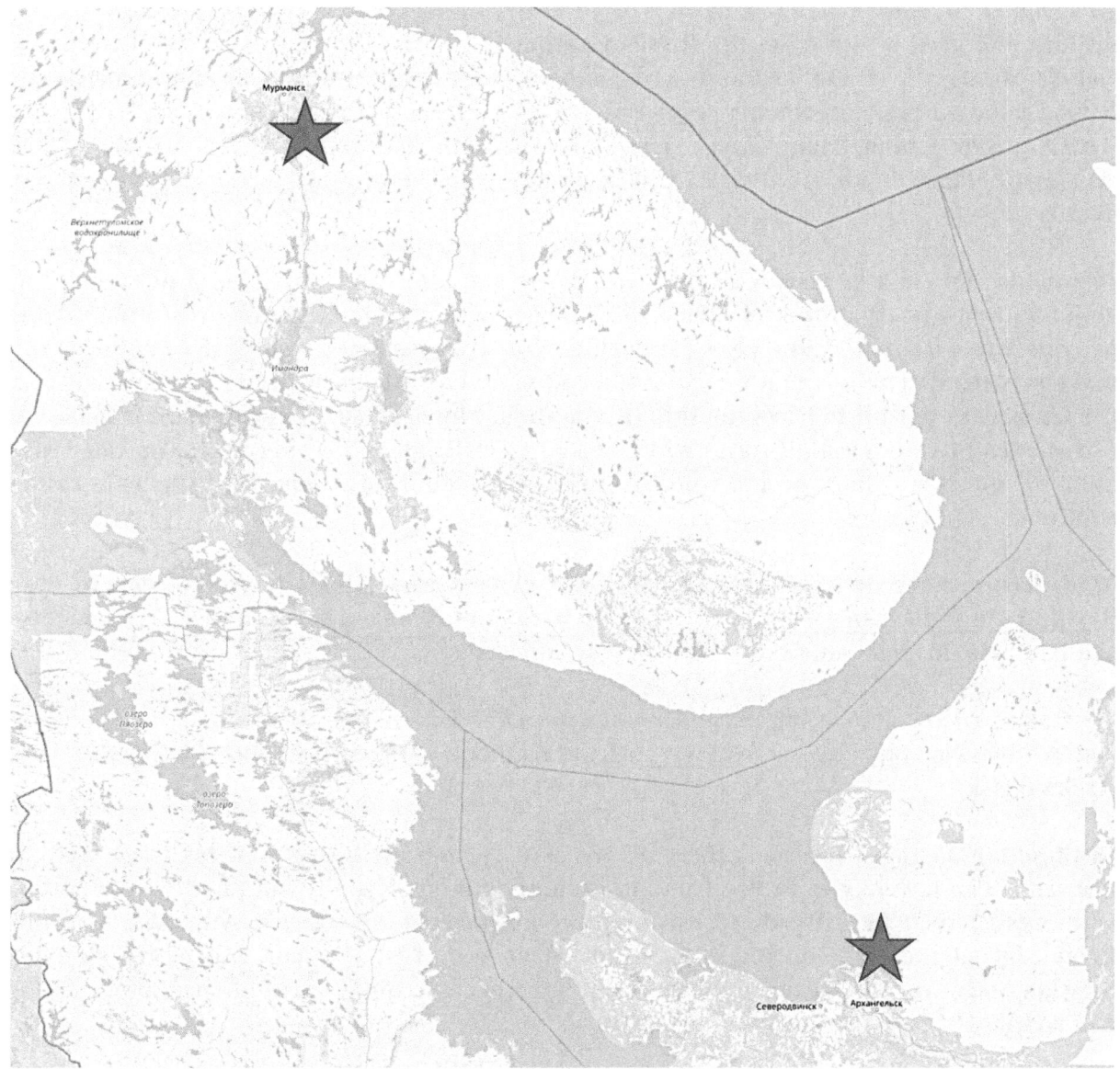

The far northwest of Russia (© OpenStreetMap contributors)

For those of you whose cruise itinerary will include a visit to Murmansk and possibly beyond to Arkhangelsk in Russia's far northern lands, this chapter will be of great value. Apart from having been to Russia 51 times, I have also had the good fortune to explore this high Arctic region of the far northwestern Arctic region. Speaking the language was a big help, as I was able to gain an insight into the lives of the people living in a region that is climatically quite severe by the standards most of us are accustomed to. No two cities in a similar environment could be as different. Murmansk is a 20th century creation that grew into a major port serving the Communist government of the Soviet Union. Arkhangelsk is a very old city whose roots go back to pioneers and missionaries that settled back in the 12th century, thus it has deep Russian roots.

IMPORTANT THINGS TO KNOW ABOUT VISITING RUSSIA: The Russian government is rather strict with regard to entry into and exit from the country. Most visitors will need a visa from the Russian authorities if they want to have the freedom to sightsee on their own. Only a handful of countries are exempt where their governments and Russia have mutual agreements regarding travel. Citizens with passports from Argentina, Brazil, Chile, China, Hong Kong, Israel, Kazakhstan are among a few nations whose passport holders do not need visas. Check on line with www.visitrussia.org.uk for current details.

If you do not have a visa, you may still leave the ship and participate in sightseeing activities that are organized by your cruise line or by tour companies that are authorized to provide you with temporary visas for each activity away from the ship. If you choose this more private alternative, make certain the company has the authority to provide you with the temporary permit to leave the ship. If you do not have a visa or if you are not from one of the exempt countries, all times when not on an official sightseeing tour, you must stay onboard the ship. Many people who like to have freedom to explore find this rule rather confining.

Many cruise lines do offer private cars with drivers and guides to enable you to have flexibility in sightseeing where you are not part of an organized group. Such arrangements can be made through your ship's shore excursion office.

To make private sightseeing arrangements you can visit on line at *www.kolatravel.*com or email them at *info@kolatravel.com* for information regarding both Murmansk and Archangelsk.

In these far northern locations there are no hop on hop off busses and taxis can only be utilized if you have a visa or are from an exempt country. Even if you qualify to be out on your own, it will be difficult to use public transportation or a taxi without a working knowledge of the Russian language, which is no easy feat. I spent four years studying Russian and it was only after a dozen trips that I became quite adept at speaking, reading and writing.

If you have a visa and go off on your own, you will find that very few people are able to speak English or other European languages. And most of the signs and informational posts are written in the Cyrillic Alphabet, so getting around is difficult on your own without having a guide. These are not cities often visited by people from outside of Russia

Credit cards can be used in most shops and restaurants, but if you are going out on your own or with a private car and driver and guide you should carry some Russian rubles, as foreign currencies are not accepted in Russia.

If you have a chance to speak with your guide or other Russians regarding their lives or their views, do not be forward in pressing them for opinions of a political nature. Most Russian people are very proud of their heritage, their country and the fact that it has emerged from its long Soviet Era. Many of us who live in the West have very strong views regarding the current Russian government and the country's president that are often rather negative. What you do not want to do is get into an argument over political or global issues when you are a visitor in their country. Even if Russians that you meet who can converse in English or your language then voice negative views, which on occasion some will do, it is best to try and remain neutral in your demeanor. Be the polite and correct visitor and in the end you will leave with pleasant memories, as Russians are very warm and giving people.

MURMANSK МУРМАНСК

The spruce and willow woodlands surrounding Murmansk

THE LOCAL GEOGRAPHY: The city of Murmansk is one of the two most important warm water ports in all of Russia. A map of the country will show you that despite having a very long Arctic and Pacific coastline, the northern latitudes mean that much of it is locked in ice for many months of the year, although the winter period is changing with global warming. Murmansk benefits from being at the far northern end of the Gulf Stream, that important warm water current that comes across from the tropical waters of North America, washes the coast of Norway and reaches Murmansk. Russia's other warm water port is Vladivostok, which is thousands of kilometers or miles to the east on the Pacific Coast close to the borders of China and North Korea. Thus Murmansk is a critical port for commercial and military uses because it is due north of the Russian heartland, which is west of the Ural Mountains.

Looking over the city center and docks at Murmansk

THE LANDSCAPE AROUND MURMANSK: The landscape is one of moderately hilly ground that is covered in a mix of tundra vegetation interspersed with groves of willow, birch and spruce, which are outliers of the dense coniferous taiga to the south. For anyone who knows their geography or climatology, they will find the amount of vegetation quite surprising for such a far northern location. But the explanation lies in the farthest reaches of the mild Gulf Stream waters that help to moderate the overall climate of the city.

The climate is essentially continental with severely cold and snowy winters. There are 138 days each winter in which some snow will fall. If it were not for the slight moderating influence of the Gulf Stream, the conditions around Murmansk would be even more severe than they are. Now global warming is also adding to the amelioration of the Murmansk climate. Still record low temperatures on occasion almost reached minus 40 degrees Celsius/Fahrenheit. And at its high latitude above the Arctic Circle, Murmansk experiences six to eight weeks of absolute total darkness each winter. With a population of over 400,000, it is the world's largest city at such a high latitude.

Residential Murmansk is primarily composed of large apartment blocks

HISTORY OF MURMANSK: Murmansk is a young city founded in 1915 because of the pressing need for a warm water port during World War I. The building of a railroad line was the key factor and Murmansk was the northern terminus because of its deep and sheltered harbor. Officially it was the last city to be grant755 0ed a charter in 1916 by Tsar Nicholas II just less than one year before he would be forced to abdicate the throne. The original name was Romanov-on-Murman, but in April 1917 the name was changed to Murmansk, as the Tsar was now no longer head of state. Romanov was the family name of all the Tsars who ruled from the time of Ivan the Terrible back in the 17th century.

In October 1917, the Bolshevik Revolution occurred in which Communist forces took control of the government in St. Petersburg. This precipitated a civil war between the Communist Red Army forces and the White Army that was loyal to the Tsar and Imperial Family. A British naval squadron occupied the harbor and city until 1920, supporting the

White Army forces in their fight to oust the Communists from the government. Ultimately, their efforts failed.

By 1922, most of the country was in the hands of the Red Army and the Union of Soviet Socialist Republics was proclaimed in December 1922. Murmansk ultimately became a part of the Soviet Union and by 1926 it had its own city soviet council. The city quickly grew, as the Soviet Union industrialized under the rule of Joseph Stalin, its warm water port being critical. But its role would heighten with the outbreak of World War II.

After Nazi Germany invaded Russia and blockaded Leningrad (formerly and again today St. Petersburg), the import of war materials, food and other vital supplies was critical to the nation's survival. The Allies organized convoys to supply the Soviets through Murmansk, and this in part is why Nazi forces considered Norway to be such a vital link since its ports could shelter U-boats that would prey upon the Allied convoys.

The heroic statue of Alyosha stands over Murmansk

German forces attempted to cut off the vital supply route, using Finland as a staging area. The Finns had given permission for Nazi troops to be stationed on their soil because the Red Army had made an attempt to recapture Finland, claiming that their 1917 independence was not valid and that they were a part of old Imperial Russia. The combination of winter weather and very stiff Red Army resistance made the capture of Murmansk impossible, but the city did suffer from severe enemy shelling that destroyed much of its vital infrastructure. Like Leningrad, Stalingrad, Minsk, Kiev and many other citie0s in the country, Murmansk was proclaimed a Heroic City by the government

following the war.4

The eternal flame and flower offerings at the base of Alyosha

Following World War II, the Soviet Union and the West became embroiled in the Cold War that essentially lasted until the fall of the Soviet system in 1991. Murmansk retained its strong military role, especially as a submarine base and also an Arctic research center given that Canada and the United States lay over the northern horizon. Today Murmansk is still the most important submarine port in all of Russia even though the Cold War is essentially over. During the Soviet Era Murmansk was essentially off limits to foreign tourists. Today it is totally open, and when your ship sails in, you will pass alongside the submarine base.

The city is filled with memorials and statues to the heroes of World Wars I and II and also the Russian Civil War. It is a city where you can feel its military significance when your tour its important sites. But most dominant of all is Alyosha, a giant statue of a soldier in a trench coat that stands 35.5 meters or 116 feet high, perched atop a hill overlooking the city. This has become a sacred site for Russians who have strong memories passed down from generation to generation with regard to World War II. Alyosha is pivotal in that remembrance.

Tributes at the base of Alyosha behind the eternal flame

THINGS TO SEE AND DO: Although I will be listing the important historic and scenic attractions, most of you will have little choice as to what you will see unless you either have a visa or hire a private car and driver/guide. The tours will have a predetermined itinerary that will not allow you any personalized choices. But hopefully you will get to see the majority of the places I have listed.

I am not giving names or addresses because in the city they would all be written in Cyrillic, which for most of you would be unreadable. I am offering opening hours, but often they are not adhered to in many instances. My recommendations for Murmansk are listed alphabetically for convenience. But if are by chance able to read the Cyrillic alphabet, there would be a different order of presentation.

* **Alyosha** is the number one attraction, as I noted above. It is a marvelous statue and has such great significance to the Russian people. He represents all the thousands of Red Army soldiers who died in defense of their country. That is why you will see fresh flowers and wreaths at the foot of Alyosha that people bring almost daily. To reach Alyosha you must be on a group tour or have private transportation. Even if you have a visa, it is too far to walk from the city center and unless you speak or read Russian, getting there on a public bus would be difficult.

* **Fine Art Museum** is not large and impressive as in St. Petersburg, but it does feature artists from the far north and the work is excellent. Russian landscape painting is done in an impressionistic style and is highly sought after in the West. The museum claims to be open from 10 AM to 5 PM except Tuesday.

The statue of the woman waiting for her husband to return from the sea

Graves of foreign merchant marines lost at sea during World War II

* **Lenin Nuclear Ice Breaker** is a very popular exhibit for most Western visitors. If you are not part of a group tour, special arrangements should be made at the time you arrange your car and driver/guide. Once again there is no wow factor, yet the ice breaker speaks for itself. It was a remarkable piece of equipment and represents a high point in Soviet Arctic exploration. The tour is conducted in Russian, but if you are part of a group or have a private guide, they will translate for you. It is one of the highlights of a visit to Murmansk.

* **Lenina Prospekt** is the main boulevard and shopping street that runs through the center of Murmansk. Most of the buildings reflect the Stalinist period in former Soviet history and give the city an arrested look of not having moved out of that 1930's period.

There has been little modern development in the downtown of Murmansk and thus the downtown area reflects primarily the architecture of the Stalinist Era.

Lenina Prospekt (avenue) in the heart of Murmansk

* **Memorial Complex to the Soldiers and Seamen Who Have Died in Peacetime** is a very somber, yet elegant memorial. It shows how important honoring those who have served their country is in Russia. The memorial and its church offer a glimpse into the devotion Russians feel for personal sacrifice. Also the location gives an outstanding view out over the city. No specific hours are posted, but if you have a private car and driver, he/she will know if you can visit.

* **Murmansk Railway Station** will not be on your group tour, but if you have a personal interest in trains, I would suggest a quick visit if you are out with a private guide. This rather ornate blue and white building typifies the attention to detail given to railway stations in the Soviet Era. And like so many other cities today, it is badly in need of repair even though the importance of rail travel has not diminished in this largest of countries in the world. If you happen to visit when a train is arriving or departing, you will find it a satisfying visit. In Russia when a train departs or arrives, the loudspeakers on the platform generally broadcast very rousing music, a carryover from the Soviet Era. And you will see quite a cross section of people, especially here in the far north where there are members of the Sami and other forest dwelling tribal groups.

The overnight train for St. Petersburg departing on its 24-hour journey

* **Murmansk Shopping Mall and Entertainment Center** on Lenina Avenue is the city's major shopping and entertainment complex. Although it may not meet standards of the glitz of the West, it is important to visit because you get a feeling for the changes taking place today in Russian retailing. It shows you a different side of this rather somber city. The mall is open daily from 10 AM to 10 PM and you will find a visit to be quite interesting.

* **Northern Fleet Naval Museum** receives mixed reviews from those who visit. The building itself is badly in need of restoration, and the exhibits are rather staid and conservative with now wow factor. But given the importance of the subject matter to the history of Murmansk, the museum does represent an important part of the city's development. The museum is open every day except Tuesday and Wednesday from 9 AM to 1 PM and again from 2 to 4 PM.

The Soviet Era Palace of Culture

* **Palace of Culture and Folk Art of Kirov Gallery** dates back to the early 20th century when the Communist government was attempting to control all aspects of daily life. This entertainment and education center was the cornerstone of social life for most Murmansk residents well into the 1980's. Architecturally it is typical of public architecture from that period found in all major cities, and emulates what dominated Moscow. The center is open daily from 9 AM to 9 PM and is definitely worth your time to visit.

* **Soviet Era residential districts** dominate most of the city of Murmansk. Since the end of the Soviet Union Murmansk has not seen the rapid modernization found in more dynamic Russian cities. Much of its residential districts still contain the massive apartment blocks that house the majority of its residents. This gives the city a look from the past, reflecting the drabness of life during much of the Soviet period. It is a window into what most cities in the former Soviet Union looked like. And also given the 20th century founding of Murmansk there is no architecture from the Imperial Ages of the tsar.

If you have a private car and driver/guide you can have a better chance of enjoying the varied landscapes of the city than on a motor coach tour where the guides rarely speak about the local architectural styles.

An example of older Soviet Era apartment blocks

There are literally dozens of monuments and memorials all over the city that represent different aspects of the role of Murmansk and those stationed here in war and peacetime. Rather than fill pages with sites you may not get to see, I simply trust that your group or private guide will point out any of the monuments you pass in your journey around the city.

DINING OUT: If you are on a group tour chances are that you will be returned to the ship for lunch if it is a morning tour. Afternoon tours will depart following lunch. However, if you are out with a private car and driver, you can stop for lunch and your guide will be there to assist. Few restaurants in Murmansk will have English menus or wait staff that will speak English or other languages. Russian food is hearty and very good. You should try it and I am sure that even in Murmansk, which is far from the major cities, you will enjoy sampling the cuisine. My four recommendations are as follows (shown alphabetically):

* **Kruzhka** – This traditional Russian restaurant with items on the menu from other Eastern European countries is located at Lenina Avenue # 34 in the Murmansk Mall. You will find this restaurant gives you a good taste of what Russian cuisine is like in all its many forms. They are open Monday through Thursday from 8 PM to 7 AM and Friday thru

Sunday from 6 PM to 7 AM. You would need to have your driver call for reservations if they are needed. Call +7 815 275 00 05.

* **Mama Mia** has an Italian name, but most of its menu is traditional Russian, but with a few Italian dishes. It is located on Egnorova Street # 14 and open for lunch at Noon. There are many very traditional Russian dishes on the menu and the quality is very good. And they do have an English menu. Your best choice if you want a good Russian meal, but count upon your guide to interpret the names of the different food choices. The restaurant is open daily from Noon to Midnight. Have your driver call +7 815 245 00 60 to book your table.

* **Restaurant Tsarskaya Okhota** – This is a very traditional Russian restaurant with an emphasis upon recipes of the far north. Seafood is high on the menu because of the availability of both freshwater and saltwater species. The cuisine is excellent, as is the service. Located at kolskiy Avenue # 86, it is a bit far from the center of town, but of course with a car and driver it is still within easy reach. Their hours are from Noon to Midnight daily. Have your driver call +7 815 225 52 24 to see if a reservation is needed.

* **Shtolle** is located on Lenina Avenue # 97 and open daily from 8 AM to 7 PM. Shtolle is a very popular chain of restaurants in St. Petersburg and other northern cities. . This is one of a popular chain of restaurants that specialize in Russian pies. But unlike what you might think of as a dessert restaurant, Russian pies are main courses. There is a great variety of meats, vegetables and yes also desserts. My favorite is a cabbage pie as the main, and then a fruit pie for dessert. It is quick, fresh and tasty and a Russian example of slow fast food. Reservations are never needed.

FINAL WORDS: Murmansk is essentially a product of the Soviet Era, having developed as an industrial warm water port with a strong military overtone. The architecture and entire ambiance of the city reflects this period and in many ways it is like going through a time machine. There are only a handful of buildings that date to the initial founding in the waning Tsarist Era. There is some modern development in the city center and in the outermost residential suburbs, but Murmansk is not a reflection of the more dynamic Russian cities that also have a long history behind them.

Because of the impact of World War II, Murmansk does strongly show the importance of patriotic fervor in the number of monuments and memorials across the entire city. The impact of the war left a strong legacy in Murmansk. Russians have long memories and having been through two world wars with a long and bloody revolution and civil war in between the two great wars, this has left a strong mark upon the people. Even the youth of modern Russia are raised with an appreciation of the sacrifices made on their behalf and strong emotions are felt by all. This is a country where even those who oppose the current government's policies still have a strong sense of patriotic spirit, something that many outsiders fail to understand.

A children's poster for carefree summer activities at the Palace of Culture today

MURMANSK MAPS
Мурманск

Greater Murmansk area

Greater Murmansk

This map is best viewed directly from OpenStreetMap.com on your personal device where it can be expanded or one specific area can be enlarged. Given the format of this book, it is impossible to display maps with the level of detail you might wish to have while actually out exploring the city. But the OpenStreetMap maps used directly are the tool I always rely upon.

CITY OF MURMANSK

City of Murmansk

This map is best viewed directly from OpenStreetMap.com on your personal device where it can be expanded or one specific area can be enlarged. Given the format of this book, it is impossible to display maps with the level of detail you might wish to have while actually out exploring the city. But the OpenStreetMap maps used directly are the tool I always rely upon.

THE CENTER OF MURMANSK

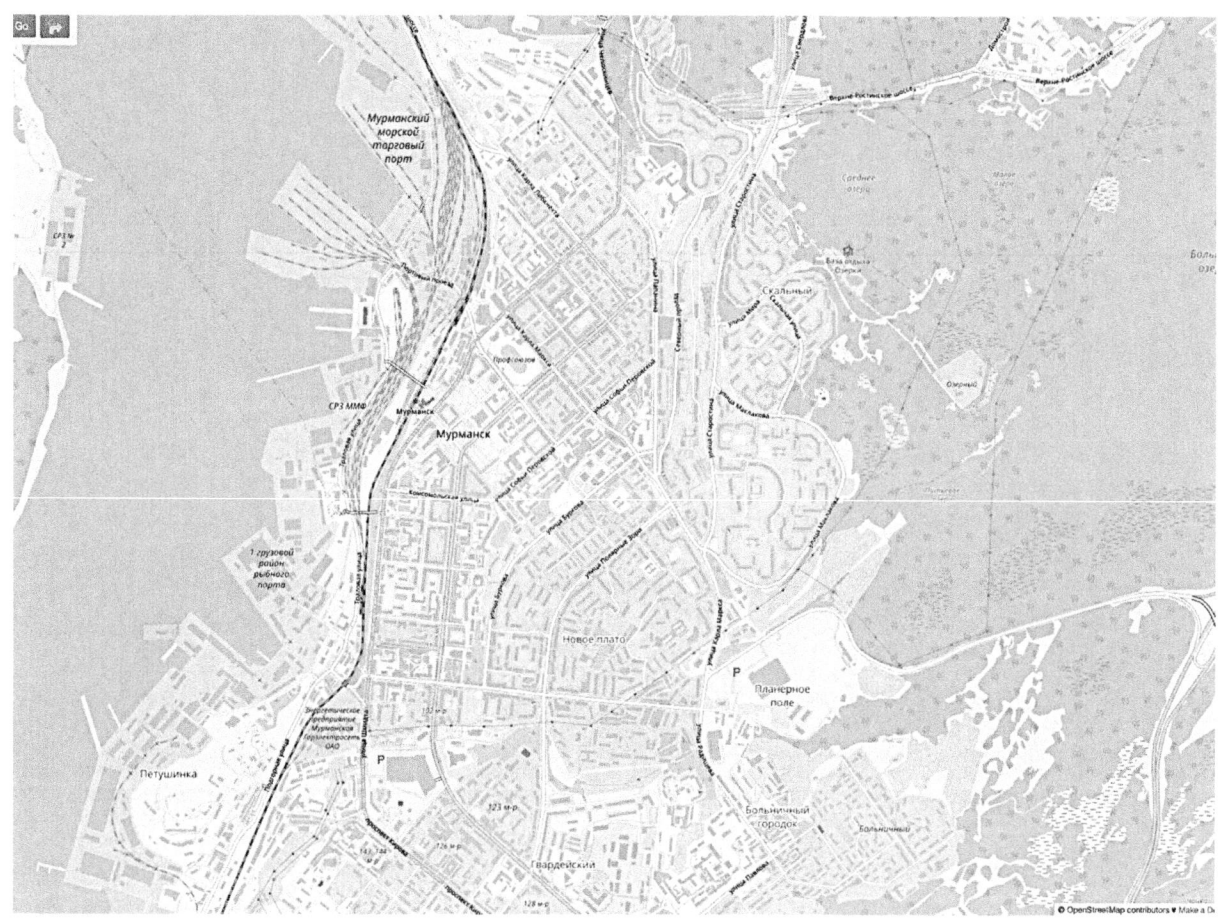

Central Murmansk

This map is best viewed directly from OpenStreetMap.com on your personal device where it can be expanded or one specific area can be enlarged. Given the format of this book, It Is impossible to display maps with the level of detail you might wish to have while actually out exploring the city. But the OpenStreetMap maps used directly are the tool I always rely upon.

ARKHANGELSK АРХАНГЕЛСК

Unlike Murmansk, Arkhangelsk is a centuries old Russian city whose origin is from well back in early tsarist times, and with a very strong religious flavor. Located near the mouth of the Severnaya Dvina River on the White Sea, it is a far northern community, but just slightly below the Arctic Circle. If your ship is visiting, the journey from Murmansk will take two nights and one full day of travel.

NATURAL SETTING: The landscape of Arkhangelsk is essentially flat to just slightly rolling and the land is right on the northern margins of the great boreal forest or taiga. Spruce, willow and birch trees dominate the countryside and the agricultural potential is severely limited by the short growing season. It is worth being out on deck early in the morning to watch the sailing up the Severnaya Dvina River for a couple of hours prior to arrival. You will catch glimpses of small villages and farms where the way of life has hardly changed, giving you an appreciation for the isolation and harshness of life in these far northern lands.

Sailing up the Severnaya Dvina River toward Arkhangelsk

The climate of Arkhangelsk is definitely continental and more like that of western Siberia, as it is too far east for the Gulf Stream to have any significant influence. Winter temperatures are well below zero Celsius, often below minus 40 degrees. And snow covers the ground for up to six months out of the year. In centuries past the major winter travel routes were the frozen rivers, and even today with global warming these ice roads are still used for several months each year. During summer, however, the rivers then served as water highways since they flow primarily north toward the Arctic Ocean. And the size and depth of the Severnaya Dvina gave Arkhangelsk its importance as a northern port dating back to medieval times.

Arriving in Arkhangelsk, the skyline is actually quite modern

As a city, Arkhangelsk is larger than Murmansk with approximately 420,000 residents, but being just slightly south of the Arctic Circle, it is not able to claim to be the most northerly large city in the world. That distinction does belong to Murmansk by just a few degrees of latitude.

Only a handful of cruise ships venture as far east as Arkhangelsk, and if your cruise itinerary includes this ancient city, you will be fortunate. It is an architectural gem with regard to its early Russian heritage. And it is also in many ways still a frontier city, but undergoing a modernization not seen in Murmansk. In Arkhangelsk you will see many 17th through 19th century wood buildings of a long ago era combined with quite modern constructs of the 21st century.

The skyline of old and new seen while docking in Arkhangelsk

BRIEF HISTORY: Arkhangelsk may have dated back to as early as the 9th century because of Viking chronicles that note a community near the mouth of what is now known to be the Severnaya Dvina River. A fortified monastery was built near the banks of the river and dedicated to the Archangel Michael during the 12th century by the then powerful kingdom centered upon what is today Veliky Novgorod, the important religious center located 200 kilometers or 120 miles south of St. Petersburg. The actual historic founding of the city of Arkhangelsk dates to 1584, when Tsar Ivan the Terrible ordered the establishment of a trade center close by to the monastery and it ultimately took its name from that religious complex, which translated into English is a reference to the Archangel Gabriel.

Trade in furs and timber in exchange for European goods became a major factor in the development of Arkhangelsk. It is believed that this was the first Russian port to trade directly with England via the Barents Sea to the waters of the North Atlantic Ocean. The importance of Arkhangelsk cannot be under estimated, as up until the founding of St. Petersburg and the assertion of Russian naval might, the Baltic Sea was not readily accessible to central Russia, as Sweden was the dominant regional power. Thus Arkhangelsk was the main trade outlet for Moscow all during the 15th and 16th centuries. It came under attack by both the Poles and Norwegians on several occasions, but it never fell to invading forces.

After 1703 with the establishment of St. Petersburg on the Gulf of Finland, the importance of Arkhangelsk diminished and it began to decline. But there was a brief resurgence of importance during the Northern War with Sweden, which was already in progress when St. Petersburg was founded. A major fortress named Novodvinsk was begun in 1701 to add to the overall defense of the river delta and secure trade. The Swedes attacked the fortress the same year it was begun, and fortunately the Russians were able to be victorious. The Swedes and other forces attempted capture of Novodvinsk, but it never fell to invaders. But this did not ultimately diminish the importance of St. Petersburg, which became the naval headquarters for the nation and overshadowed the role of Arkhangelsk, mainly because Tsar Peter the Great wanted to develop his showcase window to the west and bring Russia into the European community.

Old turn of the 20thh century wood housing

The Napoleonic Wars of the early 19th century saw Arkhangelsk serving as a vital support for supplies to reach the interior of Russia. During summer, the Severnaya Dvina became a water highway deep into the interior. In the mid 19th century, Arkhangelsk was connected to Moscow by rail, but it was still competing with St. Petersburg with regard to trade. Given its importance as the Imperial Capital and its outlet to the Baltic Sea, St. Petersburg won out over Arkhangelsk for superiority in trade.

During World War I the city was a supply point and later after the Bolshevik Revolution of

1917, it became a center of resistance, held by the White Army forces. But ultimately it fell under Communist rule, as did the entire country by 1922.

During World War II, the city served a vital role in helping to supply Russian forces fighting on the Eastern Front with many supplies, both military and domestic. Murmansk was the larger supply port, but with the 900 day's blockade of Leningrad (St. Petersburg) it was safer to ship supplies via Arkhangelsk. Nazi troops had expectations of capturing Murmansk and Arkhangelsk to totally neutralize the Allied convoy assistance, but their vision fortunately never materialized. The immensity of distance made such a plan nothing more than wishful thinking. And it was a lucky break for Allied forces since Russia's war front helped weaken the Nazi military. However, the German Air Force did conduct a bombing campaign and Arkhangelsk was heavily damaged.

The city is today a vital port for trade, exporting timber, fish and assorted minerals mined in the far north. It is also a center for Arctic research thanks to global warming enabling longer periods when the ocean is ice free. To keep the port open as long as possible, Russia has built some large icebreakers and this is vital to a longer trade season for Arkhangelsk.

The story of Nazi bombing of the city in World War II

SHIP DOCK IN ARKHANGELSK: The ship will dock alongside the great Orthodox Cathedral where there is plenty of room for tour coaches to meet guests. For anyone who has a visa or a passport that allows freedom of movement within Russia, the docking location is ideal, as it is on the southern edge of the central core of the city and within easy walking distance to so many major sights.

SIGHTS TO SEE: There are many very interesting and historic sights to be seen in Arkhangelsk. However, remember the restrictions placed upon tourists by the Russian government. You must have a visa or be from one of a handful of countries visa exempt to get out on your own. The next option to having a greater degree of freedom, if you have a visa or are from an exempt country, is to arrange through your cruise line for a car, driver and guide. You can check on line with Kola Travel at *www.koltravel.com/arkhangelsk* to see what they can offer that might be better than what your cruise line has available.

Most passengers will opt for one of the ship sponsored group tours by motor coach since they will not have either a visa or be from an exempt country. The sights I am listing in this section are what I believe to be the most important in and around the city. It will depend upon what option or tour you select as to what you will be able to see during your visit to Arkhangelsk. My recommendations are (shown alphabetically):

* **Arkhangelsk Merchant Yards Museum** is located along the river's northern embankment. This museum presents an excellent history of the city's founding and development through its many fascinating exhibits. It is open from 10 AM to 7 PM daily. Most tours of the city will include a brief stop at this museum.

* **Arkhangelsk Regional Fine Art Museum** – This small museum has a fine collection of paintings, folk art and costumes reflecting the local region. It gives you a look into the soul of this part of Russia from the religious to the secular. Many people overlook the fine quality of Russian painting, sculpture and the craft art of producing the highly elaborate lacquered boxes with their fairy tale motifs.

The collection is quite good and worthy of a visit. The museum is open from 10 AM to 7 PM Tuesday thru Sunday. It may or may not be included in the group motor coach tours of the city. For anyone who is free to explore, this museum does offer an important glimpse into the Russian creative spirit.

* **Cathedral of the Archangel Michael** - This absolutely grand and magnificent Russian Orthodox cathedral was just recently built. It took many years to complete because of the labor intensive details in recreating a style from centuries back. The cathedral reflects the emphasis once again placed upon religion after the long Soviet Era. No expense was spared in creating a monumental structure dedicated to the Russian belief in the church. You must visit just to gain an appreciation for the role religion now plays in the country.

No specific hours are shown for visitation, but when a cruise ship is in port, the cathedral will be one of the major highlights of any tour of the city. . I recommend making this your first stop if you are exploring privately, as it is adjacent to where cruise ships dock and is simply steps away from the dock.

The newly built Cathedral of the Archangel Michael , (Work of Alex1970, CC BY SA 4.0, Wikimedia.org)

* **Chumbarova-Luchinskovo Avenue** is one of the major highlights in the city center. Originally Arkhangelsk was constructed almost totally of wood. Buildings were beautifully built and highly decorated, but as the city grew into the 20th century, most were destroyed to make way for massive concrete apartment complexes. During the Soviet Era, the concept of what was then modern expansion ruined much of the historic residential architecture of the country, but here in Arkhangelsk the architecture of the pre Soviet Era is an absolute treasure.

Chumbarova-Luchinskovo Avenue is a street where dozens have been preserved and today serve as restaurants, shops and museums. The street is dedicated to pedestrians only and is the true delight of modern Arkhangelsk. Although it is becoming a tourist attraction, it has carefully preserved many of the old wood structures that otherwise would have been destroyed.

The beautiful wood architecture along Chumbarova Avenue

* **Downtown Arkhangelsk** – The central business core of the city of Arkhangelsk will come as a surprise to most visitors. This is essentially an isolated frontier city located in the far north. Yet the downtown core has shown a strong degree of modernization since the collapse of the Soviet Union. Chumbarova Avenue stands in stark contrast to many of the sleek new stores, the few high rise towers and the overall ambiance of the downtown core.

Most motor coach tours will simply drive you through the city center with little commentary. Only those guests who have a visa or have a passport allowing them freedom of movement will be able to truly enjoy exploring the heart of this unique city. This rigidity on the part of the Russian government continues to hinder the ability of so many cruise visitors to explore on their own in the country.

Apart from seeing a modern skyline, you will find that shops are well stocked with both Russian and imported merchandise. If you have the freedom to get around on your own, do take the time to browse through some of the stores to gain more of a feel for the availability of products in Russia today. The supermarket is one very good place to start. And if you have a sweet tooth, Russian dark chocolates rival those of Belgium.

The new and modern city center shopping mall

The heart of Archangelsk's main shopping area

The large Lenin statue in the downtown core

* **Malye Karely Open Air Museum** is located about an hour drive south of the city along the river. This outdoor museum has brought together examples of the historic wood architecture of the far north. It is a grand experience given that you not only see what Arkhangelsk would have been like, but local guides and personnel dressed in traditional garb and performing various tasks make this a fascinating experience. If you go in mid-summer please be sure to take with some insect repellant, as the northern mosquitos can be very pesky. The museum is open daily from 10 AM to 5 PM.

* **Northern Maritime Museum** located in the city center is a very good museum with exhibits concerned with the close ties between Arkhangelsk and the sea. Its exhibits are well crafted, but unfortunately the descriptions are primarily written in Cyrillic and you will need a guide to interpret. It is open Tuesday thru Friday from 10 AM to 6 PM and on Saturday and Sunday from 11 AM to 7 PM.

The historic old St, Nicholas Church

* **Saint Nicholas Church** is in the heart of the city and a must see venue. Built in the true Russian Orthodox style over two centuries ago, it is still an active church and you may be able to stand in the back and watch and listen to the morning liturgy, which is very inspirational.

* **Small Korela Wooden Architecture and Folk Art Museum** is right in the city, and like the Malye Korely museum, this one also features the importance of the wood architecture that was once so commonplace all across the north country and into Siberia. This small museum is not as diverse but gives much of the same experience without traveling an hour each way between the city and Malye Korely, leaving more time to enjoy the city's other sights. No specific hours are posted at the time of this writing.

* **Solovetsky Monastery** is one of the great treasures of northern Russia. It is a UNESCO World Heritage Site and especially spectacular. Built in 1436 on Solovetsky Island in the White Sea, it is accessible by air only during a one day port call in Arkhangelsk. Not all cruise lines offer a tour, as it is expensive and very few passengers are aware of the significance of this great fortress monastery.

During the Soviet Era it served as a prison and then as a labor camp and has only been restored in recent years. Since the collapse of the Soviet Union, there has been a restoration of many of the old monasteries and churches throughout the country. You can only reach this incredible monastery on a group tour because of the distance involved and the need to have a prearranged flight.. Many cruise lines will have a tour planned, generally by chartered aircraft to allow for more time on the island.

* **Victory War Monument and Eternal Flame** pays homage to World War II and is considered to be hallowed ground by local residents. It is located along the northern embankment of the river in the center of the city and is a very major stop on all group and private tours.

A classic fully restored 18th century Russian wood house

* **Wood architecture** – Much of the inner city of Arkhangelsk dates back hundreds of years and up until the late 19th century, wood was the predominant building material. There are many historic buildings throughout the heart of Arkhangelsk that represent various levels of design and ornamentation, many dating back as far as the 17th century. These are classic structures, some in great repair and others in the process of restoration. In the poor parts of the city many of these masterpieces of architecture have languished. But today there is a growing appreciation for this type of construction, which has been lost in so many of the cities during the long Soviet Era. Arkhangelsk is an architectural jewel among Russian cities for its large number of such wood houses, churches and public buildings.

There are many monuments and statues around the city that are all of historic interest. But you will not have time to visit them all. On most group or private tours, you will see a good number in passing. Important statues include; "Papa Lenin," Peter the Great, General Kuznetsov and the Monument to Russian Wives and many more.

An 18th century wood house that has not been restored, but is still lived in

DINING OUT: Most guests will not be dining out in Arkhangelsk because the majority of tours are only half day in length and then without a visa they are unable to leave the ship. For any full day tour, lunch will be included but the restaurant of choice will be predetermined. Only if you have a visa or are from an exempt country, are able to leave the ship or if you are out with a private car, driver and guide is lunch possible. I have listed several personal recommendations based upon past experience. My choices are:

* **Anrov** – Located in the city center on Severni Dvini Embankment # 71, this is a superb restaurant serving very traditional region Russian cuisine. Surprisingly they also serve many Italian dishes, which one would not expect here in Arctic Russia. Their desserts are also to be savored, so if you have lunch here, leave room for a fine pastry. They are open Monday thru Friday from 8 AM to 11 PM and Saturday and Sunday from 10 AM to 11 PM. Have your driver or guide call for a reservation. Call +7 818 248 71 71.

* **Bobroff** – Located on Ulitsa Popova # 2, this restaurant is not pretentious, but does present an excellent meal served in a simple setting. The cuisine is genuine and reflects the regional variation on Russian recipes. During summer fresh seafood is a specialty and if

Arctic char is on the menu, it would be my first choice. They are open daily from 11:30 AM to 2 AM. Have your driver or guide call for a reservation at +7 818 228 58 13.

* Pomorsky is located on Pomorskaya Ulitsa #7 on the third floor and a bit difficult to find on your own. But guides are all familiar with it because it is an outstanding place to dine. They do have an English language menu. The selections are all traditional and I strongly urge you to do a soup, entree and dessert to have the full experience. Their fish soup, borscht and all fish dishes are excellent. There are many meat dishes including chicken, pork, venison and rabbit, but in the far north fish is at its best. They are open daily from Noon to Midnight. Have your driver or guide call +7 818 220 18 58 for a reservation.

Pictures of traditional cuisine at Pomorsky (compliments of management)

* **Restaurant Pochtovaya Kontora 1786** is located along the river embankment and is open from Noon to Midnight, serving both lunch and dinner. The provide a wide array of traditional Russian dishes as well as cuisine that is more in keeping with western European tastes. The restaurant is open from Noon to Midnight daily with extended closing at 2 AM on Friday and Saturday. Have your driver or guide call +7 818240 78 40 to reserve a table.

If you are out with a driver and guide, you can seek their advice as to what other restaurants are recommended if traditional Russian cuisine is not to your taste.

FINAL WORDS: Arkhangelsk is a memorable experience, but it is a shame that more cruise ships do not make the journey this far east into the high Arctic to enable guests to have the experience. I do highly recommend that you be up early and out on deck or your verandah to watch the ship sail up the river into Arkhangelsk. This will give you an opportunity to see some of this far northern countryside.

Arkhangelsk is in many ways similar to cities in Siberia because of its remoteness and the nature of its early settlement. This is a city with a rich historic heritage that predates Saint Petersburg by centuries and is more akin to cities in the Moscow area with regard to its antiquity.

An old church bell tower survives in front of the railway station

ARCHANGELSK REGION
Архангелск

GREATER ARCHANGELSK

Archangelsk Region

This map is best viewed directly from OpenStreetMap.com on your personal device where it can be expanded or one specific area can be enlarged. Given the format of this book, it is impossible to display maps with the level of detail you might wish to have while actually out exploring the city. But the OpenStreetMap maps used directly are the tool I always rely upon.

CITY OF ARCHANGELSK

City of Archangelsk

This map is best viewed directly from OpenStreetMap.com on your personal device where it can be expanded or one specific area can be enlarged. Given the format of this book, it is impossible to display maps with the level of detail you might wish to have while actually out exploring the city. But the OpenStreetMap maps used directly are the tool I always rely upon.

HEART OF ARCHANGELSK

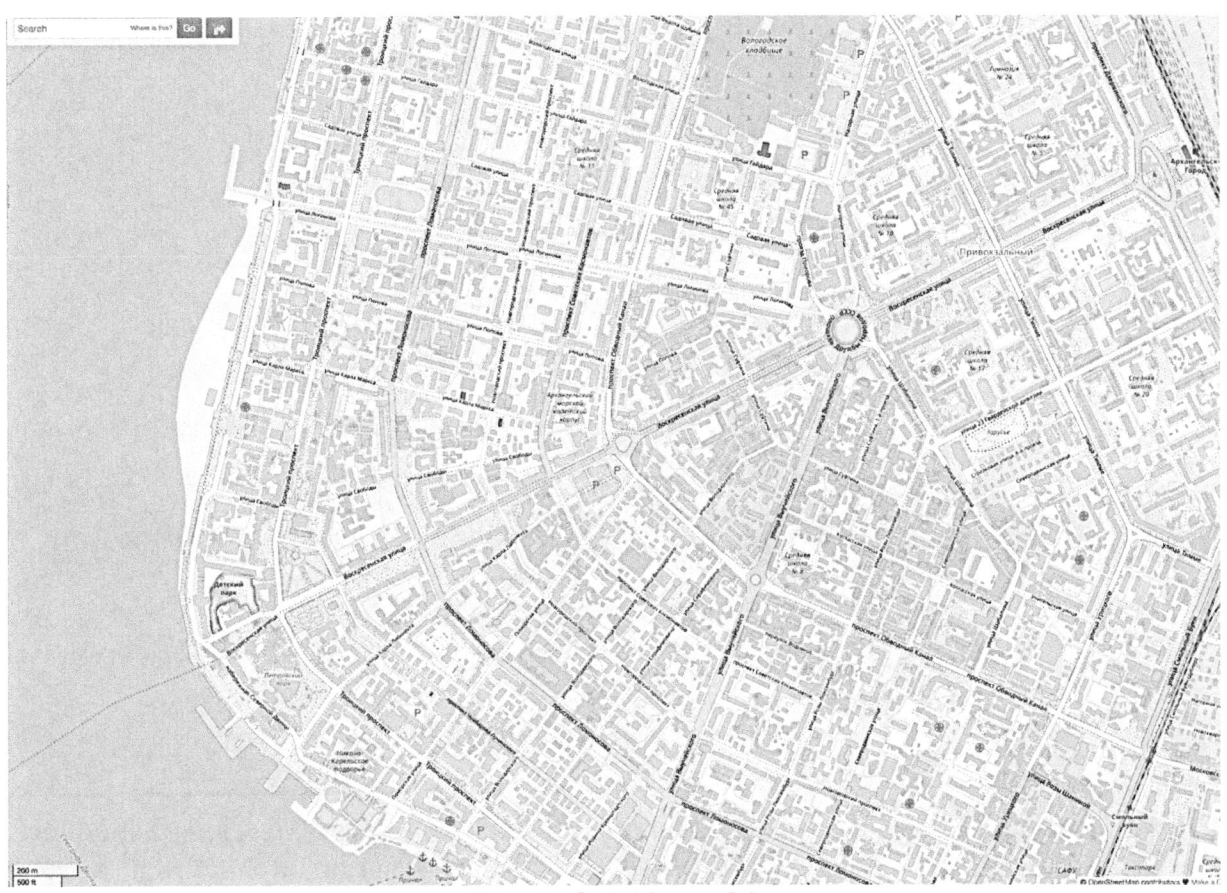

Heart of Archangelsk

This map is best viewed directly from OpenStreetMap.com on your personal device where it can be expanded or one specific area can be enlarged. Given the format of this book, it is impossible to display maps with the level of detail you might wish to have while actually out exploring the city. But the OpenStreetMap maps used directly are the tool I always rely upon.

ABOUT THE AUTHOR

Dr. Lew Deitch

I am a semi-retired professor of geography with over 46 years of teaching experience. During my distinguished career, I directed the Honors Program at Northern Arizona University and developed many programs relating to the study of contemporary world affairs. I am an honors graduate of The University of California, Los Angeles, earned my Master of Arts at The University of Arizona and completed my doctorate in geography at The University of New England in Australia. I am a globetrotter, having visited 97 countries on all continents except Antarctica. My primary focus is upon human landscapes, especially such topics as local architecture, foods, clothing and folk music. I am also a student of world politics and conflict.

I enjoy being in front of an audience, and have spoken to thousands of people at civic and professional organizations. I have been lecturing on board five-star cruise ships since 2008. I love to introduce people to exciting new places both by means of presenting vividly illustrated talks and through serving as a tour consultant for ports of call. I am also an avid writer, and for years I have written my own text books used in my university classes. Now I have turned my attention to writing travel companions, books that will introduce you to the country you are visiting, but not serving as a touring book like the major guides you find in all of the bookstores.

I also love languages, and my skills include a conversational knowledge of German, Russian and Spanish.

I was raised in California, have lived in Canada and Australia. Arizona has been his permanent home since 1974. One exciting aspect of my life was the ten-year period, during which I volunteered my time as an Arizona Highway Patrol reserve trooper, working out on the streets and highways and also developing new safety and enforcement programs for use statewide. I presently live just outside of Phoenix in the beautiful resort city of Scottsdale.

TO CONTACT ME, PLEASE CHECK OUT MY WEB PAGE FOR MORE INFORMATION AT:
http://www.doctorlew.com

Printed in Great Britain
by Amazon

42025883R00192